FAMILY DEVOTIONS WITH SCHOOL-AGE CHILDREN

By Lois E. LeBar

Children in the Bible School
Education that is Christian
Focus on People in Church Education
Family Devotions With School-Age Children

Family Devotions with School-Age Children

Creative Guidelines for Christian Parents

Lois E. LeBar

Fleming H. Revell Company
Old Tappan, New Jersey

Library of Congress Cataloging in Publication Data

LeBar, Lois Emogene, date
  Family devotions with school-age children.

  Includes bibliographical references.
  1. Family—Prayer-books and devotions—English.
I. Title.
BV255.L37   242   73–5525
ISBN 0–8007–0593–9
ISBN 0–8007–0594–7 (pbk.)

CONTENTS

TO THE PARENTS WHO USE THIS BOOK

1. To you the Lord has committed the great responsibility of Christian nurture. The Bible says,

> Children, obey your parents in the Lord:
> for this is right.
> Honour thy father and mother;
> which is the first commandment with promise;
> That it may be well with thee,
> and thou mayest live long on the earth.
> And, ye fathers, provoke not your children to wrath:
> but bring them up in the nurture and admonition of the Lord.
> Ephesians 6:1-4

In other words, bring them up with Christian discipline and instruction (ASV), in such training and correction as befits the servants of the Lord (W. J. Conybeare), with the sort of education and counsel the Lord approves (Charles B. Williams), raise them by letting the Lord train and correct them (William F. Beck). (The comments by these men may be found in The New Testament From Twenty-Six Translations published by Zondervan Publishing House.)

This responsibility cannot be relegated to church or school, though church and school may supplement home training. Only in the home can problems be dealt with when they arise. Only in the home can children see living models of Christ reflecting Him in the midst of daily living. Only in the home are there time and experience enough to mold human nature into Christian character.

2. The purpose of family devotions is not systematic Bible study but rather it is making the Lord the center of all the activities of daily living. When we see the Lord at work, we rejoice together; when conflicts and frustrations annoy, we discover the Lord's perspective on them. The lack of this kind of interaction is what creates a gap between generations and drives young people into their own inner worlds or away from home. In a family we need to relate to each other in terms of how we are feeling and loving and hurting as well as what we are thinking.

Therefore, rather than starting at the beginning of this book and taking the subjects in this order, ask yourself each day what is the particular need of your family for that day. Then look in the Index to see if that need is included. Each subject is a unit in itself, to be selected as needed. If no particular need is evident at the moment and you anticipate no definite need, use the order of subjects in the book. After using a subject, check it in the Table of Contents.

As you study the topic of the day before the family gathers, adapt it to your own circumstances. The natural way to begin is to describe the cause for rejoicing or a difficulty until all the members of the family sense its significance. Concentrate on the aspects of the problem that you are now experiencing. After you lead the family in finding the biblical answer, discuss very specifically what

you as a family should do about the problem in order to obey the Word. Whenever possible, illustrate from your own daily lives, except of course when a
person would be humiliated by the disclosure.

   3. There are usually three parts to the subject for each day:

      a. Focusing the problem until the need is keenly felt,
      b. Finding the answer to the problem in Scripture,
      c. Deciding how to obey the Lord in this matter,
        and talking to Him about it.

   Please don't hurry through the first and third parts as if they aren't really
important. Unless the members of your family feel a current need, they won't
put forth much energy to find the answer in Scripture; God's truth will just be
empty words to them. Too often the Word of God means nothing to us as individuals because it doesn't touch our lives in any way. Don't leave any idea from
Scripture up in the air without personal relevance. Unless we make definite plans
to do something during the day, it's natural for good intentions to evaporate.
If possible, check up on decisions before the day is ended, or at least once a
week.

   Guide the family in studying their own Bibles rather than telling them what
God says. Whenever you come to a question, pause to let the members of the
family find the answer in Scripture or think about it or answer from their own
experience. It is much easier for all of us to obey God if we ourselves discover
the truth rather than listen to someone preach to us. Keep the one idea for each
day sharply and clearly focused so that it will stay in your minds all day without
being clouded by details, even if they are relevant.

   4. As parents be ready to make changes as the Word speaks personally to you.
If you pretend to be perfect, in need of nothing, the children will not dare to
reveal their real inner needs. The Word of God deals with the basic problems
of human nature. As we grow older our problems become more refined and
mature, but we still have the basic problems of human nature. The children will
think more rather than less of you if you admit that you will always continue
to grow in Christlikeness. They are quick to detect phoniness. The Word admon-
ishes, "Confess your faults one to another . . ." (James 5:16).

   5. Keep family devotions from becoming routine, which is deadly. You will
be training your children in wrong attitudes if this time together is boring or
impersonal. Don't get preachy. You can make it the best hour of the day if it
becomes a part of life, not apart from life. If you don't follow the suggestions
in this book slavishly, but use them to penetrate the very inner life of your own
family, the children will think of devotions as a time to solve their personal
problems, to talk over with you their deepest frustrations. Make this time so
enjoyable and profitable that no one will want to miss it. You may start with a
short period, then extend it as the children get personally involved.

6. Don't think you've committed a crime if the family can't manage a time together every day. We need the Lord's help and guidance each day, but we can talk to Him as we walk down the street or drive in the car. Cultivate a continual communion with and reliance upon the Lord, yet keep home devotions as regular as possible. And don't think you need to cover a whole subject each day. You might profitably spend one day focusing the problem, another on the scriptural answer, and another deciding how you as a family and as individuals should obey the Word of the Lord. It takes time to relate biblical principles to one's own life. If you have only a few minutes together, it might be well to read a praise psalm, like Psalms 19, 27, 92, 96, 103.

Though many families find it very difficult to get together at any time in the day, perhaps the best time is morning as you start the day, with a discussion at the evening dinner table on how the subject of the morning worked out during the day. Or you can discuss a subject one evening and report how you carried it out the next evening before you talk about the new subject. It is as important to check on progress as to make plans for change. Good intentions will evaporate unless you establish the habit of checking up on them.

7. The suggestions in this book are beamed at junior high school level. Older teens should realize that they should identify with you, the parents, rather than with the younger children. Bible truths are so basic that all ages need to continually work on them as new levels of difficulty come along, yet they are simple enough for children to begin to comprehend. If you have an older teen and a primary child, the teen can sit by the primary to help him find the Bible portions and read a few dominant words, or read to him. The primary cannot be expected to grasp all the details, but he should get the general idea, he will probably want to be present, and he can often draw or cut out or find something that illustrates the subject of the day.

If you have only primary and preschool children, this book is not for them. They need Bible truths geared to a lower level and activities that do not require reading.

TO THE WHOLE FAMILY

The purpose of family devotions is that the Lord God may speak a personal word to each of you each day for the living of that day. Then each day can be an exciting adventure with the Maker of the universe! You can be caught up in His great plans and draw upon His power. It is just as important that you continually communicate with Him as it is to talk to your parents and brothers and sisters if you have them. God wants to talk to you about your school, your work, your play, your friends, your thoughts. He is personally interested in everything that affects you because He has given Himself for you so that you can freely give yourself back to Him. Try every day to hear some word from His Book that relates to what you are now doing.

If you are going to have a happy home, each member must be open and honest with each other member. None of us will be perfect until we see the Lord face-to-face, so now all of us want to be growing and changing. Of course, outside your home you will stand up for each other, but inside, in the presence of the Lord who understands us all, we must face reality—things as they are, our weaknesses as well as our strengths. Since there are reasons for everything we do, try to understand each other, help each other, and pray for each other, that each of you may become what you want to be. If you hide in your shell or put on a mask to protect what you don't like about yourself, you become unreal, a phony, hurting rather than helping yourself. It's a wonderful feeling to be free and transparent before God and before men. So be free to rejoice over what God does for you and also free to say *I'm sorry* when you do wrong.

In this book we assume that our typical family has four children: Jim in high school, Sue in junior high, Ted in fifth grade, and Alice in second grade. Of course different ages have different needs, but we all need God's truth and God's help, from parents down to the young child, as soon as he understands what God is saying. When a question in the book makes you think, that question is for you. If it doesn't, if it is easy for you, the older ones should let the younger ones answer it. If a question is evident to all of you, skip it and go on. A book has to be written for all kinds of families, yet this book should be made as personal as possible because only the personal makes a difference in our lives.

Each member of the family should bring his or her own Bible to family devotions. If possible each of you should work in a different version so that you can often read a verse from various versions to give it depth of meaning. Younger children will find it easier to read the paraphrased Living Bible and the New Testament's Good News For Modern Man. It would also be helpful, though not essential, to have handy a chalkboard and chalk to make notes as you go along.

Though Father or Mother leads devotions, all of you should be ready to take your part. God gives younger people as well as older people insight into His higher ways. Parents can learn from children as well as children from parents. If you have your own questions about a subject in addition to the questions asked in the book, don't hesitate to ask them. Home devotions focus on our daily lives, just as they are, difficulties as well as joys. See if you can grow stronger in some way every day.

13

KEEP CHECKING

Are we creating an atmosphere of sharing
    and discussion of common problems
        of concern to us all?

Are we making our discussions personal—
    relating what is happening each day in our lives
        to the principles of Scripture?

Do we parents acknowledge that we are human beings
    with our own problems
        as well as being responsible to God for our home?

Is each child recognized as a special creation of God
    with his own potential
        and place in the family?

Is each child getting actively involved
    in terms of his own daily living?

1 WHAT GOD WANTS FOR OUR FAMILY

The Role of the Family

IN HIS Book God says little about schools, more about churches, but much about families. God is greatly concerned about families, and He is greatly concerned about our family.

Think way back to the very beginning when there was only God—only God. After He had created a beautiful earth for people to live on, He created a man and then a woman to be his helper and to be the mother of his children. How much is a human baby able to do for himself? Not much. Baby animals can do much more and become fully grown much faster. It takes human babies years and years to grow up. Since no baby asked to be born, what does God expect parents to do for their children? It takes parents a lot of time and work and sacrifice to take good care of their children.

All of us as human beings have many kinds of needs. First we think of the needs of our bodies. What physical needs must be met if we are to keep alive and well? Yes, food, clothing, shelter, health, safety, etc. Animals need these things too. But people are more than animals. Because people are made in the very likeness of God, what other kinds of needs are just as necessary as keeping well?

Shelby is a sturdy boy who was born into a wealthy home. His parents bought for him all kinds of expensive toys and clothes. He lives on a beautiful large estate with plenty of space for games and sports. He has a horse of his own. But Shelby was lonely and bored. Yes, with all this. He had no close friends. His father was out of town a great deal; his mother was busy with many social affairs. One day Shelby ran away. Why would he run away? His parents couldn't understand. What did he want? Hadn't they given him everything a boy could want? Had they? What hadn't they given him?

Because people are human, what do they need most of all? They need to feel close to other people, and especially to the Personality who is the center of the universe. People need warm relations with other people who think and feel as they do. Shelby's parents were treating him as a thing rather than as a person. Things don't satisfy people, and we resent it when people treat us as things.

What are our needs in relation to people (our psychological needs)?

1. We want to feel love from the people in our family who are important to us.
2. We want to feel that home is the place where we belong.
3. We want others to recognize each of us as a special person with our own special abilities.
4. We want to do things that help us discover what are God's special plans for each of us.

Abraham's Responsibility—Genesis 18:18, 19

We also have important needs that relate to the Lord God, who is the very heart of the universe. What are these needs? Turn in your Bible to Genesis

18:18. Long ago God chose a man to head a long family line. What great promise did God give Abraham? In verse 19 what was Abraham's part? How would you say that in your own words?

The First Commandment—Deuteronomy 6:4-9

Now turn to Deuteronomy 6:4. This is probably the most quoted verse in the Old Testament. Through the centuries good Jewish people have repeated these words several times a day. This statement is followed by the greatest of all commandments; let's read it together. That's a lot of love!

How can we do what verse 6 asks us to do—keep God's words upon our heart? We can remember them, think often about them, work at carrying them out.

Is it enough to think about God at one time in the day when the members of our family can get together? When else should we think about the things of God? Read to yourself verse 7. When would it be natural for us to talk of God as we sit together? Yes, when we're driving in the car, when two or three of us are cooking in the kitchen, when we're watching TV together, etc. When do two or three of us walk together? Before we go to sleep, we naturally talk to the person who sleeps in our room. And at the breakfast table we could say that we're trusting God to help us with our lessons or our work during the day. During this day let's see if we talk to God and about God as naturally as we talk to each other.

Some Jewish people have tried to carry out the commands of verses 8 and 9 outwardly and literally. They have put the words of 4 and 5 in small leather cases with long leather thongs attached and put them on the inner side of their left arm next to their heart (indicate the position) and then wound the thongs around their arm seven times. As frontlets between their eyes, they have worn a small case in the center of their forehead tied there by the strings (phylacteries). To obey verse 9 they have put the great commandment in a little box tacked to the right side of their door and touched it as they came and went (mezzuzas).

How much good do you think it did those Jewish people to wear the first commandment and touch it on their doors? Not much if the customs became routines that they did without thinking. How could those customs have been helpful to them? Whenever they did these things, they could have told the Lord they loved Him and asked Him to help them show it. Real love comes from our hearts inside. Instead of wearing and touching God's words, how does He want us to show that we love Him?

Action

Just as God chose and called Abraham's family, so He has chosen and called our family, in order that He may bless us and make us a blessing to others. He wants our home to be the happiest place on earth for each of us. He Himself, the Maker of heaven and earth, will live right here with us to do what we can't if we do our part.

Our earthly father is strong, but our heavenly Father can do anything! (Even if we have no earthly father, we have a heavenly Father.)

> When we're sleeping, what will He do?
> When we're hungry, what will He do?
> When we go out, what will He do?
> When things are hard, what will He do?

He is able to do a great deal for some families, and very little for others. What does it depend on? What is our part? To love Him and keep His way. How can we keep His way? We can hear what He says in His Book, think about Him during the day, obey Him. Over and over (in the book of Deuteronomy) He says, in various ways,

> Keep My commandments,
> that it may go well with you and your children after you (4:40; 5:16, 29, 33; 6:3, 18; 12:25, 28; 22:7),
> so that I can bless you in all that you do (7:13; 14:29; 15:4, 10, 18; 16:15; 23:20; 25:19).

Do you know any of God's commandments that our family ought to be paying more attention to? Let's pray that we may do our part so that He can do everything He wants to do in our family and with our family to help others.

Deuteronomy 6:4-9 is a good passage to memorize.

The Love That God Wants in Our Family

ONE OF the first things we do in the morning is to see what the weather is. Is it hot, cold, rainy, snowy, cloudy? When we consider moving our home to another location, we ask whether the climate there is sunny, crisp, sticky, or polluted.

One of the most important things about a home is its climate, its atmosphere, the feeling you get in it. What would make a home feel sunny? How would the people act if the climate were cold? Angry? Careless? Indifferent?

Think of the various homes that you've been in. Do they all have the same climate? What kind of climate do we want in our home? Do we want what God is most concerned about? What is that? LOVE. When a house is filled with love, nothing else matters too much. The chief cause of all our troubles is lack of love. It was love that brought Father and Mother together in the first place. Love brought you children into the world.

Where does love come from? Jim, will you please read Romans 5:5, beginning with the words, "the love of God"? How much does the Lord love us? Enough to die for us, enough to give Himself, the Maker of heaven and earth, for us who are weak human creatures.

When we feel loving, all tends to go well. When we don't love, what happens? What can we do then? We can ask God for His love, which is always great enough.

Genuine Love—1 Corinthians 13:1-7

How will we act if we have God's love? Turn to the famous love chapter in the New Testament—1 Corinthians 13. The first three verses show how important God thinks love is. In my own words I might say:

> If I speak in all the many languages on earth and even in the language
>   of angels,
>   but don't have love, I won't be communicating, but only making
>   noise.
> And if I am an inspired preacher and know all God's secrets and have
>   enough faith to move mountains,
>   but don't have love, I am nothing.
> If I give away everything I have and if I am burned alive for Christ's
>   sake,
>   but don't have love, it does no good.

The next four verses tell what a loving person does. I'll write this list here on our chalkboard. Be thinking which ones we as a family need most to work on and which we as individuals need most.

Verse 4. What words shall I write for verse 4? When do we need to be more patient and kind? Have we recently been jealous or proud? Let's each examine ourselves. If we are open and honest to the Spirit of God, He will show us how we look from God's viewpoint. I confess that I was not patient when Sue was not ready to go to the city with us yesterday, and I was in a hurry. I'm sorry,

Sue. It's hard for me to wait for people, but the Lord can help me to be patient. (Give a personal example that the family can appreciate.)

Verse 5. How do our various Bible versions express verse 5? Which of these do we have most trouble with—being rude, selfish, demanding our own way, being touchy, or remembering wrongs done to us?

Verse 6. How do we feel when we hear about wrongs, even wrongs done to our enemies? Are we glad inside when anyone gets in trouble?

Verse 7. Verse 7 emphasizes all things or always, not just some things or sometimes. Do we love enough to take anything the Lord brings to us even though we don't like it? It's so natural to get discouraged. Can we keep plugging along until we finish what we start?

Action

Which of all these acts of love does our family need to work on first? No, it isn't at all natural or easy for sinful human beings to love like this. But God's love never fails. What is our part? Yes, we can ask Him to help each morning and at the very moment when we don't feel loving. Ahead of time we can think through what is best to do in hard situations.

Let's role play the time you mentioned, Ted. When Alice coughs on your stamp collection that you are carefully organizing by countries and they fly all over the floor, you naturally feel like hitting her and calling her names. But if you send up a quick little prayer for God's love, what will you do? She didn't mean to disturb your stamps. (Tear up little pieces of paper to represent stamps.)

Now as individuals let's each ask the Lord what bothers Him most about us, and listen for His answer. How can we correct this fault? Do all of you know what you can do in addition to praying for help?

Today when one of us expresses love, how would it be to thank that person for his love, recognizing that he might have been cross or impatient or selfish instead? Right now I want to thank each of you for one particular way in which you have shown love to me. Would the rest of you like to mention times when we showed love to you? Wouldn't it be wonderful if a person who steps inside our door could very soon sense our family's love because it fills the house, just as he could feel if our house was cold or hot!

As we pray, let's thank God for His amazing love that is greater than we can imagine. Then let's ask Him to help us show love today, especially in the way that is hardest for each of us. At the dinner table tonight be ready to tell us one way you showed love during the day when it wasn't natural.

(Since we'll all be working on the practice of 1 Corinthians 13 until the end of our days, this would be a good chapter to read when the family has only a very short time together, yet wants to hear a word from the Lord to start the day.)

The Joy That God Wants Our Family to Have

(IF ONE of the children would like to make a bright poster featuring the word JOY, it would center your thoughts for this subject.)

Think of a time lately when you've had fun. Fun is usually lighthearted, like playing a game that you can stop and start easily. Now think of a time when you've felt happy. What made you happy? Happiness usually depends on what happens. When we like what happens, we're happy. When we don't, we're not happy.

God wants us to have fun and to be happy, but more than that He wants us to have joy, for joy is better and deeper. How can joy be better than happiness? What can give us real joy? Can you think of a time when you felt joyful? Yes, remember how deep down joyful we all felt when Uncle Joe received Christ and stopped drinking after we had prayed for him so long (cite an instance that the family will recall).

The Joy of the Lord

Let's turn to Psalm 32:10, 11 to see what should be the spirit of God's people. Why do these verses say we should be joyful?

Where does joy come from? Look at Psalm 16:11. This psalm says *fulness* of joy for *evermore.*

What does Jesus say is one of His purposes for coming to earth? John 15:11. He doesn't do things halfway.

The Lord wants to make our home a joyful place where we like to be and other people like to come. Does that mean that He will take away all our difficulties and make life easy for us?

What kind of joy is the Lord's joy? Turn to Hebrews 12:2. What did Jesus experience before He had the joy of sitting down on His Father's throne? What does He mean when He asks us to take up our cross and follow Him? He has never said that it will be easy to follow Him. No, for then we would be shallow, superficial, weak people, unable to appreciate deep joy. But He says that we will have the joy of becoming strong people by overcoming difficulties. It will be deep down satisfying.

What does He say very realistically in John 16:22? 24? If our joy depends on things outside ourselves, they can be taken away. What might these things be? Yes, our health, money, belongings, our good times, what people think of us.

In 2 Corinthians 8:1, 2 Paul says something very interesting about the churches in Macedonia. As I read each phrase in Good News for Modern Man, let's put the ideas in our own words; it sounds complicated in some versions. How could these churches have great joy in giving generously when they were very poor and greatly troubled? Verse 5 reveals the secret of their joy. How can we give ourselves to other people if we have already given ourselves to the Lord? When He gives us His fulness, we have an overflowing life to give to others.

In Philippians 2:1-4 how does Paul tell the Philippians that they can complete his joy?

Action

The Myers family took things as they came, feeling light and happy when events went the way they wanted them to, and feeling down when they had what they called bad luck. They were happy or sad according to the way things happened—*until* son Bob was in an auto accident. When he was so badly hurt that they didn't know whether he would live or die, the whole family began to look at life in a different light. If only Bob would live, it wouldn't matter whether or not they could take the long vacation trip they had planned. They would spend that money for hospital bills. It wouldn't matter whether or not they could buy the new car they picked out if only Bob would be well enough to go some place with them. The day he came home from the hospital they experienced more love and joy than ever before. They began to realize that what happened inside people was much more important than what happened outside; that joy depended on right relationships with people, not on things.

What are the real joys that God has given our family in the past—important things that really matter in the light of all eternity? Let's see how many we can think of and what these joys cost us. To express our joy and thanks to the Lord let's sing "Joyful, Joyful We Adore Thee." In the second and third lines our hearts are compared with flowers. First visualize a flower garden with blossoms closed under a cloudy sky after a rainstorm during the night, then gradually opening as a bright sun comes out in the morning. In the song people's hearts unfold as they feel the warmth of God's love which drives away sin and sadness and doubt. What kind of gladness is *immortal* gladness? Joy that lasts forever.

Sometimes the Lord drops a miracle of joy right into our laps without our doing anything at all. That makes us glad, but it doesn't make us strong. What shall we ask the Lord to do for our family right now in order that we may rejoice in Him? What is our part—maybe a hard part? How can we be strong enough to do that hard thing? Let's talk to Him about this.

The Peace God Wants to Give Us

OUR WORLD is crying out for peace, yet there is war.

Close your eyes and see a picture that for you is a scene of peace—a beautiful colored picture. What will you put in your picture? Are there people in your scene? What makes it peaceful? Let's wait until we can see our picture very clearly.

This earth was a wonderful place as God made it. Even the ground was free of the weeds that now try to choke our grass and flowers. The animals did not kill and eat each other as they do now. In the future kingdom that the Lord will set up, how will the various kinds of animals get along with each other? Sue, read Isaiah 11:6-8. Can we tell the reason for this great change before Sue reads verse 9? In the kingdom to come instead of people's quarreling and fighting, what will they be saying? Ted, will you please read Isaiah 12:2?

Now think of a time when our home was delightfully peaceful—when we all felt good, all of us were in harmony with each other, working happily together for some purpose, or enjoying something together. What keeps us from having this peace all the time? Things happen that we don't like, we do things we don't like, we can't do what we want to do.

Even at these times Jesus says to His people, "Peace I leave with you; My peace I give to you; not as the world gives do I give to you" (John 14:27, RSV). He wants us to know His own peace, a deep calm, a serene quiet at the very center of our being, no matter how storms and pressures and struggles swirl around us. How can we have the Lord's own peace? How does this work?

Paul's Shipwreck—Acts 27:10-44

Let's see how the Apostle Paul experienced God's peace when things didn't go the way he wanted them to. He was being taken to Rome as a prisoner on a grain ship because his preaching of Jesus had stirred up a riot.

Turn to Acts 27:10. What did Paul say to the captain and owner of the ship when they decided to set out on the rough Mediterranean Sea though treacherous winter was coming? When the crew didn't pay attention to his warning, what happened, in verses 18-20?

In this desperate situation how many on board that ship probably had peace at the center of their beings?

Had Paul done all he could when he warned them? What did he say to them in verse 21?

Because they had not been wise, was no hope left? What is Paul's attitude in verse 22?

How could he say that? See verses 23 and 24. Can we expect the Lord to speak to us clearly like this in time of need?

Then in verse 25 Paul tells the secret of his peace. Do we have faith to believe the promises God has given us, in His Book and privately in our hearts? If we don't really believe Him, what will happen to our peace inside? If we do believe Him, we will be like Paul, we will take heart and not be afraid. If we find that our peace has departed, what can we do? Yes, we can look to see who this is who asks us to trust Him. He is no ordinary mortal but the mighty Creator-Redeemer Himself, who made and controls everything that is.

Because Paul did not lose his inner peace, did everything go smoothly from then on? No, he says in verse 26, ". . . we must be cast upon a certain island." Jim, read what happened when the ship drifted onto a beach—verses 41-44. Paul had peace not because things went the way he wanted them to, but even when they didn't.

Action

Things will always happen that we don't like. Will we let these happenings overcome us, conquer us, take away our inner peace? Peace is not the absence of conflict but the ability to cope with it.

Sometimes when we ask people how they are, they say, "Pretty good under the circumstances." *Under* the circumstances! If they are God's people we can ask, "What are you doing under there?" God wants to enable us to live *above* the circumstances. How can we live above the circumstances? We can face reality as it comes, look it squarely in the face, and ask the Lord, "Do You want to change these circumstances, or help me change them? If so, what shall I do?" But sometimes things cannot be changed—the ship will be broken in pieces. Then we can pray:

> God, grant me
> the serenity to accept the things I cannot change,
> courage to change the things I can, and
> wisdom to know the difference.

What circumstance is right now bothering our family, keeping us from enjoying the peace that God wants to give us? Let's ask the Lord what we can do about it and what must simply be accepted as part of life, of things as they are. Can we believe that the Lord will work this circumstance for the good of everyone concerned—even if we don't like it? Can we leave the outcome with the Lord and have peace about it in our hearts?

Right Relations

SOMETIMES OUR peace and joy are disturbed by outward circumstances, and sometimes by people. How would you finish this sentence: The most important thing in life is _____?

Rightly Related to God

In the beginning God made man different from the animals, like Himself with ability to love and choose and feel deeply, so that we can be intimately related to Him. Because He understands the whole of things from beginning to end, He gave us a guidebook to help us understand the nature of the universe that He created. What happens when we follow the guidebook? We feel good inside, for He put in us a godometer, an indicator that tells us how we're doing, called our conscience.

How do we feel when we don't follow the Book, when we think we know better than the One who created us? We feel guilty. But we don't have to keep feeling guilty. What has the Lord provided to take care of our guilt? Yes, He loved us enough to send His own Son to take the punishment that we deserve. Think of that! Then what is our part in being forgiven? "If we confess our sins"— finish this verse, Ted (1 John 1:9). Feeling guilty acts like a poison to us. Let's get rid of that feeling just as soon as it comes; let's not let it do us harm. It's a wonderful feeling to be at one with God.

Rightly Related to Ourselves

Do you ever feel like two people instead of one? Do you ever feel mad at yourself? When? Since we'll all have to live with ourselves all our lives, we better like ourselves. If we don't feel good about ourselves, we better discover the reason why we don't. It's a wonderful feeling to be at one with ourselves.

Rightly Related to Others

If we aren't rightly related to God and to ourselves, we won't be rightly related to others. But God wants to help us with all these relationships. One reason we often conflict with others is that we expect them to be just like us. We want them to like the things we like, do things the way we do them. But they won't. Why not? God made each of us different, with our own temperament, interests, abilities. Do we really respect the difference in other people, listen to what they are saying? What happens when we are not rightly related to other people? It's a wonderful feeling to be at one with others.

Jacob's Interrelations—Genesis 27—28

Jacob was a smart young man whose name means cheater or schemer. Can you tell some of his story? God said that the older brother in his family would serve the younger instead of the other way around as it usually is (Genesis 25:23) and Jacob was the younger. Jacob and his mother didn't wait for God to bring this about in His own best way and time. What did they do? Yes, by deceiving his aged father, Jacob stole the birthright from his older brother Esau. Against whom was that sin? Against God, his father, his brother, and himself.

Though he was no doubt glad he had the birthright, how else must he have felt? Guilty toward God and his father, yes and no about himself, and afraid of his brother.

What was brother Esau thinking? Read Genesis 27:41.

What did his mother Rebekah say to Jacob? Verses 42-45. So he had to start out alone on a long journey to an uncle he had never seen.

Was the Lord through with that kind of cheat, who was not rightly related to Him, or himself, his parents or his brother? When Jacob saw in his dream a ladder reaching to heaven, what did the Lord who stood above it say to him? 28:13-15.

When Jacob awoke, how did he feel? 16-18.

What did he promise the Lord? 20-22.

Action

It's a great thing to have a clean conscience—a conscience void of offense toward God and toward men (Acts 24:16)! Right now how do you feel toward God; is there anything between you and Him; do you have a quarrel with Him over anything? If so, why not straighten it out this minute, so that you may have His peace and joy? Because Christ died for our sins, He is ready to forgive just as soon as we confess our sin.

Then think about yourself. Is any kind of struggle going on inside you? Is there anything you want and don't want at the same time? How will you decide which of two things to do? Which does the Lord approve? Which is really more important? Would you like us, your family, to help you decide?

Then do you feel right with all of us and with all your friends? If we let little conflicts develop, they get worse and fester. Should any of us say we're sorry to anyone, or write a letter to anyone?

Finally when we're right with God, ourselves and others, we're free to help others. God will let us go adventuring with Him, we won't have to spend our energies worrying about ourselves, and we won't put a stumbling block in anyone's way. Let's get up in the morning and go to bed at night feeling right with the world!

> Create in me a clean heart, O God;
> and renew a right spirit within me.
> Psalm 51:10

The greatest thing in life is _____? Relationships—being rightly related to God, to myself, to others.

The Christian Life-Style

WHEN OUR non-Christian neighbors think of our family, how do they really feel toward us? Do you think they would want to be like our family? Or wouldn't they want to be like us?

Why might other people say, "No, I wouldn't want to be like the Christians I know"?

1. Yes, some Christians don't seem to have much fun. We seldom see them laughing, playing together, enjoying their friends, having the best times. How does God feel about His people having good times? He plans good times for them.

2. Some Christians are known for what they don't do instead of what they do do. People look at them and see that they don't do this and they don't do that. They don't do enough good things to be known for the good that they do.

3. Some Christians seem very narrow in their interests and concerns. All they seem to be interested in is their own family, their own friends, their own church.

4. Some Christians appear to others to be proud, feel they are better than others, "holier than thou." Other people feel that they are looking down on them because they aren't living up to all that the Christians pretend to.

Do you suppose our neighbors feel any of these attitudes toward us? How does the Lord want His people to look to others? Why did He leave us in this world after He saved us from our sins? If we're going to show others what He is like so that they will want Him too, we'll need to have contacts with them, have things in common with them.

What do we Christians have in common with our neighbors who are not Christians? Yes, we live in the same world, in the same country, in the same city. The rain falls or doesn't fall on all of us. All of us are responsible for taking care of the natural resources of land and sea that the Lord has given us. He has made beautiful things for all of us to enjoy. We all need food and homes and clothes and cars to go places. We all need to pay taxes and obey the laws of our government. We have a lot in common with all our neighbors.

The Biblical Viewpoint

But the Bible says that we Christians should be different from non-Christians in some ways too. How should we be different if we are to show others what our God is like?

1. What is the center of the Christian's life? The center of the non-Christian's life is himself. He tries to get things for himself, he is interested in other people for his own interests, he is concerned primarily about the way he feels. What does the Lord say in Jeremiah 10:23? If the way of man is not in himself, who is the center of the Christian's life? What difference does this make to us?

2. What does the Christian put first in life; what is his priority in life? How does the Lord state the first and great commandment? Let's read together Matthew 22:37. Only the Lord Himself can help us to live like this.

3. How should we feel about ourselves? Read to yourself Matthew 22:38, 39. We can love ourselves if we have our center in Christ because He loves us so

much and we are pleasing Him. Of course we're not satisfied with ourselves. How can we be? See if you can pick up the answer from Luke 2:52. We're not discouraged if we are growing in all ways as the boy Jesus grew. In what ways did He grow?

4. And how does the Christian feel about his neighbors? Matthew 22:39. Have we shown our neighbors that we love them? What can we do this week?

5. How does the Christian feel about the routines of life—the chores, the daily round of duties? They aren't always just what we would choose to do. It is very natural to feel like complaining about these duties. How does 1 Corinthians 10:31 tell us to react to them?

Action

How do we as a family measure up to this Christian life-style? How clearly do we show our neighbors what real Christians are like? In what ways are we strong? In what ways do we need to improve? Let's rate ourselves on the scale below.

enjoy good times	|—————————|	little fun
many interests	|—————————|	few interests
concern for all kinds of people	|—————————|	interest in few people
minimum time on the cares of this world	|—————————|	bogged down with the cares of this world
life centered in God	|—————————|	life centered in ourselves
routines done unto God	|—————————|	routines a bore

Which one of our needs shall we work on specifically this week? What will be the part of each one of us? What will we find hard? Let's ask the Lord to help us do these hard things. "I can do all things through Christ which strengtheneth me" (Philippians 4:13).

God's Best or Second Best?

THE HARRIS family were very comfortably settled in their suburban home. They had fixed it up with a grill in the backyard, a family room with Ping-Pong table, and separate rooms for each of the children. They liked their home now. And Father liked his work; he was specializing in business management and was receiving promotions. Then an urgent call came for a business manager from the mission society in Germany that this family was especially interested in. Father felt the pull of the call, but he agreed with the rest of the family that he hated to pull up and leave this place.

Jim hated to leave his basketball team. Sue was president of the artists' club at school. Ted had his Christian Service Brigade friends, and Alice liked her second grade teacher very much. The opening in Germany seemed to be God's call. But was it sensible to leave their home just after they got it fixed as they wanted it? Could this move be God's best for them when everything now seemed to be going so well? They couldn't visualize what life in Germany would be like. Here they were serving God in their church and in their community. Would they obey God's call even if they couldn't see what the future would hold? Would they trust God even if the move might not seem wholly sensible?

Adam and Eve—Genesis 2—3

What happened when the very first family on earth thought they knew better than God? Let's look at that first family. What kind of place did the Lord prepare for them? Read Genesis 2:9, Alice.

What was God's plan for this family, Ted? Verses 15-17.

But other voices often tempt us human beings to disobey the voice of the Lord God. Let's take parts to read Genesis 3. Alice, you take the part of the snake, Ted be Adam, Sue be Eve, and Jim, read what the Lord says. When the exact words of the people aren't given, say the idea in your own words. I'll read the story between your parts (verses 1a; 7, 8; 20, 21; 23, 24).

All the families since this first one have sinned and have had to work harder than the Lord intended they should.

Action

Why is it so hard for us human beings to trust God to know and do what is best? Yes, from our own point of view our own ways seem so sensible that we trust ourselves. What are the excuses people give for trusting themselves instead of God?

1. Yes, Alice, we can't see God and can't talk things over with Him the way we do with each other. How would you answer this excuse? How do we find out what God's best is? We listen to Him through His Book and in our own hearts when we're still enough, and we talk to Him in prayer.

2. Can you think of another reason why we don't trust God's best? Yes, we can't see ahead to what is going to happen in the future, and He can. How much better, how much higher are His ways than our ways? Turn to Isaiah 55:8, 9, and give the answer in your own words.

3. Can you think of any other reason why we don't trust God's best? Sometimes we're afraid that His higher ways won't really be for our good, that He will let us down. How would you answer that objection? Why should we be assured that He will not let us down? He created this world with all its possibilities for our home, He gave His Son who gave Himself for us, and He is preparing our future home in heaven. ". . . no good thing will he withhold from them that walk uprightly" (Psalm 84:11).

In what way do we need to trust right now that the Lord's way is best? Do we really want His best, not His second best, though it may cost us something at the moment? Can we honestly tell God three things:

First, that He wouldn't give us anything less than the best?

Second, that He knows just what is best for everyone concerned?

Third, that He knows the future when we don't?

Do you have any problems with these three beliefs? If so, let's discuss them very frankly. Then let's tell the Lord how we feel about His better ways.

Necessary Things

(IF YOUR family has a real need at the moment, start with that. If not, describe the need of another family that all of you can appreciate.) Mr. Walton in our church has not been able to find work since he had his operation, his wife has worked a little, but she is kept busy with her five children, and their money is getting very low. How would you feel if you belonged to that family? What would you do? If you asked the Lord to supply your need, would you feel sure that He would? Why?

Here on the chalkboard let's make a list of things we'd like to have in order to live a joyous Christian life. This is quite a list we have before us. God loves to give His people good things that they can use for Him. If in His great eternal wisdom God should not give us some of these things or take some away, could we still be joyous in Him, or would losing them take away our joy?

As we look through this list, Alice, will you erase the ones that aren't really necessary, leaving only the things we really need. Do we really need to be healthy? Do we know anyone who is not healthy, yet who rejoices in the Lord? Yes, Mrs. Norton lives in a wheelchair, yet is always praising and serving the Lord. But, you say, we couldn't do what we're doing now if we were sick. Very true, but might not the Lord have something else then for us to do? Yes, we need our eyes for many things, but blind people serve God too in their own way. If we're thankful for good health, eyes that see, ears that hear, being able to walk, etc., let's pause to thank God for these right now.

But some of these items on the board are necessary for life. Which are they? Yes, probably clear minds, food, home, clothes, safety. Friends? If we moved away from our friends here, would that be disastrous? If we were the right kind of people, we could make new ones. How about money, a car, a good position?

Our heavenly Father has given us a great promise about our *needs* in Philippians 4:19. Read it, Ted. But this is not a promise to supply all our *wants*. He is in control of the whole world, nothing is too hard for Him to supply. But He doesn't always do it in the way we expect.

Elijah Fed—1 Kings 17:1-16

Because God's people long ago were led to worship idols by wicked King Ahab, God told his servant Elijah to tell the king how He was going to punish the land. Turn to 1 Kings 17:1. Read what Elijah said to King Ahab, Sue.

But if it didn't rain for three years, how could Elijah get food? The Lord didn't forget His servant who obeyed Him. What did the Lord say He would do for Elijah? Verses 4, 5. How would he be fed? By ravens! Birds! Don't be silly! Suppose Elijah had thought, "I can't be fed by birds! I'll just stay where I am."

What actually happened in verse 6? But with no rain, what else soon happened? Verse 7.

Would God let His servant starve? How was He going to provide for him next? 8, 9.

As I read the story part of the next incident (10-16), Jim and Sue read the conversation between Elijah and the widow. (A widow is a woman who has lost her husband.)

The Kingdom First—Matthew 6:25-33

Alice has cut out magazine pictures to illustrate important words of the Lord Jesus, and Ted has practiced reading the words. (It would also be well if Alice had practiced showing her pictures at the right time while Ted reads.)

Repeat that last, verse 33, in your own words, Sue. How do we seek first God's kingdom and righteousness? We do everything to please God and not ourselves.

(If you have an incident about the way the Lord supplied a need for a current servant of His, share it here.)

Action

When God is the center of a home, He supplies anything a family really needs, anything necessary for them to live for Him. When we have a need, what do we do? He says, ". . . ask, and you will receive, that your joy may be full" (John 16:24, RSV). What does the Lord tell us not to do in Matthew 6:25 and 28? If we are anxious and worried, what kind of people does He call us at the end of verse 30?

What does our family really need just now—anything that we are sure the Lord wants us to have? What shall we do then? We'll ask Him and believe He will supply.

If at the present time we have all the necessary things, can we go merrily on our way? We can first thank Him for what we have. Many Christian brothers in our world do not have all the necessary things. Let's each pray for some of them.

Unnecessary Things

ON A bitter cold winter's day I asked our mailman if he wouldn't like to stop in the house for a few minutes to get warm. He was glad to step inside. I asked him if he wouldn't like a hot drink and a cookie. He said, "No, thank you, I have an ulcer, and must drink only milk." So I warmed some milk and he ate a soft cookie. He explained that he had to take two jobs in order to buy the new house he wanted and new furniture to go in it. But now he has developed this stomach sore which keeps him from eating many of the foods he likes very much. And he is so tired when he comes home at night that all he wants to do is fall into bed. He doesn't have any time for his wife or his children, or to enjoy the things he already has.

Are any of us striving, struggling to get something that we really don't need? That we would be happier without, from God's viewpoint? That will probably be hard for us to see, once we have set our heart upon something. No matter how old you are, can you remember something in the past that you thought you simply must have in order to be happy? I can. Maybe yours was a bicycle or a certain article of clothing or maybe a lawnmower so that you could earn money. At the time it seemed absolutely necessary. But as we look back now, was it really as necessary as we thought?

What happens if we stubbornly say to ourselves, "God may not think so, and other people may not think so, but I just must have this thing"? What then are we actually saying to God?

The Rich Young Ruler—10:17-31

One day as Jesus was starting on a journey, a young man clothed in rich garments came running to Him and dropped on his knees before Him on the dusty road. Though still young, this man had been chosen a ruler. What question did he ask Jesus in Mark 10:17? Jesus must have been delighted to hear him ask that most important question.

How did Jesus answer him? Verses 18, 19.

We can tell what kind of person he was by the way he replied. Verse 20. He didn't hesitate to say that he had always obeyed these commandments.

How did this make Jesus feel toward the young man? Verse 21. But there was one thing that was keeping this fine fellow from God's best. What did Jesus tell him to do?

What does verse 22 tell us about this man? Why was he sad? He really wanted eternal life, but not enough. What did he love more? So he kept his possessions and failed to obtain eternal life.

We might think everything would be easier for people who are well-to-do, who never have to worry about money. Jesus' disciples thought so, thought of course this would be so. But is it? Read on, verses 23-27. So if we don't have much money, that's an advantage—in one sense. Then Peter made a startling discovery! He realized that he and his friends had done something that rich men find very hard to do, verse 28.

In verses 29 and 30 is Jesus talking about receiving much more money than we had before, Jim? Verse 31 poses a puzzle; how can the first be last and the last first? A banker who is well known for doing good may not be as rich in the sight of God as an old woman who has very little but who gives all her time and energy to helping others.

Action

Are any of us saying no to the Lord because we want to come to Him on our own conditions? Are we trying to keep anything that He is telling us to give to Him or to others? If we put Him first and ask Him what He wants us to have, He delights to give us many good things, for we will use them in the right way.

What shall we do when we don't know whether or not we need something? We have decisions like this to make all the time. (Mention a decision you must make soon.) Right now it's when to buy a new car. We don't need one for the looks of it, but we don't want ours to break down on the road. Ted has been wanting a new baseball suit and Sue would like a new dress.

Let's each tell the Lord how we feel about Him and ask Him whether or not He wants us to have the things that seem good to us.

Possessions

Let me hold lightly
   Things of this earth;
Transient treasures,
   What are they worth?
Moths can currupt them,
   Rust can decay;
All their bright beauty
   Fades in a day.
Let me hold lightly
   Temporal things,
I, who am deathless,
   I, who wear wings!

Let me hold fast, Lord,
   Things of the skies,
Quicken my vision,
   Open my eyes!
Show me Thy riches,
   Glory and grace,
Boundless as time is,
   Endless as space!
Let me hold lightly
   Things that are mine—
Lord, Thou hast given me
   All that is Thine!

MARTHA SNELL NICHOLSON

The Authority and Humanity of Parents

NOTHING IN this world is harder than being a good Christian parent, yet nothing is more important! Parents bring into this world new lives that may be either a blessing or a curse to themselves and to others. Though children have wills of their own, their early upbringing determines largely the course of their whole future. Think of the different ways in which children are being reared and the differences in their attitudes and actions. Parents and their children can either enjoy each other or be a threat to each other.

Young people think mainly about themselves. When two of them fall in love with each other and get married, they have many adjustments to make. What happens if these two are not mature people who understand themselves and each other? When they are intimately related, tension and conflict result. They can't think only of themselves anymore. When a baby is born, he complicates the situation. Each parent has two other people to think about. And so on as more children come along. With each child come new adjustments, which may be hard to make.

God says to parents, "You take the place of Me until your children are grown." And yet parents are only human, not perfect as God is. Even though we try hard to reflect the Lord, we fail continually. Will you children try to put yourselves in the place of us parents and see what our role is? We stand between the Lord and you, responsible to both, much concerned about you both, trying to bring you two together when you are initially very different. How can we be our own real selves as frail mortals and yet represent to you the authority of God?

Responsible to God and Family—Colossians 3:12-17

Both God and you want us parents to be real and not phony. Therefore there's no use pretending to be what we aren't. We aren't God and so we make mistakes. We aren't afraid to say *I'm sorry*. Though we can't expect to be rigidly consistent, we can be dependably real. We are very thankful for God's standards in His Word. There is no question about them. We seek to maintain them for ourselves and for you. When Scripture is not definite about a problem, we'll talk it over together in the light of what is given.

Let's look at the passage beginning with Colossians 3:12 and try to get each other's point of view, you the view of us parents and we the view of you children. Since God has chosen us and called us to Himself, what attitude should we have toward each other? Which of these qualities in 12 and 13 are hardest for us to practice? Is there any situation in which we feel hardhearted toward someone because we can't feel with him, understand why he acts as he does? If we do, let's try to understand the feelings of the other fellow. Do you ever feel, "Oh, if only someone would be kind to me right now" ? When are we inclined to feel proud instead of lowly? There are times to be strong and courageous, but also times to be meek and gentle.

Let's each mention a time when we have to exercise patience and forbearance with each other. If we know what bothers other people, maybe it wouldn't be too hard for us to oblige. Often we aren't aware of what annoys others. I guess I have most trouble with patience when it is too noisy for me to carry on a telephone conversation.

Is any one of us harboring a hurt that has not yet been forgiven? Don't let any root of bitterness poison your soul. Straighten it out this minute. Is there anything you have to keep forgiving over and over? That isn't necessary.

Don't you like the way verse 14 expresses the wonder of love! Everything is so much easier with love! Everything so hard without it! How does your version word 14?

What would you say is ruling in your heart right now? Is it love? Or what verse 15 speaks about—peace, or thankfulness? Which is uppermost?

In 16 how can the Word of Christ dwell in us richly? We can ask the Lord for just the right word for every situation that we're in, and meditate on it. Do you children realize that you teach Mother and me many things, as well as we teaching you? (Mention one specific thing that you've learned from the children recently.)

In relation to 17, have we done anything recently that was not done in the name of the Lord Jesus, that we couldn't do with Him, that we couldn't thank Him for? This paragraph in Colossians gives you the spirit of what we parents are striving for in this home. When we fail, we ask your forgiveness. Pray for us, as we do for you.

To Wives, Husbands, Children—Colossians 3:18-21, Ephesians 6:1-4

Next in Colossians God speaks specifically to wives, husbands, and children. Because there can't be two heads to a family, the Lord has ordained that the father should take the lead and bear the responsibility for leading (18).

In Paul's day what did he need to warn husbands about? They are to love their wives as Christ loves the church! That is overwhelming love!

In 20 what is God's Word to children? How long are children to obey their parents? As long as they are dependent upon them.

Turn also to Ephesians 6:1. What other command to children is added in 2, 3?

Then in verse 4 is another warning to fathers. With the best of intentions, in their very attempt to see that their children obey the Lord, some parents are so strict and rigid that the children get discouraged, and give up trying to please as impossible. Do you children feel like that about anything? You see by this verse that I am responsible for bringing you up in the discipline and instruction of the Lord. I am to help and encourage you so that you want to please Him. Only as you want to please the Lord will I be pleasing Him!

"Dear Lord, may we parents keep growing in our ability to discipline and instruct our children lovingly and wisely so that they will want more than anything else to please You. Help us especially where we have been weak and have failed in the past."

2 LETTING GOD BE GOD IN OUR LIVES

God's Love

WE USE the word *love* very loosely in all kinds of ways. We say, "I love ice cream," or something else to eat that we could get along very well without. Is there any growing plant that you might say you love, like red roses? Any animal, like a dog or a horse?

Think of the people who love you. How different their kinds of love! What makes you think a good friend loves you? Maybe he waited for you when he was in a hurry to get someplace. What makes you think a favorite relative loves you; what has he done for you? What has a brother or sister done to show you love? When it comes to fathers and mothers, we step up to a different level. We can only begin to list the innumerable ways in which parents love their children whom they have brought into the world. Think of the many times that Mother has put her children's interests ahead of her own. I trust that the rest of you have felt the deep love that I have for you.

Parents, how have your children shown love to you?

God's Love in Salvation

But many people on this earth have never experienced the greatest love of all! How does God's love compare with the very greatest human love? Love never begins with us. Where does it always begin? Let's look at Jeremiah 31:3. The center of this universe is Personality, who is love.

Because God's love for all people is so great, what did He give that was very hard for Him to give? Very little is hard for God, but this was. Quote John 3:16, Alice.

And what did Christ give because He too loved us? Ephesians 5:2.

This love is far greater than any human love could be. How great is God's love to us? Look at the end of John 17:23. Think of that—God the Father loves us as He loves Christ, who is His perfect Son! Can you really feel that? It's hard for us to fathom it!

Therefore the Psalmist exclaims: "Because thy loving kindness is better than life, my lips shall praise thee" (Psalms 63:3). God's love is better than life!

What Else God's Love Does for Us

God's love not only saves us but does much more for us. Here are verses for each of you that tell what else:

Alice—Romans 8:28. God can make even the sad things in our lives turn out for good.

Ted—Romans 8:39. Nothing, no nothing, can separate us from the love of God.

Sue—1 John 4:16. God wants to make His love the very center of our lives.

Jim—1 John 4:18. God's perfect love takes fear out of our lives.

Mother—Ephesians 2:4-6. Christ already sees us as ruling with Him on His throne.

Father—Romans 5:5. Through us God radiates His love to others by His Spirit.

Let's illustrate this reflection of God's love by a series of concentric circles. (Draw them on the chalkboard, or use colored paper to make the four circles.) This universe begins with the Person of God, who is love. He loved the world He made so much that He sent His own Son into it. Christ loved us so much that He gave Himself on the cross for our sins, which separated us from God, who is holy. He sheds God's love abroad in the hearts of those of us who receive Him into our lives. Other people do not see the Lord, but they should see His love reflected in us; this should attract them to Him.

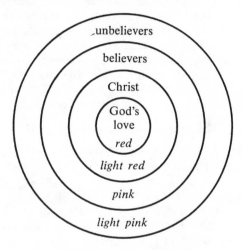

Why We Don't Always Feel God's Love

Are there any times when you don't feel God's love, which is from everlasting to everlasting? Revelation 3:19 tells what else His love does for us. Hebrews 12:5, 6 tells how we should respond to this aspect of His love. If He just let us go our own way, what kind of people would we become? Soft weaklings. He is interested not just in making us comfortable, but in making us like Himself, so that we can reflect His love.

Action

Which of these verses that we've looked at today would you like to think about each morning this week when you get up? Here is a strip of paper for you each to write your verse, so that you can put it where you'll see it each morning.

God's Sovereignty

(ASK TED if he can bring a picture of the vastness of the universe. Also bring a weighing scale with a clump of dust on it to illustrate Isaiah 40:12 and 15.)

When you sit and watch a colony of ants on an anthill, what impresses you as to the difference between ants and human beings? What you or I could do if we stepped on the anthill with one foot! How easy would it be for an ant to understand what kind of creature a human being is? Could an ant ever imagine how things look to us humans?

Now in the same way imagine the Lord God looking down on this earth with us human beings going to and fro. God created this whole universe out of nothing and will some day destroy it. Think of the vastness of outer space with its planets and stars moving in their own orbits light years apart! Stretch your thoughts to conceive of a Person who could make and control all this vastness! Can you imagine all these worlds just happening and keeping in their own places? I can't.

How is it possible for us small humans on this one planet to know anything about the almighty One who is in control? He has written and told us clearly in His Book. How does our earth look to the Person who started it all?

The Ruler of All—Isaiah 40:12-31

Turn in your Bibles to Isaiah 40:12. In verses 12 and 13 what pictures do you see in your mind? Can you imagine God measuring all the earth's oceans and rivers and lakes in His hand? Does God have hands like ours? No. Then why, Jim, does the Bible talk about His hands? The only way we can understand the Infinite whose ways are so much higher than ours is to express ideas about Him in our own terms. Imagine Him weighing all the earth's mountains on scales. (Set out the scale you brought.)

What is the answer to the questions in verses 13 and 14? The answer is no one, no one at all.

How do whole nations appear to God, in verses 15 to 17, RSV? What islands in this earth could He take up like fine dust? "Less than nothing and emptiness" are strong words.

Then God ridicules one of the silliest things that human beings have ever done. Read about it in verses 18 and 20. Why is it so silly?

Instead of tiny ants, what are humans compared to in verses 21 to 23? What are called "nothing" in 23?

When God has completed His purpose with the rulers of this earth, what does He do with them? Verse 24.

When you think of God, do you see Him in control like this? Most people's God is too small, too small to control all things, too small to help them. How does He want us to think of Him? Verses 25, 26.

But this very greatness bothers some people. How does it bother them? They think He can't be interested in their little lives. What does He say about Himself? What is He ready to do for His people? What is our part? Verses 28-31.

Action

The Creator—Redeemer—Judge of the whole universe could easily force us to obey Him. But He has allowed us to have wills of our own, to decide whether we will try to make it on our own, or whether we will get in tune with Him.

Suppose you, a human being, would say to a tiny ant, "I'll protect you and work with you if you will fit into my plans." Would it be sensible for the ant to do this? Will you be caught up into God's great purposes for our universe, or will you say to Him, "You're too big, too high, too far away from me"?

Because He is who He is and we have set up a connection with Him through Christ, what do you want to say to Him? To ask Him?

Let's sing "He's Got the Whole World in His Hands," including "He's got *our family* in His hands."

God's Power and Deliverance

WHEN RECENTLY did you feel most frustrated? Many of us are most bothered by situations we don't like but can do nothing about. What causes these difficulties? Maybe the laws of our school or our business or our government, or other people's ideas or power. If those of us who are frustrated get together and rebel, what happens? Often many people get hurt. There are some things we just have to learn to live with, that can't be changed.

But if we're a part of God's great plans for this universe, what can we expect to happen? When recently have we heard that God delivered His people who trusted Him? Jerry planned all winter to spend the summer on his uncle's ranch. He was so disappointed when he was too sick to go at the time his plane was scheduled to leave. Later he learned that this flight crashed in the mountains. Then he felt delivered rather than disappointed. Our disappointments are God's appointments. Or sometimes God delivers by letting His children narrowly escape an accident. I'm sure we don't even know all the trouble the Lord delivers us from. Since nothing is too hard for the Lord, He delivers us whenever we are part of His plans.

Alice, show us your pictures now; Alice has put markers in her Bible storybook at the pictures that show the Lord using His great power.

How can we expect the Lord to use His power to deliver us? Let's look at one outstanding example in the Old Testament and one in the New.

Deliverance from Egypt—Psalm 106:7-12

In the Old Testament God's people were worn out from working very hard as slaves in Egypt. They wanted to leave that country, but the king wanted them to keep working for him. What did God do to make the king let them leave? He sent many plagues until the king said "Go." The people were very glad to get out, but when they came to the Red Sea and saw that they were trapped, what didn't they do and what did they do? Turn to Psalm 106:7.

If the Lord had been a human person, no doubt He would have left them then and there. But why did He save them? Verse 8.

Verses 9 and 10 tell how He saved them. Imagine making a dry path through a rushing stream of water! What happened to the Egyptians in verse 11?

Finally how did the people respond to God as they should have? Verse 12.

So God brought them to Himself and gave them a land of their own. In their own land when problems arose, what should they have learned to do? Trust God to deliver them.

Christ's Resurrection—Ephesians 1:19-23

In the New Testament God gave His people another great demonstration of His power. Look at Ephesians 1. In verse 19 what does the writer Paul want the church at Ephesus to know about God's power? Where does He want to display His power today—read those important four words. "In us who believe" (RSV).

What kind of power is available to us today? 20. The same power that raised Christ from the dead!

Where is Christ now? 20, 21. This is the seat of power over the whole earth. Over what does Christ have control now? 22, 23.

Jim, will you please read this section, Ephesians 1:19-23, stressing with your voice the amazing power of Christ's resurrection so that we'll feel the force of it?

Action

To think that this tremendous power is ours to draw on! God wants to deliver us from all sin that would hurt and weaken us. To which of His people can He give this power? To no one who will use it selfishly or irresponsibly, but to those who carry out His purposes in His way.

In what ways does the Lord need to deliver our family? Are we sure that this deliverance is part of His plan? Sometimes we have to wait for His timing, which is always best. At least we can ask Him. He works "in us who believe." Do we believe that He is able to do what we are asking? And what other people we know need His deliverance? Let's also ask Him about these. For what past deliverance should we thank Him?

God's Holiness

OUR WORLD is in a pretty sorry state today. Even when many people are trying hard to improve it, humans are polluting land and sea, and worse yet, they are hurting each other. Don't you believe that many of our leaders are doing their best? Yet things seem to be worse rather than better. Can you explain why? What's wrong with the world? What are the weaknesses of human nature that we see in our community and in nations? Yes, people are selfish, they lie, they cheat, steal, are unjust, unkind.

What if the control of this vast universe were in the hands of a weak human being even though he tried to do good? Still he would have the weaknesses of being human. I'm thankful that no mortal man will have the last word, that no mortal man is the supreme Ruler, aren't you? What kind of person does the One in control need to be? He needs to be holy, perfect, just, pure. In your mind can you see the white light of God's holiness, that breaks up into all the colors? What kind of Ruler, Judge, King is the Lord God? Look at Psalm 9:8.

Even though we live in a country with a president and a congress, some of us have voluntarily put ourselves under the rule of still another, a holy God. What difference does this make? What difference does it make that our citizenship is in heaven as well as on earth? We must still obey the laws of our country, but there is a difference. Yes, our country may not give us a fair deal, but if we do everything as unto the Lord and take everything from Him, what does He say He will do? Yes, make everything work together for good, for moving us toward Christlikeness (Romans 8:28). He will see that we eventually get individual justice.

Approaching Our Holy God

Do you remember that back in the Old Testament the tabernacle had a holy place and a holy of holies that most people couldn't enter? Who could go into the holy place with its golden candlestick, its table of fresh showbread, and its altar of incense? Only the priest, who was dedicated to the Lord. And who could go into the holy of holies? Only the high priest. How often? Only once a year. For what purpose? To offer the blood of an animal on the mercy seat for the sins of the people. Sinful beings cannot approach our holy God without a blood sacrifice. Since all of us have sinned, why don't we offer blood sacrifices on altars in our churches?

Christ our sacrifice has been offered for us (1 Corinthians 5:7). Turn to Hebrews 10:4, 5, and see how you would say that truth in your own words. God prepared a body for His own holy Son so that He could give that body on the cross for us. Sue, will you please read the way Good News for Modern Man expresses Hebrews 10:11-14? Since Christ is also God and holy, He only could take the punishment that all of us deserve for our sins.

Because the Lord is holy, things related to the Lord are also holy. What things are they? Yes, His Book, His name, His day, and His Spirit who lives in His people. Because His Spirit is holy, what else does God say is holy in 1 Peter 1:16? How can He ask us to be holy when He knows that we can't be perfect? We can become more and more holy until finally when we see Him, the process will be finished, we'll be like Him! We don't get discouraged if we see that we're constantly making progress.

Relating to Our Holy God

The Old Testament priest had these words engraved on the front of his special cap: Holy to the Lord (Exodus 28:36, 37). Without these written words on us, can we still show people what kind of God we belong to? How can we? Do you know Romans 12:1 by heart? Quote it, Jim. How do we do that? It is only reasonable to give ourselves back to Him who gave Himself for us when we see who He is.

There is something else that a holy Person deserves from those whom He governs. He deserves our worship. As I read Psalm 99 (expressively) in The Living Bible, bow your head each time you hear the word "holy." Why should the nations tremble and shake before Him? A holy Person must punish sin unless people ask forgiveness. Holiness is the opposite of sin. How else does this psalm describe God? He is supreme above all rulers, He is great, He is fair and just, He is to be exalted, He speaks to His people and answers them.

As Mother reads this psalm, in our hearts let's thank Him that we are in the hands of this kind of Person.

God's Wisdom

HOW DREADFUL would be God's great power if He weren't wise enough to use it rightly! Think of human beings who have misused power to destroy, not help, others. Yes, we think of Hitler and Stalin who took the lives of many other people. What they are accountable for!

Why is it that God can be so much wiser than men? Yes, because He made everything, He keeps everything going, sees the end from the beginning, is carrying out His own purposes, is working for the good of everybody concerned, loves everything He made, etc.

Psalm 104

What does this world that God made tell us about His wisdom? The psalmist says in Psalm 104:24, "O Lord, how manifold are thy works! in wisdom hast thou made them all." So in verse 1 he sings, "Bless the Lord, O my soul! O Lord my God, Thou art very great."

What things that God created does he appreciate most? He mentions the wind, mountains and valleys, springs of water, plants, birds, animals, sun and moon, great and small fish. What would this earth be like if any one of these things were missing? The plants, for instance, or the animals?

Of all the things that God has made, what seems most wonderful, most wise to you? Let's each tell why we selected what we did. To me the human brain seems most marvelously wise. Though we are frail human creatures we can actually think God's thoughts after Him. Our brains consist of soft folds of gray and white matter and millions of minute connections that can give directions and receive directions from the rest of our bodies so that we react as a whole. Even the wisest scientists cannot explain just how the brain works. Neither can they create life or as yet cure cancer. A human person is fearfully and wonderfully made! And God thought it all up as well as created it. How great is His wisdom!

Verses from Proverbs

The Book of Proverbs has a lot to say about being wise. Here is a verse or two or three from Proverbs for each of us. Read your verse or verses, say the ideas in your own words, and think of one way to obey this verse. I'll write these directions on the chalkboard. We'll take a minute to study by ourselves, then we'll each have a turn to share our findings. If this book that I'm reading has ideas that we don't have, I'll add them.

Father: Proverbs 9:9, 10. If a man is wise, he is never satisfied, for he knows there is much more to learn. Wise people are also righteous, for they know how stupid it is to do wrong. Wisdom is based on worship of the Lord, for no one has basic understanding who doesn't know the Holy One. A way to obey these verses is to get one new truth from the Lord each day.

Mother: Proverbs 4:12, 13. The wise man goes straight to his goal letting nothing hinder him, and even when he is in a hurry, he gets there without difficulty. Get all the learning you can; don't let it escape you, for it results in a full life. I want to do this by reading more books from our church library.

Jim: Proverbs 4:25-27. Keep your eyes directed to your goal, and watch the steps you take to get there so that you won't stumble. Don't let any evil temptation divert you from your purpose. I can't let sports keep me from getting grades high enough to get into college.

Sue: Proverbs 6:6-8. If you're inclined to be lazy, watch the little ant work. Though no one is bossing her, she wisely prepares her food in summer and stores it away in the fall. I should do my homework without being prodded all the time.

Ted: Proverbs 24:5. A wise man who knows a lot can be mightier than a man who is physically strong because by his wise ideas he can outfox the strong muscles. I gotta use my head more in baseball.

Alice: Proverbs 20:11. Even a child can be known as a wise child if he or she does what is good and right. I have to take smaller pieces of cake so I won't leave any of it.

Action

Can we think of recent times when the members of our family have been wise? I thank God that Alice was wise enough to phone me when she couldn't get home as early as I expected her. I would have worried if she hadn't. And do you remember that Ted picked up all the broken glass before the car drove into the driveway?

In what ways do we need the Lord's help to be wiser than we are naturally? Sometimes it's very difficult to know which is the best of several things we might do, and sometimes nothing we can think of seems wise. But the Lord sees the future as well as the past, He is able to change things, and He knows what other people will do when we don't.

> But if any of you lacks wisdom,
> he should pray to God,
> who will give it to him;
> for God gives generously and graciously to all.
>
> James 1:5, TEV

God's Beauty

IN ALL the world of nature that God has made, what do you think is the most beautiful? Maybe other people don't think it is so wonderful, but what seems most beautiful to you? Help us to see why you enjoy it so much. God has created amazing things in this world!

When He created human nature, human beings, He meant for them to be the highest order of creation, the most beautiful, the most wonderful of all. For He made people like Himself, and He combines in Himself all the perfections of all good things. Notice all that is said about the Lord in Psalms 96:6-9, especially His beauty (read these verses slowly from the King James Version, which expresses the ideas very clearly).

Read these verses in your version, Jim.

Shut your eyes and contrast two pictures: one of street violence with angry people trying to hurt each other, and the second picture of a scene in church when all God's people are bowed before Him asking Him to make them like Him. They are saying, ". . . let the beauty of the LORD our God be upon us" (Psalm 90:17).

God's Beauty in His People

On this earth we see much in people that is not beautiful, but sometimes we catch glimpses of God's beauty in His people. Let's look at examples of God's beauty in Bible people and then see if we have noticed these same kinds in any people today.

1. Lot and his uncle Abram both had large numbers of flocks and herds and tents and servants to take care of them. Their herdsmen began to quarrel because they both wanted the same rich pasture land for their flocks. How did Abram reflect the beauty of the Lord in the way he solved this problem? Read Genesis 13:8, 9. But what happened to selfish Lot, who chose the best well-watered land? This land was near the very wicked city of Sodom, which the Lord had to destroy.

How was the beauty of the Lord shown in Abram? He was not selfish; he let Lot have his choice. When have you noticed unselfishness in some person today? The beauty of the Lord can be upon us.

2. Joseph's brothers sold him to a caravan going to Egypt and let their old father believe that an animal had killed him. Later when he was ruler and the brothers came to Egypt for food, he could have gotten even with them. What did he do instead? Read Genesis 45:7, 8 and 15. What quality of the Lord his God was he an example of? Have you seen someone today forgiving and returning good for evil?

3. When David and Jonathan were young men, they loved each other so much that when David became king and found that Jonathan had a son who was lame, what did he do? Read 2 Samuel 9:1 and 7. Do you know anyone recently who has showed special kindness to someone else?

4. When the king of Babylon was considering Daniel for the highest office in the land, the other high officers were jealous of him and tried to find something that he did wrong. When they could find nothing, do you remember what they

did to accuse Daniel? They got the king to make a law that no one could pray to anyone but to the king himself. Then what did Daniel do? Read Daniel 6:10. The king was very sad, but what had he promised would happen to anyone who disobeyed the law? How was the beauty of the Lord seen in Daniel? Do you know anyone today who has obeyed the Lord even when it was very hard to do so?

5. When Jesus' enemies were planning to kill Him because they were jealous of Him, what did a woman do who loved Him very much? Read Matthew 26:7. What did the disciples say about this? Verses 8 and 9. But what did Jesus say? 10. Do you know of anything unusual that someone has done because he loved Jesus very much?

Action

Did we see the beauty of the Lord in anyone in this house this last week? I knew the Lord prompted Sue to take time to read to Alice when she wanted to be doing her own homework.

Which people we know look beautiful to us? Is it only the ones with good-looking features and clothes? Sue and Mother were talking about a new neighbor they saw in a yard across the street. "I thought she looked beautiful," remarked Sue.

"That's strange," replied Mother, "I didn't. What was she doing when you saw her?"

Sue answered, "She was holding the baby up and smiling at her."

"Oh, that explains it," said Mother. "When I saw her, she was scolding her younger brother and threatening him."

We should say some of the things we say in front of a mirror, to get the effect. When do we most feel the need of the Lord's working His own loveliness in us? Notice the root of that word loveliness. Let's ask the Lord silently to show His beauty in us this week.

The Lord's Control of Events

IN THE Old Testament God chose the nation of Israel to show the world what He was like and to be the channel through which the Saviour of all mankind would be born in the fulness of time. Because He gave human beings wills of their own, Israel failed in the first purpose. Does the nation of Israel today reflect the Lord? No, He has had to scatter the Jewish people all over the earth and let them endure great suffering. Recently He has brought them back to their own land, and some day they will acknowledge their Messiah, Christ Jesus. In spite of Israel, God carried out His second purpose; the Saviour was born from the line of David.

In our day what is the Lord's overall purpose? He is building His church, the body of Christ. Do we know whether or not it will succeed? In spite of all its weaknesses Christ promised that the gates of hell shall not prevail against the church (Matthew 16:18). He lets evil proceed just so far and then He steps in. The greatest question for us today is: How are we relating to His plans? Are we cooperating wholeheartedly with Him, are we apathetic toward His working, or are we rebelling against Him?

And it isn't a question of our own individual lives only, for none of us lives to himself. We each influence others. Again and again we read either that the kings after David did what was right in the sight of the Lord as David had done, or they walked in the way of his son Jeroboam who made Israel sin. Which people have had a good influence on your life, and which evil?

What happens to people who do not cooperate with God's overall plans?

Jehoram's Disobedience—2 Chronicles 21

Because King Jehoshaphat of Judah followed David and not Jeroboam, God blessed him with years of peace and victory when he needed to defend his country. But what were the results of letting his son Jehoram marry the daughter of wicked King Ahab and Queen Jezebel of Israel? Turn to 2 Chronicles 21. In verse 2 how many sons did King Jehoshaphat leave when he died?

In 3 how did he treat his sons?

In 4 when Jehoram was solidly established as king, what did he do? Why? Very likely because his brothers and the princes sided with good King Jehoshaphat instead of wicked King Ahab.

In 6 why did he insist on following Ahab rather than his own father? How disastrous was that marriage! How far-reaching its consequences!

If the Lord had been thinking only of this man, what would He have done, in 7? But again we see how David's influence continued.

Then what did two nearby nations that Judah had been ruling do? Jim, read verses 8-10. And notice the reason—not because they were stronger than Judah, but because God was controlling what happened to Jehoram.

In 11 what was he even leading his people in doing?

Mother, read in 12-15 the contents of a letter that this wicked king received from Elijah the prophet.

With that fatal disease rotting away his insides, what else took place outside to torment Jehoram, in 16, 17? All his personal possessions carried away!

In 18, 19 as he died in great agony, how did his people feel toward him? Usually the nation made quite an affair of mourning for their kings. Wouldn't it be awful for people to be glad when you were gone! He was not buried as usual in the royal cemetery.

Working With the Lord or Against Him?

Have we been aware of how God has controlled the events in our lives as a family? The first important event is the fact that we are a Christian family. Think of the many husbands and wives who do not love each other, and the dear children who come into this world unwanted and yet they didn't ask to be born. They don't know what real love is, they don't know what the Bible says, they have no Christian examples, they form bad habits rather than good ones. God has special things in store for children of Christian families. Abraham, Joseph, Moses, David, Daniel and many other outstanding people could do what they did because they had such a good start in life. What is our part in carrying out the Lord's plans?

What does our part depend on? Yes, being ready to hear God tell us our part and preparing to do it. Jehoram didn't read any of the signs that God gave him. He could have repented, and switched over to following David. The Lord has purposes for all that He ordains. Have we understood all the circumstances that He has arranged for us?

Our part depends on the spiritual gifts He has given us. Have we used them this last week? To help the relatives and friends He has given us? What did we learn from them this last week? How did we help the community we live in? What is our family's influence here where we live? How has God used our strengths? Have we trusted Him to make His strength perfect in our weakness?

Sometimes when we meet opposition, it's hard to tell whether the Lord is closing a door to us or whether the enemy is putting up a barricade that we should plough through.

"Lord, we're so glad we can take everything from You and do everything to You. Help us to discern Your purpose in all our circumstances and take our place in Your great plans."

The Necessity of God's Word

IN THE basements of many school buildings are piles of old books that have been used, but have now been replaced by new ones. Why do school books and most other kinds of books become outdated? New knowledge is being discovered all the time. Only one Book is never out-of-date, the best seller of all time. Why is that? It was written by the Creator, who began all things and will bring all things to an end.

Since this one Book relates equally to all nations, the only way all the people of the world will be brought together is by accepting this Word of the Creator of all. Think of all the ways in which people disagree with each other. This world is full of disagreements. We don't have peace because people have such different ideas about how to get it. Can you think of anything important that everyone agrees on? What are some of the other things that people differ on? Yes, God, salvation, heaven, evolution, divorce, government, laws, pollution, punishing wrongdoing, how to change things you don't like, etc.

Some people even say there is no right or wrong, that everyone should do what he thinks best just so he doesn't hurt other people. Is there anything that is right for everyone, that is absolute, that is truth? The Creator of the universe, the One who is in control, says there is. But we would never know why He made this world or how it should be used unless He had written to tell us. Because we can't see Him, we would never know what kind of Person He is if He had not told us.

How would you answer a friend who says that he has his way of doing things and you can have yours—each person to his own way? The Creator of this universe is also the Judge, who will test every man's work, and He tests it by the Book He has given. What should God's Word do for us?

What God's Word Does—Nehemiah 8

For years God's people had forgotten His Book. When they went their own way instead of God's ways, they had been carried away captive to another land where they never felt at home. Then some of them returned to their own land to rebuild the house of God and city walls to protect the city. After the wall was completed, it was time to get God's viewpoint on their life in the city. The priests were called to read God's Book and a platform was built for them to stand on so that all the people could see and hear.

Turn to Nehemiah 8:5. When Ezra the priest opened the book of the law, what did all the people do?

When he blessed the Lord, what did they do? Verse 6.

How did the leaders help the people? 8.

What did the people do when they heard the words of God? 9. Why do you think they wept? They hadn't been doing what it said.

But what did Ezra tell the people to do instead of weep? 10, 11. Why?

Did the people do that? 12. Yes, because they understood God's words.

As they studied the Book, they discovered something that they were not doing that God had told them to do. 13-17. They had a great festival camping out in leafy booths for a whole week! "There was very great rejoicing" (RSV).

And what did they do every day of the week? 18. That's what the Word of God did for His people.

Why Every Day?

Will we go our own way and get into trouble, or go on our way rejoicing because we are obeying God's Word?

Is it necessary to hear God's Word every day, not only every day for one week, but for every day of the whole year—365 days? Why is it? The Bible is a guidebook to keep us on the right track. Because we are sinful human creatures, we naturally get off the track and go our own way. The Bible is like a map that we follow on our journey through life. Do you remember when we took the wrong road going to Grandfather's and didn't get there in time for the good dinner Grandmother had ready for us? A map shows us where we want to go and how to get there. Also how to get back to the right road when we get off it. We have to keep checking as we go. It's so much harder to get back on the right road than to go straight there in the first place.

Do you have any questions about what God says is right or wrong? This time of the day when our family is together is the time to talk about God's ways and to decide which of men's ways are also God's ways. God wants us to understand His ways clearly. Let's ask Him to make all His best ways plain to us.

Being Doers of the Word

(ASK ALICE ahead of time to draw two pictures of Matthew 7:24-27—a
house upon a rock that is standing amid flood and wind, and another upon
sand that has crumbled to the ground. Ask Ted to practice reading Matthew
7:24-27 as Alice shows the pictures.)

In family devotions Sam was very quick. He memorized easily, he had heard
Bible stories since he was very young, and he knew many truths from God's
Word. One morning he easily rattled off the words, "Be kind to one another,
tenderhearted, forgiving one another." After devotions his mother heard him
shout to his younger brother, "You cheat! You messed up my airplane parts
that I was building! I'll get even with you!" How did the Lord view that boy
that day?

In family devotions Nancy seemed to know more right answers than the
other children. One morning she delivered quite a mini-sermon on trusting the
Lord. "Yes," she said, agreeing with God's Word, "we ought to trust God no
matter what happens, even if things don't look right to us." That afternoon her
friends had planned a picnic. The sun was bright and warm in the morning,
but in the afternoon it began to rain. "Oh shucks," she pouted, "the rain is
going to spoil all our fun. Why didn't the Lord keep the sun shining?" How did
the Lord view that girl that day?

Which is harder, knowing what the Word of the Lord says, or doing it?
Doing is much harder. How easy it is to say the words, "Do all things without
grumbling . . ." (Philippians 2:14, RSV), but how easy is it to live without
complaining?

One reason that many unbelievers don't come to Christ is that they see so
many people who claim to be Christians but who don't follow Christ. These
Christians say, "Yes, I believe God's Word," but they don't do what it says.

Knowing What God Says

What does God say about knowing and doing His Word? We know one verse,
don't we: ". . . be ye doers of the word, and not hearers only . . ." (James 1:22).
Look up James 4:17. Whenever we don't do what we know God tells us to do,
He calls that *sin*. Sin is not to be taken lightly. Turn also to Luke 11:28.

Now look at Matthew 7:21. What does Jesus say even about some people
who call Him Lord? How would you feel if on the last great judgment day
Jesus said to you what He said to those in verses 22 and 23? People today
might say, "Lord, you know I went to church most of the time, I gave money
to the church, I did many good deeds in Your name." But Jesus may say, "You
never gave Me your real inner self. I never really knew you. Now go away, evil-
doers." Wouldn't that be dreadful!

Ted, please read verses 24-27 as Alice shows the pictures she drew of these
two houses. Either great was the fall of one house, or the other did not fall
because it was built on the rock of God's truth.

Let's make up a modern story about two boys who listened to God's Word
and obeyed it when they were at home with their family. But when they went
away, they found that most boys their age did not obey God; they did just what

they felt like doing. These two boys were tempted by the wicked things that the other boys were doing. What happened to the one boy who obeyed God? He became stronger. What happened to the other one who fell into temptation? Yes, he began to drink and take drugs, became weaker and weaker, until the family hardly knew him when he came home.

Doing What God Says

It's a serious thought that the more we know about God's Word, the more responsible we are to do everything we know. When one girl realized that, she said, "Oh, my, let's not find out anything more!" How should we feel about this truth?

A Chinese woman learned to read so that she could read the Bible. A pastor helped her and kept checking on how far she had read. She started out fine, but then she said she got stuck.

"What are you stuck on?" asked the pastor.

The woman replied, "It says here that we are blessed when people talk against us falsely. I don't feel happy when people talk against me, so I can't read on till I feel right about this."

This woman was sticking with this one verse until she could live it. What would our family be like if we lived every word of God that we read and talk about?

"But," you say, "that's too hard. God expects so much of us!" Yes, He does. How can He justly expect that much? Turn to Philippians 4:13. Because He is ready to give us His own divine power to obey His Word. The most important thing is whether or not we really want to please Him, whether or not we really mean business with Him. He doesn't expect the impossible of us, and we can work on one thing at a time. We can concentrate on one thing this week, and another next week.

What word of God seems hard for you to obey right now? Let's ask Him for His power to overcome in this respect.

Looking to the Lord

WHEN SUE changed from the elementary school to the junior high school, she passed a liquor store four times a day, going and coming in the morning, and going and coming in the afternoon. At first she looked the other way when she thought of all the accidents and tragedies caused by people who drink. But as she came and went, she soon got used to all the bottles and attractive signs in the window, and just took the liquor store for granted.

At first when Ted saw children in his room at school cheating on their papers and taking things from stores after school, he was horrified. But since he didn't want to be a tattletale, he tried to look the other way and forget what he saw. What did that do to him? He formed the habit of doing nothing about things that were wrong.

How do you suppose children feel who grow up in a neighborhood where there are always plenty of bottles, pieces of glass, pieces of paper and rubbish on the streets and in the empty lots? They look at the mess and think nothing of it. That's just the way it is. But if your neighborhood is always neat and trim, if people keep their lawns mowed and grow flowers, what do you naturally do if you see a piece of paper on the ground?

What do you often see that you don't like? First think about TV. What do you see so often on the tube that you just accept it, even if it isn't good? Do you see anything so often that it seems as real as what happens right here in your house? What do you see at school that you don't like? In this community? Even at church? Even here at home? And finally what do you see in yourself that you don't like? Are we going to accept these things? When evil is in us and all around us, what can we do to keep our thoughts from being polluted?

What Shall We Look At?

1. If we don't want to look at evil until we accept it or become evil ourselves, what shall we look at? Turn to 2 Corinthians 4:18 to find an answer to this question. How does this verse help us? It's so much easier to look at the things that are seen. How can we look at the things that are unseen? It's hard to picture the Lord God, but Jesus showed us what He is like. Where else do we see the Lord? Yes, in the Bible and in God's people when they reflect Him. In your mind's eye see the glorious throne of the Father God and Jesus sitting beside Him clothed in light. See Him watching and controlling the whole world.

2. From God's viewpoint in the unseen world that is just as real as this world, what kind of people do we often seem to be? Look at Isaiah 42:18-20. When are we often deaf? When God wants to speak to us from His Book, we don't hear. What sorts of things are we blind to? We don't see what He is doing or ways to work with Him.

3. Psalm 123:1, 2 gives an illustration of how we can look to the Lord. Servants don't understand all that their masters have in mind, so they keep watching them for cues as to what they should do. So we keep looking to the Lord to be sure we are catching all His signals.

What Happens When We Look to the Lord?

In the Old Testament when the people of Israel were in the wilderness, they complained about the lack of food and water. To punish them the Lord sent fiery snakes to bite the people (Numbers 21:4-9). When they said they were sorry for their sin, what did the Lord tell Moses to do in Numbers 21:8? In verse 9 what did the people who were bitten need to do in order to live? Only look.

In the New Testament what did Jesus use the bronze snake on the pole to illustrate? Read John 3:14-16. What picture does that make you see in your mind? The wonderful Son of God lifted up on the cruel cross to take the punishment that we deserve! When we see how He loved us and gave Himself for us, we respond by loving Him and giving ourselves to Him.

After we are saved, how are we changed from selfishness into the likeness of Christ? Turn to 2 Corinthians 3:18. When do we have open faces without a veil on them? When there is nothing between us, when we feel right toward God. Just as in a mirror, when we see in God's Word what a magnificent Person He is, what happens to us? We are gradually changed into His likeness because the Spirit of God does His inner work in our hearts. The more we look into His Word and think about Him, the more we become like Him. Let's think about these words as I read them again slowly.

Have you been thinking about the Lord only at times when our family meets together? When else do you look to Him? Do you come to Him with open face, with nothing between you and Him? Let's ask Him to help us remember to look to Him whenever we have a special joy or a need.

God's Presence

(THREE SONGS are suggested today. Two are old favorites that you may know well—the chorus of "No, Never Alone" and "I Need Thee Every Hour." If you aren't as familiar with "In the Secret of His Presence," you may want to provide songbooks or typed words.)

At night after the lights are turned off, don't you sometimes talk to the person in the next bed or in the next room? You are in the presence of this other person though you can't see him. How do you sense his presence, know that he is not asleep? He hears you and he responds to you even if you can't see him. Isn't it amazing to think that the same Person who rules this whole world can be present with each of us, each one of us! No one but the Lord God could be like this!

This is a secret that some people know nothing about. Jim, will you please read Psalm 91:1, 2 in the King James Version? And Sue, Psalms 31:20 in the same version. I have typed the words of the song that go with this Bible verse so that we can all sing them:

> In the secret of His presence, how my soul delights to hide!
> Oh, how precious are the lessons which I learn at Jesus' side!
> Earthly cares can never vex me, neither trials lay me low;
> For when Satan comes to tempt me, to the secret place I go.

The first time Ted was chosen to play a Little League game, he was delighted that his father was interested enough to come to the game. Although his father could not do more to help him than to cheer lustily, Ted knew he was up there in the bleachers, and he was conscious of his presence the whole afternoon. He did his best in the presence of his father.

How is the presence of the heavenly Father different from the presence of our earthly Father?

What Difference Does the Heavenly Father's Presence Make to Us?

1. Alice, find Genesis 28:15 and read the first part of this verse; it has been one of your memory verses. Your earthly father can't be with you much of the time. What difference does it make that your heavenly Father can always be with you? Let's sing the chorus, "No, Never Alone."

When the Lord asked Moses to do something hard, to lead His people out of Egypt, how did the Lord assure him that it wouldn't be too hard, in Exodus 33:14? And how did Moses reply in verse 15? Haven't we often felt that way—"Lord, if You don't go with us, we just can't go"?

2. What kind of experiences do we have in God's presence? Fill in the words that I leave out, the most important words in Psalm 16:11 RSV:

> Thou dost show me the path of life;
> in thy presence there is fulness of joy,
> in thy right hand are pleasures for evermore.

What kind of joys and pleasures does the Lord give? Not the kind that lasts just for a day and may leave a bad taste afterward. But the kind that lasts—people being changed from those that hurt to those that help, people doing hard things in the power of the Lord.

And when we finish this earthly life, what can we look forward to? Jude 24.

3. When we are in the presence of the Lord, what does He do for us? Isaiah 41:10. At any time, day or night, He is ready to strengthen, help and uphold.

When Can't We Count on His Presence?

If we ever feel far away from the Lord, that He doesn't hear us or answer us, what is probably the reason? Look at Isaiah 59:1, 2. Read it in The Living Bible, Sue. Our sins cut us off from God, separate us from Him, raise a barrier between us and God. If we can look to Him with an open face, with nothing to hide, and have a quarrel with Him over nothing, we will no doubt feel Him near.

How dreadful it would be if the Lord banished us forever after we had sinned, or even kept us from His presence for a month or a week! When we have sinned, a good prayer to use is found in Psalm 51. Let's look now at verses 10 to 12. In verse 10 notice the emphasis on what goes on inside us—in our heart, our thoughts, our desires.

In verse 11 what does the sinner dread?

In 12 when he is restored to the presence of the Lord, what else can happen?

If you want to be sure of God's presence, that there's nothing between you and God, repeat after me each of these lines from The Living Bible:

> Create in me a new, clean heart, O God,
> filled with clean thoughts and right desires.
> Don't toss me aside,
> banished forever from your presence.
> Don't take Your Holy Spirit from me.
> Restore to me again the joy of your salvation,
> and make me willing to obey you.
> Psalm 51:10-12 LB

Shall we close by singing "I Need Thee Every Hour"?

Worship of God

WHEN WE human creatures realize who we are and who the great Lord God of heaven and earth is, what is our natural first response? He is holy, He is perfect love, He is all powerful, He knows everything! We are weak, we are sinful, we hate and destroy. Therefore what does the Lord God deserve from us? Worship is acknowledging that He is worthy of our praise, our love, our adoration. When He does so very much for us, aren't we glad that there is something we can do to please Him? We can never repay Him for all He has done for us, but we can worship Him.

Think of a high worship experience that you have had, when you felt very close to the Lord, you appreciated Him so much in your inner being, maybe you expressed your feelings in some way or maybe you just enjoyed Him inside. This worship may have come at home, at church, in God's world of nature, or with particular people. Let's each mention what this special worship experience was like.

Isaiah's Call—Isaiah 6:1-8

If our God is not too small, we see Him in His glorious majesty. Turn to Isaiah 6:1. Good King Uzziah had ruled God's people for many years and had strengthened the kingdom. When he died, Isaiah was afraid that the next king would not be so good. With the thought of this empty throne, he looked above it to a much greater throne that was not empty. How did he see the Lord? The seraphim are some of the heavenly creatures that surround the throne of God. What did they call to each other? Verse 3.

In Isaiah's vision what effect did the voice of Him who called seem to have on our material world? 4.

When Isaiah caught this vision of the heavenly court scene, how did it make him feel? 5. We picture him bowing low before such majesty, for when we humans see the glory of the Lord, we naturally bow down, for we know what a great gap there is between His holiness and our sin.

How did Isaiah dare lift his eyes? Say in your own words what happened in verses 6 and 7. How can we today be lifted up when we too ought to bow low in worship? Who has bridged the gap for us? Yes, Christ in His death has taken away our guilt and forgiven our sin. He has made us accepted in the Beloved so that we can come directly to the Father.

When Isaiah's sin had been forgiven, what question did the Lord ask, and how did Isaiah answer? 8.

Let's show by our postures what happens in worship. First we bow our heads low on the ground before the dazzling holiness of the Lord. Then we raise our eyes to see Christ dying on the cross for our sins and we ask Him to forgive us. That allows us to stand on our feet, as accepted children of God. Finally we raise our arms to ask God how He wants us to serve with Him.

Psalms of Worship

The psalms in the Bible help us express our thoughts and feelings in beautiful language. Here is a psalm or part of one for each of you to practice reading and then read expressively to the rest of us. Tell us also what you especially appreciate about these notes of praise.

Alice	Psalms 47:1, 2
Ted	100
Sue	92:1-5
Jim	98:1-4
Mother	103:1-5
Father	96:1-6

If there is worship in our hearts, let's sing "O Worship the King."

Composing Our Own Worship Psalm

How do you feel right now about the Lord? Think of a beautiful way to express this feeling.

Let's decide which of these ideas we want to include in our own family psalm, and I'll write them on this paper. Now let's acknowledge what kind of Person the Lord has been to us. What else shall we thank Him for, as a family? Let's conclude with individual notes of praise and worship.

As I read our whole psalm, see if any part of it sounds awkward. How can we make it sound more poetic? Using our own psalm will mean more to the Lord than reading someone else's. Maybe we would like to start our family devotions with this psalm for several days.

When you have a high worship experience with the Lord, why don't you put down on paper how you feel and read it to the rest of us?

Phony Worship

SUE WENT to church with her family as usual, but her mind wasn't on what happened there. Her mind was on the quarrel that she had just had with Ellen, her best friend. They had had such good times together, buying new dresses, swimming at the beach. How could they make up when Ellen had been so unreasonable, she thought. Sue sang the words of the hymn with everyone else in church, but she wasn't thinking about the words. When the pastor led in prayer, she prayed only about Ellen. She couldn't have told you a thing the pastor said in the sermon. Since she looked very serious, nobody knew that she wasn't worshiping—nobody, that is, except God. What would He be thinking about Sue that morning? Did she worship at all? Was the Lord pleased with her prayer? Would He answer it? What was missing? She was wholly occupied with herself. She didn't get a glimpse of the Lord, she didn't acknowledge who He is, she didn't get His viewpoint, didn't ask Him what she should do or ask for forgiveness for her part of the quarrel. She just selfishly wanted her own way. She was communing with herself rather than with God. What did going to church that morning profit her? Very little.

In church that morning Sue's worship was phony, not real. Nobody likes a phony. What else have you noticed about some Christians that is not real? Even in church people sometimes say, "Yes, Lord, what You say is right." Then at home how easy is it to obey that truth? It's very hard.

What God Says about Phony Worship

Turn to Amos 5:21-23 to see how the Lord feels about people who go to church because it makes them look good, and go through the motions of worshiping Him. His language is very strong here: "I hate your show and pretense. I won't accept your music!" What does God want? Look at verse 4 in this chapter.

Now turn to Isaiah 29:13-17. What are the reasons why God hates phony worship? Have you ever praised God with your lips while your heart was far from Him, thinking about something else? How can we be sure that our hearts inside are singing what our lips outside are singing? We can think about the words before we sing them. In church we can take our hymnbooks as soon as we sit down and read the words of the songs listed in the bulletin. We can ask ourselves, "Do I really mean those words?" At home we'll try not to suggest songs unless we are ready inside to mean the words. If any of you can't honestly sing them, let's discuss why not. What does the Lord imply when He says He doesn't like our religion to be a commandment of men learned by rote? Instead of going through a routine ritual, He wants to have personal relations with us.

In verse 14 instead of wise men doing marvelous things with God, what will happen to them?

Because these wise men don't know who God is, how are they wrong in their thinking? 15.

In 16 how are they turning things upside down? They are acting as if they are the potter and the Lord the clay instead of the other way round. They are pretending that God is the kind of God they want, with no understanding, that they can control.

Keeping Our Worship Real

Where does God look for our worship? He wants our whole being to praise Him. But where does praise start? It must start inside, or the words we say outwardly will be just empty words without meaning. If praise starts within, then our words please Him.

> Bless the LORD, O my soul:
> and all that is within me,
> bless His holy name.
> Psalm 103:1

Suppose sometimes we don't feel like praising when it's time for family worship. He knows that, so we may as well be open and honest and tell Him so. In that case what would He want us to do? As a family we can try to discover what is blocking the free expression of praise. Maybe that would take all the time we have together, but it would be good use of our time. If we have any question about the words of a song here at home, let's check them before we sing.

If you wonder about anything that is done at church, if anything at church is just going through the motions for you, ask us at home about it, and we'll talk about what it can mean. If you don't understand the pastor's sermon or it doesn't meet your personal need, what can you do? You can think about any point that you do understand or memorize a verse in your Bible or pray for the people who sit around you.

Let's ask the Lord to keep every part of our worship from becoming phony, sham, routine.

Psalm 103:1-5 is an excellent passage to memorize and use in worship.

What Praise Does for Us

SOME CHRISTIANS' lives are like waves of the sea, up and down, up and down. It all depends on circumstances, on what happens. When all goes according to their liking, they are up, happy, optimistic. When they don't like what happens, they are down, low, grouchy. Their lives look like this (draw a wavy line on the chalkboard).

When we allow ourselves to feel low, how does everything else look to us? We see the worst in everything, we look at the world through dark glasses and everything looks dark because of the way we feel. On the other hand, when we feel on top, how does everything look? We can tackle the hard things, so they don't look so bad; we expect the best of people rather than the worst; everything looks rosy through our rose-tinted glasses.

Is it easier to go down or to climb back up after we've been down? It's always hard to get back up. So—how can we keep up, without going down? The Lord wants even more for us than going along on an even keel, like this (draw a level line on the chalkboard). What does He want? He wants us to keep going up continually, like this (draw a line going up).

How can we keep going steadily up without letting things get us down?

A Battle Won by Praise—2 Chronicles 20:1-30

Though King Jehoshaphat made some bad mistakes, he tried to obey God. When news was brought to him that a great horde of enemy soldiers were invading his land, he was badly shaken. He realized that only the Lord was strong enough to conquer these armies. So he announced that all his people should go without eating in order to confess their sins to the Lord and ask Him for help. From all across the nation people streamed to the temple at Jerusalem to seek the Lord.

In the temple the king led his people in prayer. As Jim reads his prayer (5-12), see if you think the Lord was pleased with his attitude. Yes, he acknowledged the Lord's power and the nation's dependence upon Him.

What was the first thing the Lord did in answer to this prayer? 13-14.

How did the man in the Spirit cheer up the people? 15.

What did the Lord tell them to do in verse 16?

But what was most amazing about the Lord's directions? 17. Put yourself in the place of those frightened people. How would you have felt when the Lord said, "You won't need to fight. Just stand still and see what I will do"? How could that possibly happen?

Verse 18 shows whether the people pooh-poohed that idea or whether they believed God. And some of the priests showed how strongly they believed, in 19.

What kind of leader did the king show himself to be in verse 20? The trusting leader that he should be.

How did the king and his officials decide to start their march early in the morning? 21. What a weird way to march into battle!

But at the moment the choir began to sing and praise, what happened? 22, 23.

So when the king's army reached the enemy, what did they find? 24, 25. How many soldiers escaped? How many days did it take them to cart away all the booty? What a victory!

Did the people then properly thank the Lord? 27, 28.

And how else did this victory help God's people? 29, 30. That's what praise does for the people of God!

Winning Our Battles by Praise

With this paper and pencil I'm giving you, each of you make a list of the things for which you praise God right now.

Now on the back of the paper list those things that have recently happened that you haven't thanked God for, because you didn't like them. God's people didn't like it when hordes of enemies invaded their land.

On this second list cross off the things that were due to sin. Let's ask God to forgive these because we are truly sorry for them.

Will we let the things that are left get us down, or will we do what good King Jehoshaphat did? If we ask the Lord to undertake for us and tell us what to do about them, is it possible for us to praise Him for them? Honestly, not just with words but with our hearts? Let's see if it is possible.

For example, we don't like Ted to be sick. I don't know any reason why it is his fault. Do you, Ted? If we praise the Lord instead of griping, what possibly might happen? We don't always understand the Lord's higher ways, but maybe He wants Ted to be quiet for a bit and listen to Him. We don't see Ted quiet very often. Can you think of any other possibility?

When the car developed engine trouble which kept us at home, could we praise for that? Yes, we might have had an accident that day, and you remember that we would have missed Aunt Jane who stopped in if we had been gone.

Sue, have you been able to praise God for anything related to your quarrel with Ellen? Could it have made you more sensitive to other people, more appreciative of your friends, less self-centered?

"In everything give thanks, give thanks in all circumstances, give thanks whatever happens, for this is God's will for you who belong to Christ Jesus" (*see* 1 Thessalonians 5:18).

If we honestly can, let's thank God for whatever else we don't like right now, and ask Him to work it out for good.

Being Thankful

THE TWO children in the Harris family had much in common of course, but they were very different in one respect—Tina seemed by nature to be glum, grumpy, sour, while Nancy was naturally outgoing, cheerful, optimistic. Their parents tried to treat the two girls the same, for they loved them both the same, but it was difficult. Can you imagine why? When they went someplace, which girl was pleasant to have along? Nancy was a good companion, interested in everything she saw. When the parents thought of buying something the girls would like, which one did they think of first? Why? Nancy would be sure to like whatever the gift was and be thankful for it. Whenever a disappointment came along, which one would bog down in a slough of despond? Tina then wouldn't feel like doing anything.

Most of us aren't either so glum as Tina or so cheerful as Nancy, but which are we inclined to be? Our heavenly Father says to all of us, "Rejoice always, always be joyful, give thanks in all circumstances, be thankful no matter what happens" (*see* 1 Thessalonians 5:16, 18). Some of us have to work harder at this than others. Let's look at one of the psalms to see some of the reasons why we should always feel thankful; then maybe you can add other reasons.

Psalm 147

Let's read the first verse in our various versions. What does it do for us to voice words of praise like this?

Do we thank the Lord for the same things as the psalmist does? Have we been grateful for what he mentions in 2, 3? How can we be thankful when we're brokenhearted and wounded? Because the Lord heals and binds up our wounds. Why may the Lord allow us to be depressed?

Look also at verse 6. To understand what sin is, to be able to help others who are low, and to appreciate the joys of feeling on top of things. But our joys should greatly overshadow our sorrows.

Look at 4, 5 and 8, 9 together. What have these verses in common? Can you think of other ways in which God is great and all-powerful? Why is His understanding beyond our imagination? He can comprehend the vast expanse of the outer universe as well as the smallest thing that concerns each of us!

Therefore the psalmist breaks into praise in verse 7.

What contrast do you see in 10, 11? We can give pleasure to our God not by outer physical strength, which must seem very puny to Him, but by our inner attitude of reverence and trust. I'm thankful that there is something all of us humans can do to give pleasure to the Lord!

Instead of the Old Testament wording of verse 12, we can say, "Praise the Lord, O Christian! Praise our God, O Martin Family!"

Instead of thanking God for strengthening the bars of our gates, for what do we thank Him? 13. For keeping us safe here at home and when we're traveling on the highways. How has He blessed our sons and daughters recently?

Where have we seen peace in our world? 14. If no place else, we should at least experience peace here at home. He has also given us plenty of fine food.

The last verses of this psalm illustrate what His Word does. In 16, 17 what does His word do? It freezes things and makes them rigid. What in 18, 19? Jim, read verses 15-20 aloud to help us get the vivid effect. Are there cold hearts that He wants to melt here in our community? We who have God's Word can assist it in running quickly.

And the last idea in 20 is "Praise the Lord, He lets us work with Him!"

Continually Being Grateful

In addition to the things mentioned in the psalm, what else do you feel thankful for at the moment? The more thankful we are, the more ready we are to receive more from the Lord. He loves to give to those who are grateful and who use His gifts for His praise.

What don't you feel thankful for? Let's see if we can get God's viewpoint on these things. If we ask Him to take charge of us in relation to the whole universe, He does all things well (Mark 7:37), and He withholds no good thing from those who walk uprightly (Psalm 84:11). Of course if we're trying to manage our problems ourselves, we can't expect to claim the Lord's promises. But if we take everything from Him, there are good reasons for all that happens.

Let's each mention one thing we don't feel thankful for, if there is one thing, and see if the rest of us can catch at least a glimmer of gratitude in the situation.

When do we thank the Lord for all His goodness to us? If we wait until evening we forget many of the little things that happened during the day. If we thank Him immediately, we're in an attitude to receive the next thing He wants to send. If something doesn't seem like a good thing from our viewpoint, we can ask immediately what we should learn from it. If we don't have to learn the same lessons again and again the hard way, the difficult situation can perhaps be removed very soon.

"Dear Lord, help us form the habit of giving thanks no matter what happens. Help us to learn our lessons the joyous way in fellowship with You, not the hard way of struggling against Your love and care."

What Prayer Does for Us

SALLY AND Daisy were identical twins. Only the people who knew them well could tell them apart. Because they enjoyed each other very much, they were almost always together. So it was a great shock to Sally when Daisy died. She felt so all alone, with no one to talk to. At first she didn't feel like doing anything because it seemed as if half of her had also died. Can you imagine what pulled her out of this stupor? It was when she realized that she wasn't alone now, but that the Lord could always be with her just as Daisy had been, and that the Lord could do anything, much more than Daisy could do with her. And she could talk to Him just as she used to talk to Daisy.

Some people talk to the Lord only when they are in trouble or need something. Suppose you had a friend who came to you only when he wanted you to do something for him. How would you feel about him? The Lord doesn't pay much attention to people like that. Have you ever had a cough or hiccups that you couldn't get rid of? Prayer should be continual, like that. God says, "Pray without ceasing" (1 Thessalonians 5:17). Asking the Lord for what you want is one kind of prayer, but not the only kind.

Think of the Lord as your mighty, holy, loving heavenly Father. When else would you want to talk to Him?

When you tell Him you love Him for the person He is,
when you rejoice with Him over something good that happened,
when you feel bad about something wrong you did,
when you don't know what to do,
when you have something hard to do,
when someone else needs His help.

What the Lord Does Through Prayer

The Lord could very easily do all that He wants to do by Himself, without considering us. In fact it would be easier for Him to work without us. But aren't we thankful that He would like us to work with Him! And He wants to do His work through us. Yes, even through us.

Turn to John 14:12. Here Jesus makes a tremendous statement that many people find unbelievable. He states, "Truly, truly, I say unto you. . . ." What does He say He will do? What kind of works did He do when He was on earth? Yes, mighty works—healing the sick, calming the waves, feeding thousands, even raising the dead! He expects us to do great things.

How can that be? Read on. What phrase is repeated in verses 13 and 14? ". . . ask in My name." He wants us to ask in His name. Why? That the Father may be glorified in the Son.

But not everyone can ask aright. In verse 15 what will the people do who work with God? In order to keep His commandments, what do we have to know? Yes, the whole Bible so that we can obey it all. And how much does He ask us to love Him? (Matthew 22:37)

Then Someone else is necessary. Whom does the Father want to give us, in John 14:17, 18? What do these words tell us about His Holy Spirit, the Counselor or Comforter or Advocate? He is to be with us forever, He is the Spirit of truth, He lives with us and is now (after Jesus' resurrection) in us. So we have God's own Spirit in us to do His work. That's why we should do great things.

Look also at the last part of John 16:24. What will be the result of talking to the Lord and working with Him?

Why We Don't Pray

When the Lord promises such joy and such great things when we ask, why don't more people pray? And why don't we pray more often? On the chalkboard are six Scriptures that give reasons why people don't pray. When you find the reasons I'll erase the references and write the reasons instead.

1. John 14:6. What reason does this verse suggest as to why people don't pray? Some people have not come to the Father in the only way possible, through receiving His Son as their Saviour. If they don't have a personal relationship with Him, they are not on talking ground. There is no connection between them.

2. Psalm 66:18. Even when we belong to the Lord, when does He not listen to us? Read this verse in The Living Bible, Ted. If we do not confess any sin that we are aware of, that comes between us and the Lord, and we don't want to pray.

3. James 4:2. Instead of asking God for what they want, what do these people do? They think they can get it themselves. They fight and kill to get it, but they don't ask God. This material world is real to them, but the unseen world of the Spirit is not real.

4. James 4:3. What is wrong with the asking here? When we ask selfishly, just to get what we want without thinking what the Lord wants, we don't get an answer, and so we don't bother to pray again.

5. Hebrews 11:6. Why don't these people pray? They don't believe that God exists because they can't see Him, and they don't believe that He answers prayer.

6. 1 John 3:21, 22. What else is necessary for a person to keep on praying? He must keep God's commandments and please Him. Otherwise nothing happens, so he stops praying.

Let's listen to hear what the Lord wants us to pray about now. Let's remove any hindrance to the answer, and then let's believe His promises.

How to Pray

TODAY LET'S think specifically about one thing that all of us are concerned about, and let's work at it. Not like a mechanical wheel with prayers written on it that a person turns so that the prayers go round and round, nor like saying prayer beads by rote, the same words over and over as if we would be heard for our constant talking. When we pray we're having a personal conversation with a Person, or rather *the most important Person* in the universe.

Do you think that anything you could do would gain you an audience with a king or a president or whatever the head of a whole nation is called? I can't visualize why a king would give any child an audience, but what kind of man might have the privilege of talking to a king? It would have to be someone very important with a very important message or errand. The king would give that person an appointment ahead of time. What would the king do if this person insisted on doing all the talking without giving him a chance to say anything? What would happen if a person tried to dash in and out of a king's presence? A guard would hustle him off in no time.

Because the King of kings allows us to come into His presence anytime, anywhere, do we fail to give Him the respect and the reverence He deserves? Do you expect to do all the talking in the presence of your King? Whose words are more important? Did you ever consider the amount of time you expect the Lord God to listen to you, who are only one person? How do you think He feels when our mind wanders when we're talking to Him? Shame on us!

Steps in Prayer

1. If we are not going to rush into the presence of the Holy One, what will we do first? See if Isaiah 55:9 gives you a clue. Since His divine ways are infinitely higher and better than our human ways, what will we do as we bow before Him? We'll *acknowledge who He is and who we are.* He wants us to be personal with Him, but that doesn't mean palsy-walsy. Though He has bridged the gap between us, He is still in heaven and we're on earth.

2. What does Romans 8:26 suggest that we do in order to pray in the will of God? If we pray according to His will, He hears us. But as human creatures, we don't always know what His will is. God's Spirit in us prays with such deep feeling that it can't be expressed in words. When we *ask the Spirit to pray in us* according to God's will, there is nothing to hinder God from working.

3. Then as the third step, not the first one, we are ready to *tell Him specifically how the situation looks to us.* He wants us to express honestly how we feel. It matters to Him how we feel. How does The Living Bible express Psalm 62:8, Ted? "Pour out your longings before Him, for He can help!" He understands as no one else can.

4. Since prayer is not a one-way affair and we are polite people and we can't help ourselves, what is the next step? Read Psalm 85:8 in the King James Version, Sue. Now we quietly *listen for His viewpoint* on the situation. His answer may come in the form of words or ideas or pictures you see in your mind or questions that you can find answers for. Don't let your mind wander; concentrate on thinking about this one thing until you get an answer. What if you don't

get one? Maybe some other things must happen before you can understand His answer.

5. What is the last step in the process of prayer? Read Isaiah 50:7 in The Living Bible, Jim. This version reads, "Because the Lord God helps me . . . I have set my face like a flint to do his will." Doing God's will often takes courage and determination. But *He will help us do it* as well as know it if we ask Him. We can't expect Him to tell us anything further unless we act on this thing today.

Prayer for a Current Need

Now let's actually take these five steps that we've talked about in order to meet a real need that all of us feel. (Work definitely on whatever family need is most pressing at the moment.) For example, let's say that our family must decide whether to move or not. We don't have to, but it might be to our advantage. How would we take the five steps above to solve this problem? We'll all pray conversationally, just one idea at a time, only a short time each, as many as wish to praying for each idea.

1. How shall we take the first step? We can thank God that He sees the end from the beginning and much more about the future than we do. He can even see whether or not we could get a good house in another city.

2. What next? We will not stubbornly say we want either to stay or to move, but we'll submit ourselves to God's Spirit to pray in us according to God's perfect will.

3. Then we'll tell Him how double-minded we feel. There are reasons for staying here and reasons for leaving. Jim wants to stay till he finishes high school, but Ted wants to have new experiences elsewhere.

4. Now we'll listen to hear God speak to us. Since we'll move as a family, we'll expect that He will tell us all the same thing, not one of us one thing and another something else. It may be easier for some members of the family to hear His answer than others.

5. Finally is there anything He wants us to do either about staying or leaving? Do we need to find out more about possibilities in another place? Are there any responsibilities keeping us here? Are we ready to do what He directs? We're thankful that we can know His best way.

Unanswered Prayer

TO WHICH of your prayers has the Lord answered *yes* recently? To which has He answered No? Strictly speaking, we shouldn't talk about unanswered prayer. Why not? God answers all prayer, but not always with *yes*. What answer other than *yes* or *no* does He sometimes give us? Often it is *wait*.

Should we feel that something is wrong with us or our prayers if God doesn't answer yes? How can we learn to pray so that He can more often answer yes to us? If we talk over our needs with Him rather than tell Him what we want, we can get His viewpoint and we can ask for the best things, the things He wants to do. He wants to work through our prayers, He wants us to pray aright, so that His cause will be advanced.

What kinds of prayers are we sure God wants to answer? That people will be saved, that right will prevail over wrong, that the best candidate will get the office, etc. But even when His Spirit is praying in us and we acknowledge that He is powerful enough to do just anything, He doesn't always say yes to these prayers. Much of the Old Testament records the yearning of God's heart through His prophets that His people would repent of their sins. He wanted to keep them in their own land in triumph over their enemies, but their sin hardened and darkened their hearts. He had to scatter His people abroad. Through the prophets God shows us how He longs to answer the right prayers! What attitude should we take toward unanswered prayer?

Jeremiah's Prayers—Jeremiah 36

Jeremiah had been saying things that the people of Israel didn't want to hear. Because he had prophesied that Babylon would take them captive, the wicked king (Jehoiakim) considered him a traitor. Jeremiah had said that if they went to Babylon, they would live, but if they stayed in Israel, they would die. He had so often urged the people to repent that the king confined him in the guard court. In Jeremiah 36:2, what did the Lord tell Jeremiah to do?

In 3 what was the Lord's purpose in this?

How did Jeremiah get the Lord's words written down on paper, in 4? Baruch was his trusted friend.

Jim, read what Jeremiah said to Baruch in 5-7. On a fast day the people should have been open to hearing a fresh word from the Lord. So Baruch read all Jeremiah's words at the entry of the New Gate in the temple.

When Michaiah heard the words of the scroll, what did he do, in 11-13?

When the princes heard about the words of disaster, what did they do, in 14, 15?

When Baruch read the words to them, how did they feel? 16. What did they say?

What did they want to be sure of, in 17, 18?

Why did the princes tell Baruch and Jeremiah to hide? 19.

How did the king respond to the report? 20, 21.

Picture the scene in 22—the king in his warm winter apartments in front of a fire.

As the words of the Lord were read to him, what did he do? 23.

How did the king and the princes feel about these threatening words of God? 24.

They didn't even take them seriously, except three of them (in the next verse) who tried to keep the king from burning the scroll. What was his order for Jeremiah and Baruch? 26. But the Lord hid them.

Then the Lord told Jeremiah to write the same prophesies again, adding more doom, and noting that the king's body would be thrown out in the street and that no son of his would sit on the throne after him.

Understanding Unanswered Prayer

Even though the Lord knew He could not answer Jeremiah's prayer, He wanted him to pray continuously just the same. What was the purpose for this? He wanted the people to feel through Jeremiah how dreadful He felt because they would not return to Him so that He could save them. He wants to give unsaved people every chance to repent, so He is long-suffering, urging them again and again. It wasn't easy for Jeremiah to be the man through whom the Lord expressed His deep longing, but that was his call and his ministry.

Why can't the Lord answer our prayers for the unsaved? He surely wants them to come to Him; there's no question about that. These prayers depend on the will of others; even the Lord will not force their wills. He wants love that is free and spontaneous. But He wants us to pray, so that people may have every chance. Some of them will come. And He wants us to understand how He feels as well as how other human beings feel.

When the Holy Spirit prays in us, we see as He sees, on a higher plane than this earth. But when we can't get His perspective, He still wants us to ask Him for what seems best to us. Sometimes He gives the assurance that what we ask will be granted.

Then there's always the question of the Lord's timing. Our lives get quite complicated, intertwined with others. This and this must happen before that will be ready. Other things must happen before the answer will be ripe. We may be sure that there are always reasons why God waits. He is not as impatient as we are. He is working from eternity to eternity. But He surely wants to manifest Himself in our day with plenty happening now.

"Dear Lord, we thank You that we can work with You in prayer. Help us keep so close to You that we can understand Your purposes and fit in with Your plans even though Your ways are higher than our ways."

God's Testings

JIM ALWAYS liked sports. When he got into high school, he went out for basketball. In his junior year he practiced and practiced, put this before many other things that he liked to do, and hoped to make the first team. He thought he was going to until just before the first games of the season when he got sick. This really got him down. He blamed God, thinking it would have been very easy for the Lord to have kept him well. But God was testing him. What might God have been trying to show him? How strong he was spiritually. It wasn't enough for him to be strong physically.

When all is going smoothly, when we praise God for the good things that He sends, when we ask Him for what we need and He supplies it, it's easy to love and trust and obey. But tests are a real part of life. We have tests in school, in business, in our spiritual lives. Tests should not weaken us, they should strengthen us so that we'll be ready for the next thing God wants to send us.

When lately has the Lord tested you? When didn't He work in the way you expected Him to? Did you pass the test, or fail it?

The Way We Feel in a Test—Psalm 142

Often when we're tested, we feel very low, and very alone, as if other people couldn't understand what we are going through. I think that's why the Lord included Psalm 142 in His one book of revelation. Have any of us felt worse than the psalmist feels here?

What does this writer do first in verses 1 and 2?

Even though he feels faint, what does he acknowledge about the Lord in verse 3?

In the end of verse 3 and in 4, how does he feel about human beings?

In the rest of the psalm, what does he ask the Lord to do? And how does he say he feels? He feels very low, weak, as if he is in prison. Have you felt like that?

The Wilderness Testings—Exodus 15—18

After God opened a path through the Red Sea for His people to escape from the Egyptians who were chasing them, they sang joyful songs of praise for His deliverance. They were glad He was leading them to a land of their own where they would no longer be slaves. But as they walked mile after mile through the bare, lonely wilderness, they didn't like the Lord's discipline as He prepared them to be His special people.

1. Look at Exodus 15:22, 23 to find their first test. How would you feel if you walked three days in the desert, then found water, but it was bitter? When the people murmured against Moses, what did the Lord do in verse 25?

2. In 16:3 what was the next test? For food the Lord supplied quails in the evening and manna in the morning. What are quails? (Small game birds.) Manna? (Small white food, like seeds.)

3. Again at the next stopping place, what was the problem? 17:3. Instead of complaining and getting angry at Moses and the Lord, what could the people have done? They could have said, "Thank You, Lord, for taking us to our own

land. Right now we need water. How will You supply it or help us find some?"

4. Next an enemy tribe came out to fight the Israelites. As chosen men fought the enemy, when did God's people win? Read verses 11 and 12. This is a picture of God's people winning as long as they hold up their arms in prayer.

What to Do in Testings

Let's make a list here on the chalkboard of what we should do when we are tested. We'll keep it here for several days to help anyone who needs it.

1. What is the first thing to do when we don't see the Lord doing what we expect Him to do? For what can we thank Him? Yes, that He is in charge of the whole situation. That human beings are not putting anything over on Him.

2. Then let's acknowledge that He knows what is best and is strong enough to do what is best. He sees what we cannot see. He sees the end from the beginning and what other people will do and what timing is best. He can do miracles to carry out His own plans.

3. How are we going to know whether or not there's anything for us to do? We'll listen to Him to find out. Maybe there isn't anything for us to do at the moment, but if there is a part for us, we want to know what it is.

4. What would be the last step? Accept what He sends without complaining. Suppose what happens seems all wrong. If He sends it to us, it is His will for us. He will work it out for good, though we may not be able to see how. He doesn't mind our asking for reasons, but complaining does no good at all. Sometimes we have to wait for developments before we can understand His reasons.

3 CHRIST JESUS OUR SAVIOUR-LORD

Unconditional Love

JERRY LOVED his father, but he was seldom sure that his father loved him. If he did exactly what his father wished, his father was very nice to him. But Jerry didn't always know what pleased his father, and sometimes when he tried he wasn't able to please him. He tried very hard; but so often he just couldn't measure up to what his father expected. One day he got so discouraged that he stopped trying. That was dreadful! His father just left him alone, without a word. Jerry cried himself to sleep.

Do you think of love like this, with an *if?* *If* you please people, they love you. *If* you don't, get out of the way? How could it be otherwise? Do you love people who do things you don't like? Have you ever loved people who displease you?

Divine Love

Turn to Jeremiah 31:3. This is what God says about His love. When does it begin? End? When does He love you? Before you were born, He said, "I love you no matter what you do. No matter what!" Can you believe that? Many people find this very difficult to believe because it is so different from human love. It is God's very nature to love, for God is love. It is not man's nature to love unselfishly like this.

God tells us in His Word that He loves us, but He also shows us His love. How? He gave His only Son who always pleased Him for us sinners who don't! And then what did Christ give because He too loved like that? To think that Christ loves us as the Father loves Him! (John 15:9) What is the most precious thing that you ever gave anyone? What is the most precious thing a human person ever gave you? Soldiers in war often have to give themselves, but they don't want to. Christ gave Himself for us before we even received Him. He even gave Himself for those who reject Him. Humans can't love like that! When I think of God's love, I'm full of exclamations!

Peter's Denial—Matthew 26:69-75, John 21:15-17

When God loves us like this, what happens when we sin? Does nothing happen? What happened when Peter in the Bible sinned? Turn to Matthew 26:69. Near the end of Jesus' life on earth after He was arrested and taken before the Jewish Supreme Court, Peter sat around a fire with soldiers in the courtyard, waiting to see what would be done with Jesus. As he waited, three people came up and accused him of being with Jesus. Jim, read what Peter said, and Sue, the first person who talked to him. I'll read the connecting narrative.

The first girl noticed his speech—that he had a north country accent. Peter answered her loudly and angrily.

Ted, in verse 71, what did another girl say to him? And what did Peter answer—the Peter who had followed Jesus, seen His miracles, heard His amazing teaching, and insisted a short time before that he would die rather than desert his Master! What did this Peter say to a girl whom he didn't know? This is the love of human nature.

Soon what did another bystander say to Peter? 73. Then how did Peter show his love for Jesus, Ted?

When the cock crowed, what did Peter remember, and how did he feel? 75.

What did Peter's sin do to him? It hurt him deeply. What did it do to Jesus? Did Jesus stop loving him? Turn to John 21 to find out. After Jesus' death and resurrection, Peter was on the lake fishing in the early morning when he saw Jesus on the shore fixing breakfast on a charcoal fire. On the shore Jesus talked to Peter.

Jim, will you still be Peter, and Mother, read the words of the Lord. Again I'll read the story part. Begin with verse 15.

Why did Jesus ask Peter three times if he loved Him? After denying the Lord three times, Peter had a chance to counteract it three times. Did Jesus get angry? Had he ceased to love Peter? How do you think the Lord felt? He still loved Peter even though He didn't like what he did. His love made Peter love Him more.

Our Response to Divine Love

Do you really believe, really accept in your mind the fact that the Lord loves you no matter what you do? He tells us so in His Word and He shows us in a multitude of ways. How many ways can you think of?

The next question is harder: can you *feel* that the Lord loves you? Though we can't depend on our feelings, the Lord wants us to experience His love. It is like warm sunshine on a cold day; it makes everything seem warmer and brighter.

How does Jesus' love make us feel about sin? We become more sensitive to it, we're more careful to avoid it for we know how much it hurts everybody. If we do sin, we confess it immediately and right the wrong.

How do we respond to the Lord's love for us? We love Him back. "We love him, because he first loved us" (1 John 4:19).

Wouldn't we like to sing the choruses of "Isn't He Wonderful" and "Jesus Never Fails"?

The Wonderful Grace of Jesus

SOME PEOPLE'S names have a rich background of meaning. Some are Bible words. In some cultures people are even named Jesus, though that seems wrong to us. Have you heard of anyone's being named Love? Joy? Yes, that is rather common. Peace? Faith? Grace?

Grace is a common name for girls and one of the most important words in the Bible. We can tell how God's people feel about it by the songs they have written. How would you say they feel about God's grace from the words of these songs, and why is grace so important?

> Amazing grace! how sweet the sound, That saved a wretch like me!
> I once was lost, but now am found, Was blind, but now I see.

> Wonderful grace of Jesus, greater than all my sin;
> How shall my tongue describe it, Where shall its praise begin?

> Grace! 'tis a charming sound, Harmonious to mine ear!
> Heaven with the echo shall resound, And all the earth shall hear.
> Saved by grace alone! This is all my plea:
> Jesus died for all mankind, And Jesus died for me.

Free

In our world we get used to paying for everything we get. When we see something we want, we naturally ask, "How much is it?" When we are paid wages, we expect to earn what we get. The government tries to pass fair trade laws. When people try to do something gracious to us, we try to pay them back.

In these following Bible verses, what is emphasized about God's grace? Romans 3:24. Jesus takes away our sins freely, as a gift.

Romans 8:32. With His Son, God gives us everything else.

1 Corinthians 2:12. The Spirit of God that we have received helps us understand all that God gives.

Revelation 22:17. All those who are thirsty for spiritual things are invited to come and drink freely without paying.

Undeserved—Ephesians 2:4-10

In school, teachers try to give their pupils the grades they deserve. We're angry when we don't get a square deal, when we get cheated. We seldom get more than we deserve, more than we expect. But what does God's grace give us?

Turn to Ephesians 2:4. After reading the several versions of each verse in this paragraph, let's make our own version in words that mean most to us. How might we say the first idea? Yes, Sue, God loved us so much that He made us alive spiritually when we were spiritually dead.

That next little phrase is very important. In your words how would you say that it was by grace that you have been saved? I like that, Ted, that there's nothing you could do to save yourself from sin; God had to do it all.

What does verse 6 mean to us? When we belong to Christ, God sees us in Christ, sitting with Him in heaven.

Verse 7: God can always show how tremendously kind He has been to us who belong to Christ.

Verse 8: Since we are saved by believing, it is always a gift, never earned.

Verse 9: If we earned our salvation, we could boast of how good we were.

Now, Jim, will you please read this section from The Living Bible to help us feel the full effect of the idea of God's grace?

So because we are saved freely by God's grace, what is our part? Faith. Believing that Jesus paid the price for our sins that we couldn't pay.

Our Response

Verse 10 tells what should happen after we have received Christ as our Saviour. He saved us for a purpose, in order to show others what He is like and to do His good works in us. People don't see Him but they see us who are called by His name, *Christians.* Are we fulfilling the purpose for which Christ saved us?

When the Lord thinks of us, is He glad that He bestowed His grace on us because we are doing His good works? When you think that you could never have earned salvation, never been good enough, what do you want to say to the Lord? When you think of other people who haven't yet heard about the grace of God, what do you want to say to Him about them? About our Christian home? How does God's grace make you feel about yourself? We don't need to prove ourselves to anybody, but since God's grace has reached us, we can relax in His kindness and be our real selves. He wants to be just as gracious to us as we will allow Him to be.

Don't you feel like singing "Amazing Grace"?

Ephesians 2:8-10 is an excellent passage to memorize.

The New Birth

ALICE WAS always a happy child. She always appreciated her home, her parents, her sister and brothers. She never remembered the time when she didn't love Jesus and try to please Him. When she went from kindergarten to first grade, she felt much older, she felt that she was now a responsible person, almost on her own. One thing she wanted to do in first grade was to show that she belonged to the Lord. But when Harry splashed mud on her new dress, she got very angry at him and said things she was sorry for afterward. She asked the Lord to forgive her and even Harry to forgive her, but after that she didn't feel quite so good about herself. The next week she forgot to tell her mother what she had promised her teacher she would tell her, and that of course bothered her. Then one day after school she hurried home to bake cookies even though she saw a kindergartener crying with no one to help her. "Will I always be like this?" she asked herself. "I want to please the Lord but I just can't seem to."

In the Bible Paul felt like this too, and expressed it this way: "When I want to do good, I don't; and when I try not to do wrong, I do it anyway" (Romans 7:19 LB).

What was Alice's real problem? What did she need to do? Jesus had always been her Friend, but she needed Him also to be her Saviour. What is the difference? As Friend, Jesus was with her; as Saviour, He comes to live His life in her by His Spirit. What difference would that make? She herself couldn't be better and stronger and more loving, but Jesus in her was better and stronger and more loving. He wants to be our very life in us!

Jesus' Part

Jesus has a part in saving us and we have a part. Whose part is greater, harder? By very much! He did His part a long time ago, and is waiting for us to do our part. What is His part?

Look at 1 Corinthians 15:3, 4 beginning with the word Christ. Why did Christ have to die for our sins? Because no one who sins can come to our holy God. All sinners deserve to be punished in hell. How many of us have sinned? Romans 3:23. Every one of us. So the only way we can escape destruction is for someone who is Himself holy to take the punishment that we deserve. Who is holy and yet loves us enough to take punishment for us? The only way we could be saved is for Jesus to die in our place. Close your eyes and see Him suffering cruelly on the cross for you! What if He hadn't loved us that much? But He does! Let's thank Him this minute that He does.

But what kind of Saviour would a dead Saviour be? Read verse 4 again. What does His resurrection mean to us? Because He lives, we shall live also! And what is He doing for us right now? Praying for us, helping us, getting heaven ready for us.

Another way of expressing Christ's part in salvation is given in Ephesians 5:2. How does this idea relate to the Old Testament? Before Christ came, God asked His people to sacrifice the blood of animals for their sins, and to keep doing this. After Christ gave Himself on the cross, there is no more sacrifice; He offered Himself once for all time.

Our Part

Even a child can be saved as soon as he understands the cross because our part is so little compared with Christ's. What must happen to us? See John 3:3. How can a person be born anew, born again, born a second time? Even wise old Nicodemus asked that question. Yes, we are born the first time into this world, the second time into the world of the Spirit, the heavenly world that is unseen but just as real, where the Lord lives.

What must we do in order to have a second birthday? Turn to Romans 10:9. Even a child can tell others that Jesus is Lord and believe in his heart that God raised Him from the dead.

Now look at Romans 12:1, 2. If a sinner means business with the Lord, he will also respond to the Lord's sacrifice. Just as Jesus gave Himself for us, so we will give ourselves back to Him. He is a living sacrifice for us, and we can be a living sacrifice for Him, which is only reasonable. Then He can make us holy and acceptable to God.

What happens when we give Him control of us? Do you want to be so transformed that you can prove what is the good and acceptable and perfect will of God? That's what He wants, and He is mighty enough in you to do it. Do you have any problems about doing that?

Results

What else happens when we give ourselves to the Lord? 2 Corinthians 5:17. When Alice received Christ, she said she felt more spritely and chipper. She felt more ready to do hard things instead of trying to get out of them. The Lord helped her do things she had never done before. The Bible calls this walking "in newness of life" (Romans 6:4).

Of course things weren't as different for her as they are for the drunken bum who stumbles into a mission and receives Christ, though they both come to Him in the same way. Why not?

Does Alice's salvation mean that now she will be perfect? No, none of us will be holy until we see the Lord face-to-face in heaven. How will she keep from being discouraged when she makes mistakes? Look at 1 John 1:9. She is now more sensitive to sin, and asks God to forgive her immediately. And gradually she is being transformed, becoming more and more like Christ.

What then is the essence of the good news of Christ? What is so great about the gospel? How would you tell a friend?

Christ Changes Us

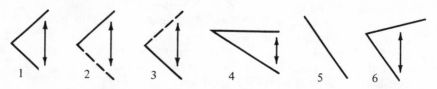

EVEN AFTER we receive Christ, we still have our old nature in us. Because we were born in sin, it is easier for us to obey the old nature than the new nature that Christ gives us. (Draw these simple diagrams on the chalkboard as you talk about them.)

1. Our new spiritual nature seeks the things that are above, where Christ sits on the heavenly throne, and so I draw one line going upward. I also draw a line going downward but not so far downward because Christ has cut the power of the old nature. It's not so strong in us as it used to be. But since our old nature has not been eradicated, we still feel its pull.

2. When we let the Spirit of the Lord control our behavior, the upward pull is so strong that the downward can't have much effect on us. It grows weaker and weaker.

3. Even in us Christians, if we don't keep submitting ourselves to the Lord for His empowering, the lower nature may gain control until we are acting as if we didn't belong to Him.

4. This is the average non-Christian whose old nature is strong and who is pleased if he can keep his conduct on an even keel though he has no higher power to help him.

5. Often he succumbs to his lower nature, gets into trouble, and grows to hate himself as well as others. Sometimes he feels so low that he can't even live with himself.

6. Even when the unbeliever tries very hard to be unselfish and to help others, he still can't reach the plane of the Christian in the Spirit. He may be very helpful to humanity, but he doesn't know what real life is, fulness of life, spiritual life.

What Changed in Paul—Acts 8—9

When Christ is given control of us, what changes in us? He gives us His own new spiritual nature, but we still have our old nature and our basic personality. Let's see what changed when the Lord very dramatically changed Saul into Paul—even changed his name. Open your Bibles to Acts 8:1. Stephen, full of grace and power, had just been stoned. What happened to the other believers?

What was Saul doing in verse 3? Whatever he did, he did wholeheartedly.

Still breathing threats and murder, threatening with every breath, breathing murderous warnings against the disciples of the Lord, what did Saul do in 9:1, 2? What is meant by *the way?* Jesus' way.

Dealing with Saul as aggressively as Saul was dealing with Christians, how did the Lord stop him in 3? Usually He deals with us according to our own personalities.

Falling to the ground Saul heard a voice speaking to Him. Jim, read what the Lord said, and Sue, what Saul said in verses 4-6. This was the first time Saul had listened to or spoken to the Lord.

What confounded the men who were with Saul? 7.

What had the bright light of the glory of the Lord done to Saul? 8, 9.

When he regained his sight, how was he changed, in 18? He saw things very differently now. Imagine his wanting to be baptized in the name of Jesus before!

In verses 19 and 22 what idea is emphasized? He was strengthened physically and spiritually. What was he doing in 20 instead of persecuting the church?

What was greatly changed in 23-25? What a turnabout! His former friends were now his enemies, and Jesus' disciples now protected him.

Let's list here on the board the things that changed in Paul's life when he was converted. Yes, his relation to the Lord, the way he saw things, his strength, his friends, and his interests.

How the Lord Changes Us—Psalm 27

How does the Lord work His transformation in us? Not often in a blazing light from heaven. It is not natural for people to change. It is easier to go along in the way we start. And it's not just superficial changes that the Lord wants to make in us, but deep permanent changes.

Psalm 27 is a fine one to read when you're alone with the Lord. Let's all read the first verse together.

Now drop down to verse 4, since our time is limited. Why was David the man of God that he was; how did he focus his life? He didn't play around with this one thing, he went after it. Did he mean that he preferred to live in the temple rather than in his palace? Not literally. How does The Living Bible read, Sue? David wanted to be conscious of the Lord's presence, thinking about His perfections, discovering more about Him.

Look at verse 8. What does it mean to seek the Lord's face? Suppose a person your age moved next door to you. You wouldn't be content merely to hear about him. You'd want to see him, talk to him, and get to know him. Do we know the Lord like this, intimately, face-to-face?

Look at verse 14. It's hard for all of us to wait. We get impatient because changes don't come faster. But if the Lord changed us too fast, we would hurt and suffer. So He works with us slowly as we are ready. He knows just how much we can take.

How We Should Change

How does your old nature try to gain control over you? When are you strongest in overcoming it? When are you weakest? Let's ask the Lord individually to strengthen that part of our life so that the new nature will keep the old in its place.

The Holy Spirit

HOW DO you use the word *spirit* in ordinary conversation? What does Grandmother mean when she says, "I'm so sorry I can't come to your birthday dinner, but I'll be with you in spirit"? When a piano teacher says, "You didn't get all the notes right, but you caught the spirit of the piece"?

When Jesus told us to baptize all nations in the name of the Father, Son and Holy Spirit, why did He add the Holy Spirit to the names of the Father and Son? The Holy Spirit is God, just as the Father and Son are God. Scripture teaches a Trinity—three persons in one God. Just as I am Mother's husband, and I am my father's son, and I am the father of Jim and Ted, but I am still one person.

When we received Christ, the Bible says that His Holy Spirit came to live in us (John 14:17). How can that be? People who understand only material things cannot conceive of this. Though it is hard to put into words, can you imagine the Spirit of Christ uniting very intimately with your own spirit at the very center of your being, and quickening it so that it is alive to God? The word "spirit" means breath or wind, the unseen reality of living beings. When you see a dead bird, what is missing? The feathers, the head, the feet, are all there, but the unseen life of it is gone.

Can you begin to take in the fact that the Lord's own Holy Spirit lives in you? Surely it is too good to be true, yet it is! The Bible states it very clearly. Deeper than thought or feeling, He lives in us. He is necessary if we are to obey the Lord, for we could never become like the Lord if we depended on ourselves. The Spirit has to take control for us. When God asks us to do things that are not natural for us, He supernaturally provides the power by His Spirit. This is one of the astounding things about Christianity.

What the Spirit Does for Us

In our Bibles let's find some of the things that the Holy Spirit wants to do for us.

1. Turn to John 14:26. Jesus said these words to His disciples before He returned to His Father in heaven. Do you realize that you have your own private tutor? Why is He the very best Teacher? Since He is God, He knows all the deep things of God. And since He lives in you and me, He knows exactly what we need, and He fits God's answer to our need.

Long ago the Spirit helped the disciples remember what Jesus had told them. What does He help us remember? The things Jesus tells us in His Book. The other day as I was sharing with a friend He brought to my mind an idea from the Word that I had forgotten I knew. (Cite your own experiences as examples of scriptural truths.)

2. Now look at John 16:8. The Holy Spirit does things that we humans find impossible to do. Why is it hard to convince people of their sin? We close our ears to the idea that we are sinning. We want our own way but we also want to pretend that we are all right.

Whose righteousness will the Holy Spirit convince people of? What is the only way that we can become right with God? Read Galatians 5:21, Jim.

What will happen to the people who say that this world is all there is, there is no spiritual world that we can't see, no God who rules over all? They will be judged according to what they did with Christ. The Spirit convinces the world of sin, of righteousness, of judgment.

3. Look at Galatians 5:22, 23. When we allow the Spirit to control our lives, what do other people see in us? Which of these nine virtues do we need the Spirit to work in us right now? I need self-control in order to stick to my financial reports until I finish them.

4. What does the Spirit want to do for us in Romans 8:14? Often when people ask me what would be best to do, I don't know. There are so many things to be considered and I can't see the future. But the Spirit knows everything—all that has happened and all that will happen. Sometimes we don't hear Him because He speaks in a still, small voice. What else might keep us from hearing Him? We won't hear if we aren't ready to obey.

5. And Romans 8:26, 27. When we have a need, something tremendous happens in our innermost being, with feeling deeper than words. What else is special about the Spirit's praying for us?

Our Part

With the Holy Spirit ready to do all those great things for us, what is our part? What do we read in Ephesians 4:30? Since the Spirit is a Person, we can make Him sad, hurt Him, grieve Him. That makes us sad too. In verse 31 what does He help us keep out of our lives, and instead what does He help us cultivate?

In the next chapter is a very interesting comparison, in Ephesians 5:18. How does a person who is filled with alcohol act? The alcohol makes him do silly wicked things because it has control of him. What does the Christian do when he is filled with the Spirit, when the Spirit is in control of him? 19, 20. So there's one way to be always and in everything giving thanks to the Lord—be filled with the Spirit.

How are we filled with the Spirit? Most people are so full of themselves that there is no room for the Spirit. Jesus said (in John 7:37), "If any man thirst, let him come unto me and drink." In relation to the Spirit, we could say, "If any one is thirsty for more of God, for His fulness, let him come to the Lord and receive from Him, breathe Him in, exchange our life for His life." Do you want to exchange your weakness for His strength? Tell Him so. Your ignorance for His wisdom? Tell Him that. Your sin for His holiness? Your selfishness for His love?

> If you [fathers] then, who are evil,
> know how to give good gifts to your children,
> how much more will the heavenly Father
> give the Holy Spirit to those who ask him.
> Luke 11:13, RSV

Receiving from the Lord

ANDY GREW up in a Christian home with a great deal of love for the Lord and for the members of his family. He always knew how much the Lord had done for him, he always went along with what the rest of the family did, he never rejected any of the family's Christian activities. Being of a tractable temperament he didn't have much trouble obeying what he was asked to do because the commands seemed sensible to him—*until* he got in with a gang at school who were not used to obeying anyone. They found excitement in disobeying parents and school rules and laws of the land. And Andy went along with them. How could he do that? How could he be weak enough to change like that?

Some people go to church, they talk about Jesus, they read the Bible, they pray, but little seems to happen. All this seems to make little difference in their lives. They seem to be so near the Lord in one sense, and so far away from Him in another. Have you ever felt like this? What is the reason for it? What is the real problem?

Outward Profession—Matthew 7:21-23

Matthew 7:21 talks about this problem of a lot of people who call themselves Christian. How do our various Bible versions word the first negative idea? These are people who say, "Lord, Lord," who sound religious, who do religious things. What does Jesus say is their real situation? Why don't they do the Lord's will when they call Him Lord? Yes, it is harder to obey than to talk, and maybe they have never received His divine life.

It's like the family who was willed ten thousand dollars by a dead relative. They put the money in the bank where it kept drawing interest and making more money. They liked the idea of having a little more all the time. They often talked about their bank account, but they never used it for anything. It never did anything for them because they never used it. All they had was a bank statement on paper.

Like that, some people like to think of God's promises on the pages of His Book, but they have never used them, never received what the Lord has promised.

On the last day when these people stand before the Lord's judgment seat, what will He say to them, in verse 22? Why did they think they would have a good reward? They may have thought they were doing all these things in Jesus' name, but they weren't doing them in His will or in His power.

In verse 23, what will Jesus answer them? Wouldn't it be awful to think you were doing things in Jesus' name, and then to hear Him say at the end, "I never knew you. Go away. You did evil, not good"!

Expecting to Receive—Matthew 7:7-11

Now turn back to verses 7 and 8 in this same chapter. If we really believe what God says, what will we do after we ask Him for something? Mother, read these verses with me; I'll read the first phrase of each idea which tells what we should do, and you read the last phrase that tells what will happen. We'll expect to receive, we'll be ready to receive.

Next Jesus compares what a good earthly father will do to what the great heavenly Father will do. Read verse 9 and decide what tone of voice to read it in. How would you read it, Ted? Read verse 10 to yourself and then aloud, Alice. When you try to show with your voice the force of verse 11, how will you read it, Jim? Yes, *how much more* will your Father in heaven give you! Why will He give so much more? He loves us most, He is able to do anything, He knows all our needs.

Therefore when we ask something of the Lord, will we be ready to receive from Him? Can we see clearly now why Andy could so easily switch from obeying the Lord to disobeying Him? He had talked about the Lord and been where the Lord was, but he himself had not received from the Lord.

Receiving Right Now

Jesus says to us today, ". . . ask, and ye shall receive, that your joy may be full" (John 16:24). What does each of us need most right now? Let's ask and be ready to receive. How do we get ready to receive?

First let's be sure we are in tune with the Lord, are right with Him. Do we know of any sin that has not been forgiven? Can we say, "Lord, I want to do Your will"? Is there a clear connection between you and the Lord with nothing between?

Do we come to the Lord as a Person, not an idea? Though you can't see Him, is He as real to you as I am? Are you face-to-face with the Almighty who made heaven and earth and yet who knows and loves you as one individual human creature?

If you meet these first two conditions, ask definitely for your need as you see it. This will be a human perspective and it may need to be revised, but be honest about the way you see it.

Then wait quietly to receive what you asked for. This may take a minute or a few minutes or longer. Keep concentrating on the Lord. Does He want you to know something? Listen for it. Does He want you to do something? Does He want to change your feelings? Does He want to give you something? The greatest thing would be to give you more of Himself, His Spirit. Perhaps you'd like to go to your own room in order to continue in His presence to receive all that He has for you.

Matthew 7:7-11 is a good passage to memorize.

The Call to Discipleship

MANY VOICES in our world are calling young people today. Some respond to the call of the sea, some to the open road, some to the call of the wild, some to learning, some to pleasure. What call gives the person the most deep-down personal satisfaction and is worth most to the world?

The Patrick of St. Patrick's Day was neither Irish nor Catholic. He was born of Christian parents in Britain way back about A.D. 389, but was taken captive to Ireland in his teens. There he experienced a genuine conversion to Christ. After slaving for six years he escaped and returned home. But he couldn't stay home, for he heard the voice of God calling him back to the people of Ireland who had never heard of Christ. His task was not easy, for the people worshiped the sun, moon, wind, and lightning. Yet he adopted the customs of the country and did not seem a foreigner. His life was often in danger from robbers and soldiers. He spent thirty-five years there, baptizing thousands of converts, establishing hundreds of churches, and ordaining many young men to preach the gospel. A hundred years later Ireland was predominantly Christian. He was never sorry that he had answered the call of God.

Think of the thousands of people who thanked God for the life of Patrick. When the people who live for themselves get old and gray, and look back over their lives, I wonder if they don't regret being so selfish, just living for themselves. Many of these people commit suicide because they get lonely and bored. When we in our family have lived our lives, how many people will thank God that we have lived? Which of the many voices that are calling to us will we answer?

Jesus' Call—Mark 1:16-20

Read to yourself what happened to four fishermen on the Sea of Galilee in Mark 1:16-20. Read it again to decide what stands out to you in the incident. Yes, both pairs of brothers immediately left their boats and followed Jesus. Would you immediately leave what you were doing and go after any person who said to you, "Follow me"? What must have impressed the men about Jesus?

What else stands out in this incident? What kind of men did Jesus choose to make His team? Men who were already hard at work, who were used to going after something and getting it. How would fishing for fish compare with fishing for the souls of people? Both were exciting, both take stick-to-itiveness and patience, both take working with the Creator. Which would be harder? Why? People have wills that say *no* as well as *yes,* and they can't be taken by force.

These men were commercial fishermen who earned their living by fishing. When they immediately left their everyday work, what does this say about them? Did this call mean that they would never fish again for fish? Not necessarily. What did it mean? What does it mean for us to follow Jesus? To put Him first, before anything else. Are we ready to do that?

His Purpose—1 Peter 2:9

How does the Lord feel about the people He calls to follow Him, and how should we feel about our call? Look at 1 Peter 2:9 RSV. I bet you didn't know you were such an important person! Especially chosen by God! Out of all the people in this world, you have been chosen by the Creator Himself. A royal priesthood. In what sense are we royal? We belong to the King of kings. In what sense are we priests? We have been given direct access to God so that we can help others to come to Him. A holy dedicated nation. A people claimed by God for His own. That's what He thinks of us. Doesn't it make you want to live up to His expectations?

For what purpose did the Lord call us? Read the last part of the verse in your versions. Notice the superlative words: His *wonderful* deeds and His *marvelous* light. He wants even us to show forth His wonderful deeds and His marvelous light.

The Sign of Discipleship—John 13:34, 35

Jesus said that even outsiders have a right to judge whether or not we belong to Him. That there is one sign by which they should be able to tell. Turn to John 13:34, 35 to find what it is. It is a new commandment because the Old Testament stressed loving God, but now we who follow Jesus become members of His body the church. How much are we to love each other? Even as Jesus has loved us! How much is that? Enough to give Himself for us! How can we manage so much love? Only as He loves in us.

When things are going smoothly, we find it easy to love each other, don't we? But when is it hard to love? I wonder if we sometimes make it hard for others to love us without realizing it. Is there something I do that bothers any of you, that keeps you from loving me? Maybe I'd be glad to stop doing that or do something else if I realized what it is. If I'm open enough to ask you this question, can you be open enough to answer me, honestly but tactfully? You can say it in such a way that I won't feel too bad. If it's something that I feel I should do, maybe it will help you if I explain why I must do it.

Do you think our neighbors and friends know that we love each other? Do they see or hear anything that does not look or sound like love?

Let's thank the Lord that He has called us to Himself and that He has great expectations for us. Let's ask for His own love to love each other especially when something annoys or disturbs us.

The Cost of Discipleship

HOW CAN we explain the fact that communism has spread over the world so fast when it is less than two hundred years old and Christianity is over nineteen hundred years old? What is it about communism that is so strong? No doubt it is the communists' zeal, their dedication to the cause, their willingness to sacrifice. Their party leaders make big demands, and get them. They don't just talk; they act; they are an active campaigning group. They teach their members what the party stands for and then require them to use the teaching. Even at the beginning they send new members right out into the thick of things, where real problems are being battled, where they feel the need of more training. The members get together in small cells to strengthen each other, and they also care about others as people, not just as new members. They say as well as show that there is nothing too good for the party.

How does the communist attitude compare with Christianity's? Yes, this is exactly what Christ asks of His people. Why don't we take Christianity as seriously as the communists take their cause? Do we as individuals care as much as they do?

No one can be a communist unless he is ready to be a real disciple. Should Christ expect less of His disciples? Why should He expect more?

Taking Our Cross—Mark 8:31-37

After Peter recognized that Jesus was the promised Messiah that the Jews had been looking for so long, Jesus began to tell the disciples what terrible things He would suffer, and that he would be rejected by the Jewish leaders, be killed, and rise again the third day. He had hinted at this before, but now that they knew who He was. He told them plainly. Peter couldn't put these two ideas together—that He would have to suffer when He was the Saviour of Israel that God had promised.

So in verse 33 what did Peter do, and how did Jesus answer? Who was Peter to tell Jesus what He should do? Why did Jesus call him Satan, the devil? Because Peter was tempting Jesus to bypass the cross with all its suffering. Men would find some easier way of salvation than the cross, but God knew it was necessary.

Then Jesus called the crowds with the disciples to hear something they needed to hear but would not want to hear. Read this next sentence in all the versions. Jesus is saying, "If you follow Me, not only will your Leader have a cross, but you too will have a cross." Jesus died on a wooden cross, but we don't have that kind. What does it mean for us to deny ourselves and take up our cross daily and follow Him? To put aside our own selfish desires and die to any self-interests that interfere with His interests.

Verse 35 is a riddle. Let's read it in the various versions. When we try to keep our own lives, we lose them, but when we give them up to Christ, we find what it means to really live.

Verse 36 in the New English Bible reads: "What does a man gain by winning the whole world at the cost of his true self?" And 37 implies: Once you lose yourself, what do you have left?

Free and Easy—John 8:31, 32, Matthew 11:28-30

Do those words of Jesus sound hard to you? Too hard? "The servant is not greater than his lord" (John 15:20). Even though we expect a cross when we follow Jesus, He says too that the life He gives can be free and easy. How can our lives be free and easy with a cross?

Turn to John 8:31, 32. When will we be free? How do we continue in Jesus' Word? Live according to the Scriptures. How does that truth make us free? Sin makes us a slave to things and people outside ourselves. The truth enables us to develop our real selves and use all our powers to respond to the Lord of life.

Turn to Matthew 11:28 for the way in which our lives can be easy. What is a yoke? A wooden bar that unites two animals like oxen so that they can pull together. How is it that Jesus' yoke for us is easy and the burden we pull light? His yoke fits us exactly for it was made just for each of us, and when we are yoked to Him, He does the hard part. So it seems light to us. He is not a harsh master who demands more than we can give, but He knows exactly how much we can take.

So if we decide to be yoked with Him, our cross will never be too much for us. For our cross we always have His resurrection power.

Making Our Decision

Jesus tells things as they are. He doesn't make His call sound easier than it is. He tells us frankly just what is involved. He had a cross and we'll have a cross—we'll have to die to soft things that weaken us, to our own selfish interests and pleasures. But if we answer His call, we can go adventuring with the Captain of our salvation who does great exploits. We can make all our efforts count for eternity and make many people glad that we lived. Instead of drifting along and living under the circumstances, we discover His purpose for our lives and begin to head in that direction using His resources. It's exhilarating to show forth the wonderful deeds of Him who called us out of darkness into His marvelous light!

Would anyone like to sing with me "I Have Decided to Follow Jesus." And:

> Who is on the Lord's side? Who will serve the King?
> Who will be His helpers, Other lives to bring?
> Who will leave the world's side? Who will face the foe?
> Who is on the Lord's side? Who for Him will go?
> By Thy call of mercy, By Thy grace divine,
> We are on the Lord's side, Saviour, we are Thine.

Obeying Authority

ONE RULE of the Martin family was that everyone was to be home at 6 P.M. for dinner, unless of course there were good reasons for being absent. Ted had been growing very lax about the dinner hour, had been sliding into his chair at 6:10 or 6:15, but since he ate fast, he usually finished with the others. One evening the family finished eating at 6:30, but still no Ted. Instead of leaving food on the table for him, Mother and Sue cleared the table and washed the dishes. When Ted finally came—he had not wanted to leave his ball game—he got no meal that night.

Sue was making herself a dress from a beautiful piece of material. She wanted to change the pattern a bit, and so she cut the material in a place where the pattern didn't say to cut. The result was that she spoiled a large piece of the material.

What is there in human nature that doesn't want to obey? When someone tells me to do something, why is it that I often feel like doing just the opposite? I guess it's because we each want to keep control of ourselves, and not be pushed around by others. When one person in a group says to me, "Why don't you do so and so?" I feel like replying, "Why don't you? Why ask me to do it?"

In our world there have to be legitimate, proper authorities. What would happen if we had no government, no laws? We're just wasting our energies straining against them, like knocking our heads against a wall. What authorities are legitimate? Yes, first the Creator who made and understands all things, then duly elected governments, schools, and parents. Both authorities and the people under them are responsible to God. If we don't think the laws are fair, there are means of changing some of them.

The God-Man Obeying—Luke 2:41-51

If we find it hard to obey, what about the boy Jesus, who was God as well as man? How would He fit into our earthly system of authorities? When a Jewish boy became twelve years old, he was considered a member of the adult community. When Jesus was twelve, He went for the first time with Mary and Joseph in the caravans to the great city of Jerusalem for the Passover Feast. Read Luke 2:43-46. Why do you suppose Mary and Joseph had not checked to see that Jesus was with them when they left the city? No doubt He had always been very responsible. But when they didn't find Him in the city, they must have been very worried as they searched for Him for three days! What kind of youth listens to adults and asks them questions about important matters?

But the boy Jesus did more than listen and ask questions. Read verse 47. The things that the teachers in the temple talked about were the things He was most interested in. Mother, read verse 48. I wonder where Mary and Joseph expected to find Jesus.

If they were astonished to find Him in the temple, how did He feel about their astonishment? What else would He be interested in but His heavenly Father's business!

In verse 50, why didn't they understand what Jesus meant?

In verse 51, even though He was having a great time in the temple with the teachers, what did He do? Without any delay, without any argument.

The Temple Tax—Matthew 17:24-27

When the collectors of the temple tax came to Peter and asked him, "Does not your teacher pay the tax?" (RSV) what did Peter answer quickly in Matthew 17:25?

As soon as Jesus saw Peter, He asked him a question about taxes, in 25. Jim and Sue, read the conversation between Jesus and Peter; Jim be Jesus and Sue, Peter. Why did Jesus imply that He didn't need to pay the tax? As Lord and owner of the temple, He was free from the tax. But to keep from offending anyone, He would pay it just like all the other citizens.

Praying for Authorities—1 Timothy 2:1, 2

Instead of rebelling against the authorities in our world, what does Paul tell us to do in 1 Timothy 2:1, 2? In addition to supplications, prayers, and intercessions for people in official positions, what else does he add? Even thanksgiving. If they didn't take their responsibility seriously, people wouldn't be able to lead a quiet, peaceful life, worshiping as they like and keeping standards of morality.

Instead of griping about the people we have to obey, have we been praying for them? Not very much. What people should we include? Yes, our president and his cabinet, our congress, our governor, mayor, yes, my boss, you children's teachers, and yes, do pray for us, your parents. If you pray every day for us, we are sure to be better parents and give you less trouble in obeying.

What rules do we as a family find most difficult to obey? Let's see if they are all necessary and why they are necessary. Maybe some of them could be changed or revised. Every rule should have good reasons behind it, but probably few rules will seem sensible to everyone. Yet the need for obedience is built into the structure of the universe.

> Although he was a Son,
> [Jesus] learned obedience through what he suffered;
> and being made perfect he became the source
> of eternal salvation to all who obey him.
>
> Hebrews 5:8 RSV

Being Mature, Not Perfect

AT EACH age level an individual should be mature for his level of development. No one expects Alice to have the personal qualities of a ten year old; neither do we expect her to act like a baby. Can you think of a primary child who doesn't act his or her age? We don't expect Ted to act like a thirteen year old, but like a mature healthy ten year old. Ted, who among your friends is an especially mature ten year old? The mature people usually stand out as the leaders in their peer groups. Sue, what makes a friend of yours mature at thirteen? A rosebud has not yet matured into a flower, yet it is beautiful in its own right, and so is a child if he is mature for his own level.

To be mature is not to be perfect. Because the Lord sets very high standards for His people and then gives us His own divine power to meet them, some Christians get discouraged because they are not perfect. His goal for us is nothing less than "the measure of the stature of the fulness of Christ," maturity that is full-grown in Christ (Ephesians 4:13). Yet we won't attain that goal until we see the Lord face-to-face. Then how can we keep from discouragement now? If we see that we are constantly making progress, constantly improving in some way, we have courage to go on.

A Man After God's Own Heart—Psalm 40:1-3

Do you know which person in the Bible is called a man after God's own heart (1 Samuel 13:14, Acts 13:22)? The Bible also states that the heart of Solomon, David's son, "was not wholly true to the LORD his God, as was the heart of David his father" (1 Kings 11:4 RSV). No wonder so many of David's psalms were recorded in the Bible and have blessed so many multitudes of people!

Let's study the first part of Psalm 40 to discover what a mature person is like. For about three minutes let's each by ourselves examine the first three verses of this psalm. What do these verses tell you about the mature person?

Now let's share our findings. Yes, the mature person waits patiently when he can't get what he wants immediately. He realizes he needs the Lord's help. He goes through very difficult experiences, he doesn't expect everything to be smooth and easy, he knows how it feels to be alone, he feels secure in the Lord, he sings new songs of praise when the Lord delivers him, and he tells others what the Lord does for him, for he is concerned about others as well as himself.

Not Perfection—2 Samuel 11:14-17, Psalm 51:1-3

Can you remember some of the exciting things that the Lord helped David to do? Was David perfect? See what he did in 2 Samuel 11:14-17. Because he wanted Uriah's wife, what did he tell his army commander to do? In other words, he had one of his best soldiers murdered! And this wasn't the only sin he committed. How then could David be considered a man after God's own heart?

Look at Psalm 51 to see how he felt when he realized how great was his sin. The Living Bible says, in verses 1-3:

Have pity upon me and take away the awful stain of my transgressions.
Oh, wash me, cleanse me from this guilt.

Let me be pure again.
For I admit my shameful deed—
it haunts me day and night.

David was far from perfect, but his heart was right. He wanted to please God and he praised Him with his whole being. He was a frail human being, like the rest of us. So he gives us hope that we too can please God even though we make mistakes and sin.

We'll never know the joy and the relaxation that Christ wants us to enjoy if we're satisfied with nothing less than perfection. Ever since the first man sinned, the things of this earth come with built-in blemishes. Sin has marred the whole human situation in which we find ourselves. The mature person sets high goals and continually gets nearer and nearer to them, but he doesn't punish himself when he doesn't reach them. He does his best in the power of the Spirit and accepts what cannot be changed.

Testing Our Maturity

(You may read the qualities below or duplicate a copy for each member of the family.) Which aspect of maturity shall each of us work on this week? See where you rate yourself—at the low end of each continuum, at the high end, or near the middle.

selfish	⊢————————————⊣————————————————⊣	unselfish
goals too high or low	⊢————————————————⊣————————————⊣	realistic goals
impatient	⊢————————————⊣————————————⊣	patient
often irritated	⊢————————————————⊣————————————⊣	optimistic
moody	⊢————————————————⊣————————————————⊣	steady, consistent
undependable	⊢————————————⊣————————————⊣	dependable
closed to change	⊢————————————————⊣————————————⊣	open to improvement
suspicious, doubting	⊢————————————————⊣————————————⊣	trusting

Let's each talk to the Lord silently about the weakness that bothers us most.

Adventuring with Jesus

WITH ALL their energy and ideas, how is it that young people so often feel
bored and empty? They are not turned on by the goals of the older generation;
they don't see that the adults' material success has brought them happiness or
peace. Youths are looking for roles as well as goals—they want exciting experiences now. Who knows what the future will hold—if there is a future for this
violent world. Are the massed forces so strongly entrenched that an individual
can't make much difference, no matter what he does? Is the individual at the
mercy of systems that treat men like things?

Is there any way an individual can make his efforts really count? Yes, he can
join the greatest force of all, the Force that started this universe and will end it,
for nothing can defeat the purpose of the Creator Himself. The Lord says in
Isaiah 46:11:

> Mark this; I have spoken, and I will bring it about,
> I have a plan to carry out, and carry it out, I will (NEB).

Will each of us drift along through life, or make our own plans and take a
chance on what will become of them, or will we enlist in the one cause that is
sure of eternal success?

What to Expect—Peter in Acts

What kind of experience can we expect if we go adventuring with the Lord?
The kinds of things that happened to Peter in the Book of Acts. After Jesus'
disciples were filled with the Spirit on the day of Pentecost, Peter preached a
strong sermon about the Saviour. What were the results of that special day?
Turn to Acts 2:43.

In the next verses what were the Christians' attitudes toward each other?
What a high moment that was for all involved—praising together, eating together, sharing what they had with each other! They were having such a great
time that they attracted many other people who wanted to get what these disciples had. Wouldn't you like to be part of a group like that!

As Peter and John were going to the temple through the Beautiful Gate, what
kind of person accosted them? Acts 3:2 What did he want from them? He was
begging in order to live.

Instead of giving the beggar what he expected, what did Peter say to him in 6?
How did Peter dare say that to the man? Filled with the Spirit, he knew what the
Lord wanted to do. And what happened? No wonder the people who saw the
beggar sitting crippled were filled with wonder and amazement. When God fills
us with His Spirit, He does things through us that are amazing!

If we go adventuring with Jesus, would we expect to see the Lord do miracles?
One of the greatest miracles is the salvation of human souls from spiritual death
to spiritual life. The Lord is not at all limited by us; He specializes in the impossible.

But those miracles in the Book of Acts aroused persecution. The religious
leaders of that time could not do wonderful things and so they were jealous of
anyone who could. In Acts 12:1-4 what did the king do to James the brother

of John and to Peter? But Peter was not a loner; the Christian community was concerned about him. What did they do in verse 5?

Jim, read how the Lord answered the prayer of these early Christians from verses 6 to 11.

When Peter got free, where did he naturally go? 12. Sue, finish the story through verse 17.

Is anybody looking for excitement? What may you experience if you go where Jesus goes? We're not surprised at opposition, for Jesus says, "I am the only way to God," and many people want their own way. Then the persecution is overshadowed by the deliverance of the Lord.

How to Prepare

If we want to team up with the Lord, how can we get ready even now? After being filled with the Spirit at Pentecost, Peter became a strong character. Do you remember what kind of person he was before that in the gospel stories? He was wishy-washy, up and down. When his brother Andrew brought him to Jesus, the first thing Jesus said to Peter was, "So you are Simon? You shall be Peter, which means Rock." At that time Peter was anything but solid and dependable. But later when Jesus asked His disciples, "Who do men say that I am?" and then "Who do you say that I am?" Peter answered, "You are the Christ, the Son of the living God." And Jesus replied, "Blessed are you, for the Father has revealed this truth to you. You are now Rock, for you have identified yourself with who I really am, the true Rock, the only One you can depend on" (*see* Matthew 16:13-18).

Do you remember other ways in which Peter showed his weakness? Yes, he contradicted Jesus when the Lord said He would have to die (Mark 8:32). Later when Jesus said that all His friends would forsake Him, Peter boasted that he was ready to go with his Master to prison and to death (Mark 14:27-31, Luke 22:33), then shortly after he three times denied that he even knew the Lord.

In the Garden of Gethsemane when Jesus asked His disciples to watch and pray with Him, what did they do (Mark 14:32-42)?

But Peter learned from his mistakes, and he learned much just from being with Jesus, and being a member of His team. What would he see about Jesus that was different from any human man? Yes, He always relied on the Father, He loved all kinds of people and met all kinds of needs, He did not get discouraged when He was opposed, He was always calm and steady, etc.

Jesus is ready to make us too into strong characters even if now we are very conscious of our weakness. How can we be preparing to go adventuring with Him? We can live with Him each day, watch how He works, and work with Him. Let's pray that each of us will be ready for the Lord's best.

Confessing Christ

DO YOU know which people in your school are Christians? Do I know which ones in my business are? Do we know which ones on our street are? We don't expect Christians to *look* different from other people—not much different anyway, though they don't usually go to extremes.

How do we tell whether or not people belong to Christ? Yes, they should both show it and tell it. How do the people you contact show they love the Lord? Don't those who are not Christians do nice things? Yes, they do. So when people look out for others instead of being self-centered, we may *think* they are Christians. But what makes us *know* so? When they get a chance, they also say so. ". . . every knee should bow, . . . in heaven, and . . . in earth, and . . . under the earth; and . . . every tongue should confess that Jesus Christ is Lord, to the glory of God the Father" (Philippians 2:11). How important is it for us to confess Christ?

Have you heard of any secret believers who would be persecuted if they confessed that they belonged to the Lord? I suppose Jewish people more than others have been banished from their homes when they made it known that they loved Jesus. Is it all right to be a secret believer in that case? When Peter in the Bible denied that he knew the Lord because he thought his life was in danger, he lied when he denied. Is it all right just to keep quiet without saying anything?

The Need of Confessing

Scripture speaks very definitely about confessing Christ. Turn first to Matthew 10:32, 33. Why is it so important that Christ acknowledge us before the Father? He said, ". . . no man cometh unto the Father, but by me" (John 14:6). He is the Judge as to whether a person merely knows about Him or truly has been united to Him. If a believer does not acknowledge Christ before others, what does that say about his spiritual life? Of course it may take a new believer a little while to realize what happened to him and to stand firmly on his own feet. If he asks the Lord for guidance, the Lord will show him the best time and situation to speak about Him graciously and tactfully.

In Jesus' day what had the Jewish leaders decided to do? Look at John 9:22. Why were they so opposed to Jesus? They were jealous because He did things they could not do, and since they had the upper hand, they wanted things to continue as they were. They didn't know what spiritual reality was.

What does John 12:42, 43 tell us about some of these Jewish leaders or authorities? Some of them were secret believers, but why didn't they confess Christ? They loved the praise of men more than the praise of God! They would have been barred from the synagogue, which was the center of Jewish life. So here on earth they were honored by men. What happened when they came to the judgment in heaven?

In Romans 10:9 what is it that God asks us to believe and confess? What does it mean for Jesus to be Lord of our lives? He has His way with us, He is the center of our lives, not we ourselves. We have stepped off the throne and given it to Him. Then what does He promise even when the going gets rough? Look at verse 11. We will never be put to shame or disappointed.

Finally what is the test of whether or not a message or confession is from God? There are false prophets as well as those who speak from the Holy Spirit. See 1 John 4:2, 3. The spirits must confess that God's own Son came down to earth and took a human body. Therefore He is truly God and truly Man.

How to Confess

Few of us today get persecuted when we confess Christ. Why is it then that some of us don't do it very often? Those who are antagonistic may sneer or ridicule or give us a superior smile. Even if they don't agree with our ideas, how can we keep the respect of these people? We can practice confessing Christ graciously and tactfully.

Suppose an aggressive Jehovah's Witness tried to win you over to his way of thinking. How would you react if every time he saw you he stopped to talk and kept you waiting till he finished his spiel? How could he possibly get you to listen appreciatively to what he was saying? Yes, he'd have to gain your admiration for him as a person, show that he respected you and your viewpoint, use a natural opportunity when the talking was appropriate, not when you were in a hurry to do something else. Then you might be interested in what his religion means to him personally.

Let's role play a couple of these opportunities for confessing Christ to give us practice that isn't for keeps. Mother, be Sue's friend Barb who is sitting with her in the school lounge. Barb is talking about a shindig that is being held that evening. Finish the conversation that starts like this:

BARB   I know I should obey my parents, but they're old fogies. They don't ever want me to have fun, or try anything new.

SUE   I sometimes feel like that—pulled in two directions.

BARB   I wonder what to do.

Here's a second role play. Ted, be Harry, a high schooler whom Jim knows. Finish this conversation:

HARRY   I just gotta get a good grade in this test, so I can get into college.

JIM   Don't you think you will?

HARRY   I'm scary about it. Think I better take notes along.

JIM   Do you need to? That's scary too.

HARRY   What else?

Maybe Sue and Jim would like to try several endings to the conversations, to see which one makes the best impression on their friends. Can they cause their friends to want to hear about Christ?

Dead to Self, Alive to God

HUMAN CREATURES go about from day to day with varying degrees of life and liveliness. From God's viewpoint many of them are dead. In what sense are they dead? Dead in sin, dead spiritually. The whole top dimension of them, that should control the rest, is missing. They have never received spiritual life. Some of us who have received Christ and become new creations in Him are not living fully. What would be meant by that? His higher nature in us is not directing and empowering the rest. Our lower nature is partially in control. So we are half-alive, we might say.

How alive were we spiritually this past week? Doesn't it seem silly to be going about half-alive when tremendous provision has been made for us to live fully, on top of everything that comes? What provision has been made for us to live the Christ life? At first there was a great gap between our holy God and us in our sin. How was that gulf bridged? How could God be true to His own nature, be both loving and just? Our sin deserved punishment. But He Himself took the hurt of our sins! He suffered in our place. He paid the price Himself, at awful cost! On the cross Jesus gave the greatest of all sacrifices! The bridge was built not by those who made the gap, but by God.

Because the Lord Himself has done all this, how can He complete the process by living His life in us?

Crucified with Christ—Galatians 2:20, Philippians 3:7-10

Look first at Galatians 2:20. "I am crucified with Christ." Have you been crucified with Christ? How does that happen? In a definite act of commitment we give ourselves to death on the cross where Jesus died. We say to Him, "Lord, put to death my own will which is stubborn, my own mind which distorts the truth, my own feelings which are selfish. Take my body as Your dwelling, and do what You please with it." Romans 12:1 says, ". . . present your bodies a living sacrifice, holy, acceptable unto God, which is your reasonable service."

Now look at the rest of Galatians 2:20. If we give ourselves to be crucified with Christ, what will He do? As we exercise faith, He lives His own divine life in us! That is really living! That is out of this world, or living on Cloud Nine, or how would you express it? It is the top high that humans can experience!

As a young man the Apostle Paul had great prestige among his Jewish friends. He was born a Roman citizen with its distinction and advantages, of purest Jewish blood, son of a Pharisee and a Pharisee himself, he studied in Jerusalem under the famous teacher Gamaliel, was an acknowledged leader in Judaism, and led the persecution of Christians. Turn to Philippians 3:7, 8. How did he feel about all these advantages in relation to Christ? Think of the persecution and the suffering he was willing to endure for Christ's sake.

In verse 9, when Paul was under the old Jewish covenant how did he expect to be right with God? By obeying the law. But though he was very strict, no human has ever perfectly obeyed the law. What now under the new covenant was he depending on for his righteousness?

In 10, what now was his aim in life? To think that the Lord of heaven and earth wants us to know Him and the power of His resurrection! That is the Christ life He wants to work in us! That may also mean the sharing of His sufferings, which are never worthy to be compared with the glory that will later be ours.

Exchanging Our Life for Christ's Life

Will you keep control of your life, or give it to Christ to make you fully alive? He wants to make the very most of you and your abilities. He wants to make your life count for eternity.

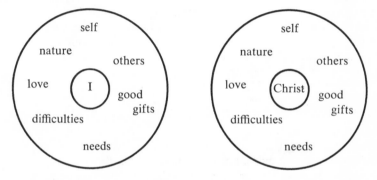

Let's try to visualize what difference it will make if the Lord is the center of our life instead of our sinful selves. How will we see ourselves? Instead of trying to make it on our own, we are now controlled by Christ, who lives through our unique personality. What difference does this make in relation to others? Instead of using them to help ourselves, we share with them in order that they may live fully. Instead of taking for granted the good things in life as our rights and grumbling if we don't have everything, we thank God for what we do have. Instead of struggling to supply all our needs that we can, we trust the Lord to give us what is best. Instead of being overwhelmed by difficulties, we line up with the great Deliverer from difficulties. Instead of loving ourselves, we love God and others, and experience a lot of love coming back to us. Instead of polluting nature for our own purposes, we conserve and protect it for future use.

Christ's Second Coming

MANY PEOPLE believe that the world is not getting any better, and many say that it is getting worse. The people who are uncertain as to how it will all end feel very uneasy. Haven't you noticed that when you feel insecure, you're inclined to feel, "Who cares? What does it matter?"

But this isn't the way an informed Christian feels. Why not? The Bible tells us what is going to happen at the end time. The Lord is going to finish what He started, and finish in a bang-up way. He tells us a great deal about the end of the world, but one thing He has not told us—when it will be. The Book of 2 Peter says it will come like a thief in the night when no one expects it (3:10). Jesus said that neither He nor the angels in heaven but only the Father knows when it will be (Mark 13:32).

What We Know from Scripture

Let's look at some of the questions for which the Bible gives us answers. The first one might be: how will Jesus return? What do you visualize as you read Acts 1: 9-12? We see from verse 12 that Jesus had asked His disciples to meet Him on the Mount of Olives, the highest mountain east of Jerusalem.

After He told them what He expected them to do, what happened in verse 9? You can imagine with what astonishment they kept gazing into heaven! Until two men in white took their attention. What did the men say? Since Jesus went to heaven as a bodily Person, He will return as a Person.

Our next question might be: What will happen to us when Jesus comes? Turn to 1 Thessalonians 4:15. Those who have fallen asleep are the dead believers, who are considered to be asleep in Jesus. We wonder who will hear the command, the call and the trumpet in verse 16—everyone, or only those who belong to the Lord. Won't that be quite a summons! How thrilling for all our loved ones who have died and all our friends who believe to meet the Lord in the air! And so shall we ever be with the Lord! What a day that will be, and what a life that will be! We will live in the places He has been preparing for us.

What does 2 Thessalonians 2:3 imply about the end time? What blasphemous thing does the man of sin do? He is called dreadful names—what in your version? Man of lawlessness, man of rebellion, son of hell, wickedness revealed in human form! The Holy Spirit is now holding him back. In verse 8 what will the Lord Jesus do to him? Who really will be working through this lawless man? The devil himself, the prince of darkness, the archenemy of God.

What will happen to the nations which are left on earth after we have gone? When Jesus returned to heaven from earth, He went quietly, alone. When He returns, what will be different? Look at Matthew 25:31.

This will be the judgment of the nations. With which animals does God compare the nations? 32. Jim, read what He will say to the sheep at His right hand, and Sue, be the righteous people who answer Him. Mother, read what He will say to the goats on His left hand, and Ted, read the answer of those nations.

Does it hurt you when you read verse 46? That human beings made in the image of God for a special purpose never achieve that purpose, but have to go away into everlasting punishment, when they were meant for eternal life?

When the Lord promised to return to earth hundreds of years ago, why hasn't He come sooner? In the last days scoffers will say, "Where is the promise of his coming? for . . . all things continue as they were from the beginning of creation" (2 Peter 3:4). How does the Lord answer this in 2 Peter 3:9? How would you say that in your own words? He is giving sinners more time to repent. In verse 10, when the day of the Lord does come like a thief, how will our earth end? The Creator who started all things will have the last word.

What This Should Do for Us

If the Lord should come today and your life on earth would be ended, would you feel satisfied with it? Would you answer the trumpet call with a glad shout? Suppose you knew that you had one week more to live, would it make any difference in what you did? When we get to heaven, we'll never have need merely to trust the Lord again, for there we'll not walk by faith but by sight, for we'll see the Lord face-to-face. If you never had a chance to do anything more for the Lord down here, would that be all right with you?

What about our relatives and friends? If the Lord should come today, which of them would be left? If we don't know, don't you think we ought to find out whether or not they have received Christ? Are we doing all we can to rescue them from eternal punishment?

Peter says to us very warmly in his second letter:

> Dear friends, while you are waiting for these things to happen
> and for him to come,
> try hard to live without sinning;
> and be at peace with everyone
> so that he will be pleased with you when he returns.
> And remember why he is waiting.
> He is giving us time to get
> his message of salvation out to others.
>
> 2 Peter 3:14, 15 LB

4 ACCEPTING OURSELVES AS WE ARE

Made As God Wanted Us

MANY OF us wish we had been made differently. We see girls who are beautiful, and wonder why we can't be beautiful. We see men who are strong and handsome, and we aren't. Because we can't change our physical make-up, we may blame God for making us this way.

What happens if we feel bitter toward Him for the way He made us? Have you noticed when people look their very best, their most attractive? Yes, it's when they are happy, enthusiastic, eager, not when they are feeling glum, sour, depressed. When we're feeling down, we don't even look as nice as we could. Are we making ourselves look better than we might, or worse?

Are the people who seem outwardly to have the most going for them the happiest? Many of the people who commit suicide are ones who seem to have so much more than most of us. God had reasons, and good reasons, for making each of us just the way we are. It wasn't just hit-and-miss chance that we came out the way we are. How well does God know us?

Handsome and Wealthy Saul—1 Samuel 9:1, 2, 16:1, 7

At first God was the real king of Israel, and He chose judges to rule His people with Him. Samuel was a good judge. But his sons who succeeded him were not good; they were selfish, took bribes, and perverted justice (8:1-22). So the leaders came to Samuel and asked him for a king like the other nations. Samuel went to the Lord, who told him that the people had not rejected him but that they had rejected the Lord from ruling over them. He warned the nation that they would have to give their sons to the king for his service and their belongings for his upkeep, but still they wanted a king.

To see what kind of person the first king was, look at 1 Samuel 9:1, 2. Handsome and wealthy, a man who stood a head taller than the rest. What more could you want—if you were looking on the outward appearance? But what was God concerned about? 16:7.

After a short time what else did the Lord tell Samuel about Saul? 16:1. Who was it that the Lord chose to be king? David was "a man after [God's] own heart" (1 Samuel 13:14).

The Lord's Knowledge of Us—Psalm 139

Did you ever feel that no one really knows the problems you have with yourself? Turn to Psalm 139. David says, "What You God know about me is unbelievable! It is more than I can humanly comprehend! It is too wonderful for me" (see Psalm 139:6).

Read the first five verses to see what seems most wonderful to you about the Lord's knowledge. Yes, He knows everything we think as well as what we do, and every word we say, and He guards us before and behind! He knows exactly how we feel about ourselves and about Him. He searches us out and examines us. Just as if He holds us in the palm of His hand to see through us.

When did the Lord begin to know us like this? Look at verse 13. He says that He formed our features before we breathed.

How does David respond to this knowledge in verse 14?

In 15 and 16 notice the care and the skill that the Lord lavished on the forming of our beings in our mother's womb before we were born. What was being formed out of sight, He saw and guided for His own purposes.

From your various versions read the exclamations of David in verses 17 and 18 when he thinks how intimately the Lord knows him.

Now drop down to the last two verses. Since the Lord knows us so thoroughly, what is our chief concern, as it was David's? We don't want Him to find sin even in our inmost being, for that hurts Him as well as us. When we doubt and wonder why we aren't made differently, it is easy to let our thoughts blame God instead of praising Him. And David finished the psalm by asking the Lord to lead him just as he is in the ways of eternal life, not just human life.

Working with the Lord

In your inmost being can you accept this revelation of God, that He very carefully made you just as He wants you to be? That He gave you just the features you need to fulfill His purpose, to fit into His plans, to take your place in the body of Christ, to become like Himself?

Let's thank Him for the things we like about ourselves. It is likely that the rest of us have discovered good qualities about each of us that we don't realize we have. Let's mention one good quality that each of us may not realize we have. These things can be a temptation. We can rely on good qualities instead of working on the weaker ones. We can become proud of what we are and have.

Now let's talk to the Lord about the things we don't like. He is just—He doesn't give some people all the nice things and some all the difficulties. Ask Him how you can work with Him to make the most of your strong points and strengthen the weak ones. It's in working with Him that we develop character.

Psalm 139:1-6 is a good passage to memorize.

Different Temperaments

THE FOUR Martin children were so different that their parents made a study of the disposition of each one. Because the children responded so differently, the parents had to deal with each one differently. See which of these people you are most like.

Jim in high school was a quiet, sensitive, thoughtful person. He liked to think through problems deeply and thoroughly. He could always be depended upon to take responsibility and carry it out very well. It bothered him if he couldn't do things just right. If he didn't, he would brood over the difficulties, get depressed, and be ready to quit.

Quite the opposite, the other son Ted, in fifth grade, was the life of the party wherever he was. Something was always going on where Ted was. He was warm, outgoing, spontaneous, jovial, and ready to join anyone else having a good time. It was fun to have Ted around except when there was work to be done. Then Ted wasn't much help. He would flit from one thing to another, didn't think before he acted, was not organized, and often didn't carry out decisions he made.

Sue was the person who got things done. She decided what she wanted to do and went straight ahead and did it. Try to stop her when she got an idea. And don't get in her way or she might run right over you or tell you what to do. Hers were good ideas too, for she had a keen mind and good disciplined habits. But don't expect her to wait for anything.

Young Alice was everyone's favorite. She was so good-natured, always calm and steady, just takings things as they came. She didn't get involved in scrapes or try to do things she couldn't or tease for things she couldn't have. At times she stuck to her own way, but usually she just went along on an even keel.

How would these four different temperaments get along with each other and with their parents in one home? It wasn't easy, or natural. Their parents often wished they could shake them up together and make them more alike. But our temperaments are so basic to our nature that if we tried to eradicate them and make over our essential natures, we would lose our naturalness, our heartiness. We would lose what is essentially our selves.

When we are so different, it's easy to judge the other person. "Why, if I did that, it would be sin," thinks Sue to herself about something that Jim is doing. Yes, it would be for Sue, but may not be for Jim. When Jim sees how carefree and casual Ted is, he thinks, "How stupid!"

Yet how did we get these different temperaments? God made each of us just as He wanted us to be. So when we accept our various dispositions, how can we learn to appreciate the others and live in harmony with them?

Not Judging—Romans 14:10-13

For the first thing we'll learn to do look at Romans 14:10. When we judge the other fellow, he feels that we are looking down on him, despising him, holding him in contempt, for we're judging him by our own standards, not his. He naturally wants to get back at us, and so a fight begins.

When we're inclined to criticize, what should each of us do? See verse 13. We better see if we're doing what we can.

If we're not careful, what will we do that is sin? 14. Our criticism may lead us into sin. What can we do when something seems wrong to us? We can try to find some way to help the other person do what seems right to us. If we ask him why he is doing what he is, the whole situation may look different to us.

Living in Harmony—Romans 15:5, 6

In our conflicts what is God ready to give us? See Romans 15:5. That first word is steadfastness, steadiness, patience, fortitude. It's so easy to fly off the handle, make a sarcastic retort, say something we're sorry for, strike back. So often a quarrel begins with some small trifle of no real consequence that makes us mad. Can we stay steady and patient so we will see what the real difficulty is?

Secondly, God is the source of encouragement. So many things in life discourage that one of the greatest things we can do is to look for ways to encourage. Who of us needs encouragement right now? Let's see if the rest of us can give it.

Because the Lord gives us patience and encouragement, how does He expect us to live with each other? We don't have to agree on small matters, but on the important matters we can agree even if we are different.

What will be the result of agreement in verse 6? It's very evident when we come together for family devotions if one of us isn't in a mood to praise God. Then our praise isn't complete. What words of praise could all of us with all our differences use now to praise the God and Father of our Lord Jesus Christ?

Strengthening Our Weaknesses

All the various temperaments have points of strength and points of weakness. What is naturally strong about the way God made you? What is inclined to be weak? Do you know what to do to strengthen your weaknesses? If you don't, let's discuss the problem. If you do, let's ask the Lord to help us form good habits.

Easy for You, Hard for Me

JIM SHOWED his disgust whenever he went past Ted's room, for it was always messy while his room was neat and orderly. It bothered Sue that Ted never carried through his part of a family project that they were all working on. The result was that Ted spent more and more time away from home with friends who appreciated his humor and his outgoing nature. His parents became much concerned that he couldn't enjoy his own family.

Sue could understand Jim's wanting to do everything just right, but it bothered her that he would sit and brood instead of getting up and getting things done. When the family planned their vacation trip, she had the route all sketched while he was pondering the best course over one small section. And he wasn't satisfied to call the job done.

It's natural for Jim to think, "Why doesn't Ted have any sense of organization; it's easy." It's easy for Jim, but hard for Ted. It's easy for Sue to finish her projects, but hard for Jim because he has such high standards. It's easy for Ted to praise the Lord because he forgets the difficulties, but it's hard for Jim. What is easy for one is hard for another.

Will we let these differences disrupt our family life so that we don't appreciate each other? Will we let the hard things discourage us so that we give up and don't try any longer? Will we say, "That's just the way I am," and let it go at that? What will we do?

What Was Hard for Young Timothy

The Apostle Paul had a young convert who was very dear to him. Some things were hard and some were easy for this young man. What did Paul tell Timothy to do about these hard things?

We'll look for answers in the two letters that Paul wrote to Timothy as well as in the other Bible books. We'll find his first difficulty implied in 2 Timothy 1:7. Timothy was naturally shy and timid. It was hard for a shy young man to perform all the public ministries that Paul asked him to do.

Just before that in verse 6 what Paul tells Timothy to do suggests that he had let something go that he shouldn't have. He should keep his gift of God kindled and burning brightly.

Before that in verse 5 Paul commends Timothy for something that doesn't seem too hard for him. Sincere faith is very important.

Then look in 1 Timothy 5:23 for something else that was hard for him. He was often sick physically; especially did he have trouble with his stomach. It's hard to be faithful and optimistic when you're feeling low physically.

Something else Paul urged is hard for all of us, young and old. Look at 1 Timothy 4:12. What kind of example do we set in speech, conduct, love, faith and purity? That's a big order, and I'm sure Timothy felt the magnitude of it. And in verse 13 note what Timothy was to do before large groups. Finish that chapter to see how much Paul expected.

Even though Timothy was weak physically, what did Paul urge in 2 Timothy 2:1-6? He should be ready for his share of suffering like a good soldier, compete according to rules like an athlete, and work as hard as a farmer. That is being strong! Paul didn't expect life would be easy for Timothy.

What Was Easier for Timothy

Yet many good qualities seemed to be more natural for Timothy. In 1 Corinthians 4:17 what does Paul say to the church at Corinth about young Timothy? He calls him beloved and faithful.

And in Philippians 2:19-23? It's pretty strong language when Paul says that he has no one like him. What's the matter with the other believers? The inference is that only Timothy is unselfish enough to look out for the interests of the church rather than his own. That's saying a lot.

How is Paul praising Timothy when he says that Timothy served with him as a son with a father?

In 1 Thessalonians 3:2,3 what is Paul sending Timothy to Thessalonica to do? That's a very responsible mission. So Timothy has many good qualities.

Supporting Others

In 1 Corinthians 16:10 Paul asks the Corinthians to put Timothy at ease when he comes. He wants the church at Corinth to support and strengthen Timothy. And Sue, read what he asks the Thessalonians to do in 1 Thessalonians 5:14.

Can we do that right here in our family? Instead of leaving a person alone to battle the difficulties by himself, can't we discuss them with him and help each other? Instead of saying, "Pooh, why can't you do that; that's easy," can we say, "What's easy for me may be hard for you. So I ought to be able to help you"?

How would it be this week if instead of giving up on the hard things, we would call for help? Right at the moment when we're tempted to call it quits, instead we call out loudly, "This is hard! Help!" Then whoever hears the call can rush to the rescue. We'll see if we can help the person in need help himself to do the hard thing. If he can't, we'll do it for him, so he won't get discouraged. How many of us will try to be supporters this week?

Let's ask the Lord to strengthen both the people who need help and the supporters.

Liking Ourselves

HOW DO you feel about yourself right now—do you hate yourself, tolerate yourself, love yourself or really like yourself? Do any of you both like yourself and dislike yourself? As dreadful as are the wars that go on between countries, the worst wars are those that go on inside individual people. Is any kind of struggle going on inside you? When don't you like yourself? Do you enjoy being by yourself as well as with others?

Some people can't believe on Christ or make decisions because they can't pull all the parts of themselves together enough to focus on one thing. The parts of them scatter in many directions. These people don't feel right about themselves. What happens when a person hates himself? Often he tries desperately to find a substitute, like gaining money or power or pleasure or fame. And he projects his hatred of himself onto other people, so his neighbor better beware. If he makes himself a zero, he has nothing to give to others.

The Lord tells us to deny anything that keeps us from putting Him first, but how does He say we should feel about ourselves? He says, ". . . love your neighbor as yourself" (Matthew 22:39 RSV). He takes it for granted that we should love ourselves because He loves us so much. If we feel easy and comfortable about ourselves, we are free to help others. Loving ourselves doesn't mean selfishness, conceit, or egotism, but respect and acceptance for what God has planned.

When is it hard for you to like yourself? Often it's when we or someone else expects too much of us—more than we can manage. When we see ourselves as a certain kind of person, but we fail to act like this kind of person, we're upset. Suppose a new person your age moves on our street. You make friends with him and want to show him what a Christian is like so that he too will want to receive Christ. But one day as you are working together, you do something so selfish that he blurts out, "I wish you were a Christian. A Christian wouldn't do that!" Then it's hard to like yourself. What do we do in a case like that?

God's Answer in Scripture—Romans 7:15-19, 8:2-4

Don't think you're the only person who doesn't like yourself at times. All of us have this experience. Even the great Apostle Paul in the Bible. Turn to the paragraph that begins with Romans 7:15. Even Paul did not understand his own actions. Why does he feel torn apart?

Is his problem that he is rebelling against the law? No, he acknowledges that the law is good. What is the root of his trouble?

When Paul says that nothing good dwells in his flesh, he doesn't mean that he can't do anything right, but that he can't do anything that will justify him as a sinner in God's sight—anything that will bring him to God.

Read that important verse 19 in the various versions. Did you ever get up in the morning thinking to yourself, "Now I want to make this a good day. I'm going to do everything I know I should this day." What usually happens? I have the best of intentions, but I discover that I am not strong enough to carry them out.

Drop down to verses 24, 25 to feel the cry of every poor human soul.

O wretched man that I am!
who shall deliver me from the body of this death?
I thank God through Jesus Christ our Lord. . . .

Then chapter 8 explains how Christ delivers us from this struggle. There is only one way to get free; read verse 2. We're living either under the law of the Spirit of life in Christ Jesus or the law of sin and death.

In verse 3 how did God Himself condemn sin in our human nature? God sent His own Son to take the condemnation that sin deserves.

In verse 4 when do we have the power to do the good that we really want to do? When we walk in the Spirit, when the Lord has control of our lives.

At the end of chapter 8 Paul assures us that we can be more than conquerors through Him who loved us, for nothing can separate us from Him. 37-39.

God's Answer in Our Lives

So then if Christ died for us and lives for us and prays for us and gives us His own power to obey Him, how should we feel about ourselves? If we are so important to Him, we should be important to ourselves. We can continuously keep breathing in His own divine life with its resurrection power.

Let's see how this truth will work out in our daily lives. Sue is used to getting high grades in school because she is a keen person and she works. When she gets sick and has to stay out of school for two weeks, she finds on returning that she is far behind. Because she feels so far behind, she can't concentrate on her studies, which gets her even further behind.

What can she do when she feels torn apart by what she expects of herself and what she actually does? She can face the reality that it will take maybe weeks to catch up and won't expect to do it overnight. Though she is used to doing things quickly, the Lord can help her to plod along a little at a time patiently, though this is not her natural life-style.

Ted used to be the best batter on his baseball team. But when a new boy joined the team, he began getting an even higher average than Ted. This has soured Ted on the season's games. What is really the trouble, though Ted has not acknowledged it? How can he get over his jealousy? If he calls it sin and asks the Lord to take it away, he can acknowledge the fact that there will always be people who are better than we are. Are we going to let that fact spoil our good times?

In his hurry to get home one night on his bicycle, Jim hit a small child who was playing in the street. It didn't hurt the child much, but Jim couldn't forgive himself for being so careless. How could we help him? If God forgives him and the child's family forgives him, the Lord can help him to forgive himself.

Hiding from Ourselves

WILL THE real *you* please stand up? Do you feel just the same and act just the same when you are here at home, when you're at school, when you're at church, when you're with your friends at play, when you're with your best friend? Why do we act differently in different situations? When do you feel most truly yourself? Which people see you as you really are, your real inner self? Does anyone? How well do you know yourself? One of the most important discoveries we can make is our own real selves. Many people do not know themselves, even many adults after living with themselves for many years.

Why don't we know ourselves? Wouldn't you think that would be the first thing we would know? But some people are afraid to take a good look at themselves. They are uptight, knotted up and anxious about so many things that they seem like several people instead of one.

When they are with those who have authority over them, they put on the front of being humble and submissive. When they are at home with people they live with, they use sarcastic language about their bosses. When they are with people they like, they are pleasant and agreeable. With people they consider their enemies, they are hostile and bitter. They put on different masks for the different occasions. Much of the time they are putting on an act, trying to impress people or live up to other people's expectations.

But it is very wearing to be a phony. We have to keep changing all the time, wondering what the other fellow is thinking and what we should do. Basically it is dishonest, for we are pretending to be what we are not, and deceiving not only others but ourselves as well. We can't act spontaneously and naturally, for we always have to wonder how we are being received.

If we want to experience reality in this world and not the phony, we have to start with ourselves. Who are we, right now, as we are? We can't move to what we want to be until we know what we are now. When we relate to people, we want to know their real selves, not their masks. What separates us from others is our secrets, for what I must keep secret poisons me. We are not whole persons until we are open to the world, not afraid to know the truth about ourselves or let others know. What are we hiding from ourselves? How can we discover who we really are?

The Biblical Pharisees—Matthew 23

The Pharisees were people in the Bible who didn't know who they were. Even today there are people who won't have anything to do with the church because they say it is full of Pharisees. How did they deceive themselves?

In Matthew 23:3 see how they were double-minded. It is always so much easier to say what we should do than to do it.

Though the Pharisees were the religious leaders of the Jews who considered themselves superior because they kept the law very strictly, how did they treat others, in verse 4? They made even stricter rules than God made, but wouldn't help the common people obey them.

Jim, in verses 5-7 of The Living Bible read the way they liked to be honored. What does this show about them? They were proud.

At the beginning of paragraphs in this chapter note how many times Jesus warns the Pharisees, "Woe unto you!" Look at verses 13, 16, 23, 25, 27, and 29.

Then He tells them why they are in danger of judgment even if they are such sticklers for detail.

In verse 23 you know what mint is. Dill is a garden herb used to season dill pickles. Cummin is also a spice. What is Jesus' point in this verse? The Pharisees were very fussy about giving the Lord a tenth of their garden produce, but were entirely neglecting the really important matters of the law—justice, mercy, and faith. As if they strained a tiny insect from their wine but swallowed a camel!

Verses 25, 26 give us the Pharisees' chief error. What are the significant words here? Outside and inside. Outwardly they looked religious and holy. Instead they were greedy and grasping. What the Lord said to them He also says to us: first make the inside clean that the outside may be also. The Lord works inside out. If we have a strong inner center for our lives, the outside will look right.

In verses 27, 28 Jesus said the Pharisees were not only dirty inside, but what else? Even dead in sin. When they should have helped the rest of the people receive Jesus as their promised Messiah-Saviour, what did He have to say about them? Sue, will you please read verses 37-39? They thought they knew who they were, but they didn't.

Knowing Who We Are

Can each of us get all the ideas about ourselves pulled together? First that the Lord accepts us just as we are. He doesn't wait until we reach any level of goodness because we can't do it ourselves. He says, "Come to Me and I will make you." He has loved us with an everlasting love, more than anyone else, and has given Himself for us. He made us just as He wanted us to be, and has a special place in His plans for each of us. Next we ought to be sure of our family's love and concern and acceptance.

Then can we accept ourselves just as we are, with our strong points and our weak points? Without trying to hide anything? Even the worst about us? We don't need to stay the way we are, but we need to know where we are. We have to start here. If we are honest about this, we can move to where we want to be. Let's ask the Lord to show us what we're trying to hide so that we can bring it out into the open and deal with it.

Then we can be our real selves when we relate to other people. We won't just be trying to impress others or live up to their expectations. We know who we are and what kind of person we want to become.

Being Accepted by Others

RAY WANTED very much to be in with his gang at school. He spent a great deal of time in school affairs and he wanted badly to be accepted as part of the crowd. And he also wanted to stay in with the church people with whom he had grown up. He didn't want to leave the church, but he didn't want to be an outsider at school. What he did was to try to be two people—a Christian at church and a buddy to his pals at school. At church he was honest in his heart when he said he loved the Lord, but during the week he did things with the gang that he would not admit in church. He tried to keep the church people from knowing what else he did.

How would you evaluate this teen-ager? What is right about his conduct, and what is wrong? How does he feel about it himself?

Is it wrong for him to want to be part of his school crowd? Not at all. We all want to belong to groups that we like, that do things we enjoy doing. Young people live in their own world with their own kind. And it was good that Ray didn't want to leave the church, still wanted to be accepted by church people. What is wrong with Ray? He shouldn't be dishonest and deceitful, and he shouldn't disobey the Lord.

How shall we relate to people our own age who are not Christians? Why not just stay away from them? Natural contacts with them are opportunities of helping them see that they need the Lord. Must we do all that they do in order to be friends with them? How can we be friends without disobeying the Lord?

Ray thought that he was getting the best of both worlds when he tried to keep in with both. What kind of life is the half-and-half life—half on earth and half in heaven? Usually the enticements of the world and the lusts of our sinful nature clamor louder than the still, small voice of God. It's like trying to walk a tightrope.

Neither Hot Nor Cold—Revelation 3:15-22

What does the Lord say about this stance, with one foot on earth and one in heaven? Turn to Revelation 3:15. You know how tasty mashed potatoes are when they get cold, and how we enjoy a hot cold drink when we're warm. We want hot food hot and cold food cold, not lukewarm. Though Ray would like to hold onto the Lord, the Lord will spit him out of His mouth! That's putting it straight.

When Ray thinks he's pretty smart for living two lives, how does the Lord see him, in verse 17?

In 18 the Lord isn't talking about literal money and clothes and eye salve. What does He mean that we should get from Him? Will you explain that verse, Mother? He's talking about the real values contrasted with the sham values of the world, a person's integrity, and eternal realities.

In 19 why is the Lord using these harsh words? Because He loves us, so that we will repent.

In 20 what is it that He wants most? To have intimate fellowship with us, for us to invite Him into our lives so that we'll get really excited about Him. Once we have personal dealings with Him, we won't be cold or lukewarm anymore.

In 21 He talks about the person who conquers. What does Ray have to conquer in his situation? Our temptation is to think that we're missing something if we don't do everything other people are doing. No doubt we are missing some very distressing experiences.

In the World, Not of the World

When we were saved, the Lord left us in the world for a purpose, though we are not of the world. What is His prayer for us in Philippians 1:9, 10? This world needs His love through us. We must be close enough to people for them to feel His love. But note the next phrase. Why is it necessary that knowledge and all discernment go with that love? So that we'll know what to approve and what not to approve, so that in all our contacts we will be pure and blameless for the day of Christ.

And in Romans 12:2 RSV he says, "Do not be conformed to this world but be transformed. . . ." In our relation with our friends, how can we be transformed, not conforming, and show them love with discernment that approves what is excellent? Still maintaining our own center in Christ, how can we show them love without conforming?

Yes, first we can enjoy together what we have in common, what both of us enjoy and approve. What do our friends like that we also like? Since Christ helps us do all things well, we can have lots of fun and do some things so well that people will like to have us around. We can gain their respect as real people, not as phonies. We can show we care about them as people, not just as things.

And where we differ from them because we are obeying the Lord, what will we do? We can explain to them tactfully and graciously the reasons, without a holier-than-thou attitude. When they are uncertain and confused about many things, we know who we are and where we are going.

What is often the result of the things they do but we don't? Often the result is anything but fun. What happens in their drinking parties, their drug sessions, their adventures in stealing, their cute pranks? The next day they wish they hadn't done them. If it takes that sort of thing to be popular, who wants to be popular? If it's a question of being accepted by the crowd or by the Lord, which will we choose?

Let's ask the Lord to give us His own love for all our contacts and also His discernment to know what to approve.

Fear

THINK OF the last time you felt afraid. What was the reason for the fear? Were you afraid you'd get hurt? Did you feel guilty? Did you feel inadequate, that you couldn't do something? Or was there another reason? How did this fear affect you as a person? Did you freeze, feel rigid? Did it keep you from acting, concentrating?

Think of other things that you have been afraid of. Don't think that it is childish to have fears. All of us have them, even the strongest people—we just have different kinds. Children may be afraid of thunder and lightning, teens may be afraid of being left out of something they want to be in on, and adults may fear that the plans they have worked on for years will fail. I confess that I was afraid to begin my new work in a brand-new company. There is fear even in love, for we're always wondering if the one we love will reject us, but the Bible says that perfect love casts out fear (1 John 4:18).

The Bible tells us both to fear and not to fear, using the word in two ways—a healthy way and a harmful way. Three hundred sixty-five times, once for each day in the year, the Bible says, "Fear not."

Two Kinds of Fear

God created us with an instinct for self-preservation, fear that is a warning in time of danger. It prompts us to flee or fight, to get away from danger.

There is also another sense in which we are to fear. Look at Psalm 33:8. What kind of fear is this? Awe and reverence because of who God is—Creator, Redeemer, and Judge of all. It is great respect for His authority and might and love and holiness, and for His ways that art infinitely higher than our ways. Instead of the word "fear" in this verse, substitute the word "reverence" as you read it, Jim. If we don't reverence the Lord God, we better watch out!

Turn to Proverbs 9:10. In what other sense do we need to fear the Lord? If we don't start by respecting the absolute truth of the Lord, we have no foundation for our thinking. We have no valid base to begin with. His wisdom gives us insight into what is right and wrong. If we don't fear evil, it will hurt us. So we are to reverence the Lord for Himself and for the start of all our thinking.

In the New Testament we often hear Jesus saying, "Fear not." Turn to Matthew 10:28. Think of the multitudes of people who live in fear that their outer bodies will be killed, but don't even realize that their souls, their real selves, are dead now, were never alive. It is hard for many people to believe the next verse.

What conclusion do you draw from verse 30?

Since the Lord watches every sparrow and knows exactly how many hairs are on our heads, how does He sum up His care of us in verse 31? If we revere the Lord as He deserves, why should we fear anything else? We can't be our best selves when we feel threatened, bound by dread, aware only of the fear and not of the whole situation.

Stilling the Storm—Matthew 8:18, 23-27

When we find ourselves caught in the throes of fear, what shall we do? We can't wish it away; it won't go. Even when we try to reason it away, it doesn't always go. But one thing always helps.

Turn to Matthew 8:18 for the setting of a Bible incident, then drop down to verse 23. When we are afraid, we feel as if a storm is raging inside us.

What was Jesus doing during the storm on the lake? Even though waves were breaking over the sides of the boat!

But the disciples weren't asleep. What did they do?

What did Jesus' answer imply? Did the disciples have reason to be afraid? If they had had more faith, what could they have done? If Jesus can rebuke a storm on the treacherous sea, can't He rebuke the storms that go on inside us? What is our part? To cry out to Him as did the disciples. Not to assume that we can rebuke them ourselves.

In verse 27 should the disciples have marvelled that even the winds and the sea obey Jesus? They were amazed that a Man who could do this was in their boat with them!

Evaluating Our Fears

Is any kind of storm brewing inside us just now—even a little storm? Let's not be afraid to look it squarely in the face and call it fear if it is fear. What happens if we try to repress it, pretend it isn't there, and push it down where we forget it? It usually comes out in worse ways, maybe making us lie about it. If we really believe that Jesus can calm the fear, we will call upon Him to do it. Let's ask right now.

If we have any questions about our fears, let's talk about them. Do we as a family have any healthy fears—fears we should have for our protection? Yes, fear of disobeying traffic rules, of lying to each other, of cheating in school, of failing to do our part in the community and nation.

Suppose we have a sneaking suspicion that we're guilty about something. What shall we do? Let's not let that kind of fear bother us for a minute. We can immediately ask forgiveness of the Lord and of anyone else involved.

Suppose we feel afraid of being inadequate in some way. What can we do then? Yes, we can be realistic about our abilities and recognize our weaknesses. Maybe we are expecting too much. Maybe we're so proud that we feel we must always be strong. No one is always strong. Or if we should do something difficult, how can we improve our ability or our skill or our insight? We can find out from people who know what preparation is necessary.

In closing, Jim, will you please read Psalm 46:1-3.

The Christian's Strength and Weakness

TODAY'S SUBJECT is a riddle to many people because it is one of the paradoxes, apparent contradictions, the yes-no of the Christian life. We'll expect to understand it more and more as we grow in grace. So let's pause a minute at the beginning of our time together to ask the Spirit's discernment in our thinking.

The subject is being strong and weak at the same time. How do most people think of a strong person? Yes, one who has what he wants and can do what he wants. Sometimes in contrast to this, a Christian seems weak. In what ways did Christ seem strong when He was on earth? Only He knew about the Father and the spiritual realities, He spoke as no man spoke, He did miracles, even raised the dead, and He Himself rose from the dead. How did He seem weak to some people? He did not what He willed but what the Father willed, He wanted no possessions of His own, and let His enemies nail Him to the cross.

We can't do what Christ did, but in what ways should we be strong today? Would we also expect to be weak in some ways, or not? When is a Christian strong?

Paul's Strength—2 Corinthians 11:24—12:10

When we think of the Apostle Paul, what kind of person comes to our minds? A very strong character. How was he strong? He was the first missionary, he gave us much of the New Testament, did many miracles, dared to say "Imitate me as I do Christ," made many converts and started many churches! Do you visualize everything going smoothly for this strong character because of his faith and obedience? Turn to 2 Corinthians 11. Jim, will you please read verses 24-27 and also 32, 33? Why was Paul willing to endure all those sufferings? They didn't make him bitter, only stronger.

In 28 what else was on his mind and heart? The churches he had started needed a lot of care and strengthening.

If Paul were to boast of one thing out of all his experiences, what do you think it might be? What does he say in 30? In the next chapter he explains this strange statement.

In addition to all his other adventures with the Lord, he was privileged to have an amazing experience that no other human being has had. Sue, read 12:1-4. He was taken up into the heavenly realm where God dwells and he heard things he couldn't describe in words, for they were literally "out of this world"!

That truly was something to boast about! How did he feel about it, in verse 5? Instead of being proud, he again spoke of his weakness.

Let's read verse 7 in our various versions. We are not told just what this was; some scholars think it was weak eyes.

Since God had done so many other wonderful things for him, what was his attitude toward this complaint that bothered him? 8.

What was God's answer in 9? How could God's power be made perfect in Paul's weakness? God loves to show what He can do in very weak instruments. His power can overcome and overshadow any form of weakness! His power shows up best in weak people!

So what is Paul's conclusion in the last part of 9? When he is weak, when he doesn't show off his own strength, the power of Christ is demonstrated.

Can we say verse 10 with Paul and mean it? Can we be content with anything that Christ sends us, for if we're not counting on ourselves, we can count on Him?

Becoming Strong

How do you explain our riddle about being strong and weak at the same time? Like Paul each of us has special strengths. The very fact that we are a Christian family who discuss God's Word together is a privilege that many don't have. What suffering has the Lord asked us to endure? Where do we feel weak right now? Are we taking these hard experiences as Paul did, asking the Lord to demonstrate His strength in our weakness? Do we feel weak in ourselves, but strong in the Lord? Or do we feel bitter about our weakness and blame the Lord? Then He can't help us and nothing good comes of it.

When Wayne first landed in the hospital after his car accident, he felt pretty bad, and kept asking, "Why did this have to happen to me?" Then one day a blind man visited him and gave him a game that he had thought up and made. That opened Wayne's eyes to things that he could do in bed. He read some books he hadn't had time for, got to know people in a deeper way, and he prayed for people all over the world. When he was given some artists' clay, he modeled a dog that won an award. After five weeks in the hospital, he went home a much stronger character, though his body was still weak. The little things that used to bother him no longer seemed to matter.

Let's each take one of our weaknesses and ask the Lord to show His power through this weakness. Let's also listen to the Lord to see if He wants us to do anything in relation to it.

5 DEVELOPING OUR POTENTIAL

Growing All Round

A BABY is very sweet, but not a five year old who acts like a baby. We call that kind of development retarded. Sometimes a child's body grows normally but his brain does not develop as it should. Then we are disappointed with his responses, for he looks large enough to act much more mature than he does. That kind of child is abnormal in his growth.

When we built our house, we set out small trees and bushes around it. At first they looked too small for the house, but year after year they grew until they looked just right. But they didn't stop growing. They grew until they got too big for the house, and spread where we didn't want them. A healthy living thing does not stop growing—it keeps on and on.

And the things we plant aren't the only things that grow. Weeds grow faster than grass and flowers. Weeds take over if we don't continually keep killing them. We have an everlasting battle with the weeds.

We too are to keep growing till the end of our days, never stopping. Of course we may grow faster during some seasons than others, but continual growth should be evident to everyone who knows us.

Growing Like Trees—Psalm 92:12-14

Psalm 92 compares growing people and growing trees. What two kinds of trees are mentioned in verse 12? What do you like about a palm tree? It is shapely, evergreen, slender, straight and tall. It sometimes bears dates. The cedar of Lebanon is a magnificent tree, larger and thicker than the palm; it exudes a fragrant gum, is a warm red tone, solid and free from knots.

Read the wording of verse 13 from The Living Bible, Ted.

How long will these trees be green and growing? 14.

Rounded Growth—Luke 2:52

The boy Jesus grew up in the land of palm and cedar trees. Can you picture what his life was like when He was growing up in the village of Nazareth? What did He often do with Joseph? Work in the carpenter shop. What did He do for His mother? Probably brought water from the village well..

Though He was God as well as man, in what four ways did He grow? Look at Luke 2:52. What kind of wisdom did He study in His school? Probably it was mostly the Hebrew language and the Old Testament. He grew taller just as other boys grow. He was always in favor with His Father God and the better people knew Him the better they liked Him. Can we say that about ourselves?

Balanced Maturity—2 Peter 1:5-8

Another part of the Bible will help us decide whether or not our growth is rounded and balanced. Turn to 2 Peter 1:5. Before that Peter says that God has given us everything we need to become strong characters—He has given us great and precious promises and His own life inside, His own Spirit, made us partakers of His very nature. So we start with faith in Him, coming to Him on His own terms, believing that He has exchanged our sin for the righteousness of Christ.

1. *Moral maturity.* Then Peter, who formerly was up and down, outlines the various kinds of growth that we should be experiencing, beginning with virtue, which is moral maturity. Let's check to see if we are growing steadily in these six ways. Moral maturity means knowing and doing what is right rather than what is wrong. What questions of right or wrong may we have trouble with? How do we respond to friends who expect us to cheat and lie? How can we refuse to drink liquor and yet be friendly to people who do? Shall we report a drug peddler even though it may get us in trouble?

2. *Mental maturity.* In verse 5 what shall we add to our virtue? When we're going to school, teachers see to it that we are growing in knowledge. Do you children try to get all the knowledge you can, not merely what is required, but all the fascinating insights you can into the way this complex world operates? And we parents can't stop learning when we're out of school. Often it's hard for me to get time to read in order to keep up, but Mother and I must keep reading in our time budgets.

3. *Emotional maturity.* What is the next kind of growth in verse 6? When do we in this family need to exercise self-control? Yes, Mother, it must be hard for you when you have dinner hot and ready, and we aren't ready to sit down to it. Alice, you need plenty of control when Ted teases you. Next time you are tempted, send up a quick little SOS to the Lord, "Help me control my feelings."

4. *Physical maturity.* After self-control comes steadfastness, fortitude, temperance. Are we doing anything that hinders our physical growth, that keeps us from being in the pink of condition? Yes, too much candy or snacks or reading too late at night. I must swim more regularly, and not find so many excuses to keep me from it.

5. *Spiritual maturity.* Then how fast are we growing in godliness? Is our relation to the Lord closer than it was last year? Do we feel that we have more of His fulness today than last month? What are our problems in relation to the Lord?

6. *Social maturity.* In verse 7 what is the last kind of growth? Is our love for people growing? Is it easier for us to get along with people because we love them more? Love is the bond that unites all these other kinds of growth. Think of one person who needs your love right now. How can you give it to him?

Sue, read verse 8 in The Living Bible. It is the Lord's plan that we grow in all these ways. In which of these are you strongest? In which weakest? Let's ask the Lord how we can strengthen our weaknesses and ask for His divine power to do it.

Spiritual Gifts

EVERY PERSON is born with certain abilities; every person who is born again has been given special spiritual abilities—gifts of the Spirit (1 Peter 4:10, Ephesians 4:7). But many Christians live and die without realizing this great fact. If they don't know they have a spiritual gift, they are not likely to develop it and use it as fully as God intended. We are living fully only when we fulfill the purpose for which we were created.

We hate to see anything going to waste, whether it is money in the bank not being used for good, or a plot of land that is just growing up to weeds, or machinery that is rusting away unused, or people's abilities that the world needs. Oliver Wendell Holmes lamented that some people never sing, but die with all their music still in them. Are we making the most of what we've been given?

What Are Spiritual Gifts—1 Corinthians 12:4-11, 28

Beginning with 1 Corinthians 12:4, what is different about the gifts of the Spirit that we have been given, and what is the same? There are varieties of gifts, of service, and of working, but the same source for all of them.

I'll write on the chalkboard the gifts that are mentioned here. Paul isn't trying to list all of them. What does he begin with, in verse 8? Do we know anyone who has the gift of wisdom and knowledge? Yes, no doubt our pastor has this gift. Anyone not in a position of leadership? Usually those with this gift use it as a leader.

What is the next gift mentioned? Who seems to have special faith? Yes, Mrs. Eck gets tremendous answers to her prayers, apparently because she has great faith.

Sometimes faith is manifested especially in healing and miracles. Many kinds of miracles are needed in our day. Not only physical healing of the body, but emotional healing of damaged souls and people's inner beings that are torn apart by personal problems. Every person needs the miracle of being born anew.

What spirits do we need to distinguish in our day? Both the Spirit of God and the spirit of the evil one speak to us in a still, small voice. Sometimes it's hard to tell which is which.

Some people are greatly inspired by speaking in new languages they have never learned, and some are given the ability to interpret these other languages.

Who decides what our individual gift is? Look at verse 11. The Holy Spirit knows just which gift is best for each of us.

Now drop down to verse 28. What other gifts are listed here? Jesus' first disciples were called apostles. Do we have prophets today? The people who teach and warn us today don't have the same ministry as the ones in Old Testament times because now we have the whole Bible, which reveals God's plans for us.

Teachers are very important; most churches have few pastors but many teachers. Helpers are also very important. Very many kinds of help are continually needed. And administrators need to organize so that time and ability are not wasted. So we see many different kinds of spiritual gifts.

Why Given—1 Corinthians 12:14-26, Ephesians 4:11, 12

What are God's reasons for giving these gifts of the Spirit to His people? He tells us in the paragraph beginning with 1 Corinthians 12:14. The church as a whole is the body of Christ, who is the head; so it can be compared with our physical bodies. Let's take parts reading this section. That will help us get the effect of verse 14, that the body of Christ consists of many members. Ted, read what the feet should not say in verse 15. And Alice, what shouldn't the ear say in 16?

Sue, read the questions and God's answer in verses 17-21. The whole body needs every one of its members, the church needs every one of its members, and our family needs every one of its members.

Jim, read how we ought to treat any member who seems to be weak or inferior, 22-24.

And Mother, how should all of us feel about each other, 25, 26?

Then Jim, read Ephesians 4:11, 12 in the New English Bible to get the purpose of the gifts stated very concisely. ". . . to equip God's people for work in his service, to the building up of the body of Christ." Each of us is to make our own unique contribution.

Our Part—Romans 12:6-8

What now is our part in the use of our gifts? Turn to Romans 12:6-8. Sue, let's you and I read these verses, in the Revised Standard Version, as a litany, I starting each phrase, and you finishing it:

I   Having gifts that differ according to the grace given to us,
YOU let us use them:
I   If prophecy,
YOU in proportion to our faith;
I   If service,
YOU in our serving, etc.

We are to use our gifts, and in order to obey that command, we have to develop them. What gifts has the Lord given members of our family? Ask yourself these questions:

> What kinds of ministries does my spiritual nature seem drawn toward?
> In what kinds of ways has the Lord already used me?
> What abilities have others noticed in me?
> What new areas would I like to have a chance to explore?

Since spiritual gifts are for body or team ministries, other people can often see them more clearly than we can. Does any one of us seem to have unusual faith? Wisdom? Organizing ability? Ability to help? Musical ability? Writing?

What can we each do to develop what we've been given?

Let's thank the Lord that we've each been given a gift or gifts, and ask Him to help us discern them, develop them and use them fully for His own name's sake.

Use of Our Time and Talents

AS WE look back over the past week, are we satisfied with the way we used our time and talents? How much time did we waste? Did we accomplish what we wanted to? What did we learn from our experience—what would we do again, and what wouldn't we?

Time is one thing we all have the same amount of, yet people use it so differently. Some get so much value from it, some so little.

> I have only just a minute,
> Only sixty seconds in it.
> Forced upon me—can't refuse it.
> But it's up to me to use it.
> I must suffer if I lose it.
> Give account if I abuse it.
> Just a tiny little minute,
> But eternity is in it.
>
> ANONYMOUS

Sue's friends envied her because she had such cute clothes. When she was eight years old, she asked her mother to teach her to sew, and she made sewing a hobby through the years until with Mother's help, she could make her own clothes. The other girls would sometimes sit and talk and watch her sew, but it was Sue who had the clothes—because she made them.

Instead of spending what money he had on small items, Jim saved his money until he had enough to buy a good camera. Then he studied light effects and scene design until he took exceptional pictures. He was the photographer of the school yearbook and some of his photos were used by the local newspaper.

How does the Lord expect us to use our time and talents?

Parable of the Money—Matthew 25:14-29

As Jesus was preparing His followers for His departure from this world, He told the parable of the man going abroad who called his servants and entrusted his money to them according to their abilities. To one he gave $5000, to another $2000, and a third $1000. His money was called talents or bags of gold. A talent or a bag of gold would be about a thousand dollars. Start to read at Matthew 25:16. What did the servant with the $5000 do?

And the one with the $2000, in 17?

And the one with the $1000? 18. No doubt he hid the money to keep it safe.

After a long time when the master returned to settle his accounts with his servants, what did the servant to whom he had entrusted $5000 bring him, in 20? And what was the master's response to him? 21. Let's read verse 21 from our various versions.

In 22 what did the servant with the $2000 bring the master? And what was the master's response to him in 23?

In 24, 25 what did the servant bring who had had the $1000? What was his excuse? How often is this our excuse when we don't make good use of our abilities? What is more often our excuse?

How did the master reply to this, in 26-28? Was it fair to give this man's $1000 to the one who had $5000 and now has $10,000?

Read the general principle in verse 29. Our abilities are raw potential, not worth too much in the beginning, but capable of amazing development. What we have is God's gift to us; what we make of it is our gift to Him. The more we develop what we have, the more we are ready to receive from Him.

Being Good Stewards

How does this principle work out for us today? The more we use what we have, the more ability God gives us. Our first duty is to concentrate on our responsibilities until we do them well, just the best we are capable of. And we never know what we can do until we give ourselves wholly to them. Sue didn't sew until she had her school work done. Then she knew how much time she had left, and felt free to sew. If we dawdle over our duties, we won't have much time left to choose what we want to do.

Some people keep switching from one interest to another all their lives. Young people need to explore many interests until they discover which one or ones the Lord wishes to use. Then they should specialize in that interest. We want to be able to do some things well. Is each of you exploring various possibilities, or have you found your chief interest and ability?

Have we been truly enjoying our leisure time? Our play isn't supposed to be work, yet many of us work at our hobbies because we enjoy them so much. How do we evaluate our time spent with TV? Has it been enjoyable and profitable? Which programs seem to be a waste of time? Seeing some of them once is enough—just enough to know what they are like.

Let's also evaluate how we have been spending Sunday, the Lord's day. What is the purpose of keeping one day different from the rest? For worship and refreshing. Has Sunday been refreshing for us? Even machines wear out when operated continously. It's great to have one day a week when we don't feel that we must do anything. God wouldn't set aside one day a week if He wouldn't help us get our necessary work done on the other days.

"Dear Lord, help us to be good stewards of the time and talents You've given us. May we discover which abilities You want to use and concentrate on developing them fully."

Creativity

THE LORD intends that we should be creative people, yes, each one of us. Christians should be the most colorful, resourceful, original of all people. Why? We're made in the image of the Great Original, the Creator Himself. In order to carry out His great purposes in our world, He wants to work through us. Of course He could do it all Himself, but how thrilling that He takes us up into His tremendous plans! In order to obey His commands for our world, we have to be creative.

What person you know is most creative, with fresh new ideas and ways, not content to do the same thing in the same way? What makes this person creative? The most productive creators are those who are dead to sin but fully alive in Christ, who see things many people do not see, who can put things together in new combinations.

What the Lord asks us to do today is to take the principles He has given us in His Word, and use them in new ways to meet the changing needs of our world. This takes some doing. We can't just copy what has been done in the past because conditions are so different. We still have the great commandment, to go into all the world and show forth God's salvation to all people, but we don't travel as David and Paul did, and we don't use the same methods and means of communication that they did. We have to reach our world by means of today's media.

The Lord Creating in Us

How does the Lord do His work today through us? Turn to Philippians 2:12, 13. In these verses most translations emphasize the contrast between *out* and *in*. Does the one you have? Read the two verses in your version, Jim. Work out your salvation for it is God who works in you. God works in as we work out.

Now notice what is God's part and what is our part. Read your version, Sue. What does God do? The first word is that he *wills,* He inspires our will, energizes and creates in us the desire to carry out His purpose. The second word is that He *works,* helps us obey Him, gives us the power to do what He wants done.

What is our part? To finish the work God has begun in us, to achieve His goals. *Fear* in this sense is reverence and awe, being fearful of displeasing Him, of failing to do our part, of doing anything that might hurt His cause.

Read verses 12, 13 in your version to summarize, Ted.

Now look at Ephesians 2:10. Read this in your versions, Mother and Sue. We are God's design, His handiwork, made as He wanted us to be. Because we are united to Him, He can do His good works in us. He has planned certain responsibilities for each of us that will carry out His purpose, that will fulfill our individual lives. Will we fully cooperate with Him?

See if you can catch the spirit of what it means to be creative in these adaptations of three other Scriptures:

Don't imitate the worldlings around you,
but be lifted above the things of earth by letting the Spirit kindle your
    mind,
that you know by experience what is God's very best for you (Romans
    12:2).

Whoever is refreshed by the Spirit shall never feel unsatisfied,
but the fulness of the Spirit shall become in him a fountain of over-
    flowing freshness,
bubbling up into the life of God (John 4:14).

They that make melody as well as they that rejoice shall say,
All my fresh springs, all my fresh ideas are in Thee (Psalm 87:7).

Our Family Creating Together

The more creative and personal our family devotions are, the more they will mean to us. Instead of following someone else's ideas, why not make up our own, that are beamed to the particular people that we are? First we might focus on a family need, problem, joy or interest that we are experiencing at the moment. Then we decide what each member of the family would like to do to see this need or interest in the light of the Lord, get His divine perspective on it. Would we like to bring in Scripture, music, poetry, current events, art, drawing, imagination, etc.? Shall we talk over what we'll do or surprise the others next time?

Here are other suggestions that we might enjoy as we ask the Lord to create in us:

1. Ahead of time ask each individual to bring something He has produced that helps him relate to the Lord, and explain it to the rest of us.

2. Bring manipulative material of some kind that all the members can use to make something on the spot that relates to the Lord in some way, like crayons, paint, clay.

3. Plan to make something together as a family during the week.

What can we expect the creative process to be like? First it takes a vision, an idea, a need. Then experimenting, often with frustration and perspiration as well as inspiration. But if the Lord is working in us and we keep at it, we may be amazed at what He does through us.

Feeling Free

Oh that I had the wings of a dove
to fly away and be at rest!
Psalm 55:6, NEB

Do you ever feel like that? Cooped up, hemmed in, circumscribed? Just for a minute you'd like to leave it all behind and escape? Be free? Probably we won't be able to get away. Do we need to escape in order to feel free? The opposite of freedom is bondage, slavery. Is it necessary to feel bound in our everyday living?

Wayne loved his father, admired him, and tried to please him. His father was a doctor. It was fun to work with him, hand him instruments, try experiments with him. "Maybe some day you'll be a doctor," his father had remarked. Wayne liked science, but he also developed another interest—writing. His teachers were very complimentary about his stories. People told him what a good news report he gave of the fire in the school basement. He was beginning to think that he'd rather study journalism than science. What would his father think about that? Was he free to move in the direction he felt like going? He didn't feel free until his father said, "Of course, Son, develop all the gifts God has given you. You can't be a doctor just because I am. You have to find God's special plan for your life." Then Wayne felt so relieved! He felt free.

When have you felt free? When bound? Let's each share one of these times, or both. Fathers often feel bound by the workings of today's business world, with its marketplace mentality, its false values, its competition. Mothers can't get to the sewing they'd like to do because there's so much cleaning and cooking and mending and housekeeping to do. Jim can't work on his hobbies because he has classes and assignments and football practice. Alice has to come in the house to bed before she's finished playing.

Are we as free as God wants us to be, or are we bound when we shouldn't be, when we don't need to be? Most people chafe against the authorities in our world that make rules and enforce rules. Our nation has rules, our state, our city has rules, our home has rules, our school, our roads have rules. Rules, rules, rules! But what would happen if we had none? Would we be happier if all of us did just as we like?

Beneficial Structures

Sue, will you please read Romans 13:1-7 to see what God says about these rules. If we don't think that laws or rules are good ones, what can we do? There are proper ways to change them. But what about the rules we can't change? To many of the things that limit us, we may as well say, "That's the way things are. It'll do me no good to rebel against them. I'll just waste my time and energy." Most of them are needed.

The Creator of our universe hasn't left us in the dark about the way He structured it. He tells us how we can get in tune with this world, how our inner being can be in harmony with the whole of outer nature. Let's look at John 8:31, 32 to see why God's own people sometimes don't feel free. How do the various versions translate the first phrase of what Jesus said? "If you abide in

My Word, are faithful to what I have said, live in My Word, hold fast to My teaching." Jesus came to set His people free.

Freedom in the Spirit—Galatians 5:13-23

Paul wrote the Book of Galatians to show the Galatian Christians that God meant them to be free, to counteract the false teachers who tried to get them back under the multitude of burdensome Jewish laws. Look at Galatians 5:13 NEB. Paul says, "You . . . were called to be free men." How are some people abusing their freedom? Turning it into license for their lower nature. What is our lower nature? Our natural ways before Christ gave us His higher nature. What would be an example of license? Yes, or eating all the candy in the family dish because I was hungry.

Is Paul contradicting himself when he next says, ". . . be servants to one another in love"? How can we be free if we are servants? Think of the Christian you know who seems most free. Is he always thinking about himself or about others?

Instead of many Jewish laws about relations with other people, how did Jesus sum them all up, in verse 14?

In 15, if we don't love our neighbor, what happens?

In 16, how do we keep control over our lower nature? What does it mean to "walk by the Spirit," or "be guided by the Spirit"? Each morning we ask the Lord to take charge of our day, to keep us listening to His voice and obeying.

If we don't do this, what kind of battle goes on inside us, 16, 17?

In our house how often do we experience the dreadful things mentioned in 19-21?

In 22, 23 which of these fruits of the Spirit do we need most as a family?

Action

Though there are limitations upon all of us, are we as free as God intends us to be? Are we ready to say, "Lord, help me accept the restrictions that You in infinite wisdom put upon Your human creatures? Help me accept the legitimate restrictions that governments put upon us. But free me from unnecessary bonds that I myself am responsible for." Are there times when you're not sure whether or not you should feel free? Let's discuss these times as a family. Sometimes we keep other members of our family from feeling free without even knowing we do or intending to. Just as God knows what He is doing in His commands and He has reasons, so parents should have good reasons for what they ask. Do any of you have questions about the demands that I make? The wishes of any of the rest of us? If we know that someone else feels bound by what we do, we might want to change.

For instance, Jim could feel free to bring friends home after a Saturday night game if we could depend on him to baby-sit Tuesday evening when Sue is out.

"If you continue in my word, you are truly my disciples, and you will know the truth, and the truth will make you free" (John 8:31, 32, RSV).

Discipline

AL IS a very talented young man. He is naturally athletic. When he went out for track, the coach thought he had good possibilities but he didn't make the team because he just didn't get to regular practice. He has a keen mind, but because he can get by without studying, he never shows up very well. He failed to get a scholarship in high school, his family has little money, and so he couldn't go to college. He plays the piano by ear, but is not in the band or in a rock group because he is always doing his own thing; he doesn't know how to work as a member of a team with others. Al could probably be a top-notch athlete, student or maybe even pianist *if*. If what?

What can we each be or do *if* we have what it takes to develop what we've got?

Of course life disciplines us to a certain extent. If we aren't wise, it knocks us around and trims off the rough edges in its own harsh way. But I'd rather discipline myself than let someone or something else do it. The word discipline has the same root as disciple. Each of us as a disciple of Christ has been given a spiritual gift. What we have is His gift to us; what we do with it is our gift to Him.

Our self-discipline is often a question of two words that are very short but very great in their results. What are they? Yes and no. The many decisions we make during the course of a day determine whether we are becoming strong or weak characters.

Daniel's Self-control—Daniel 1:8-20

When the great king of Babylon conquered the city of Jerusalem, he ordered his assistant to find the very best Jewish young men to serve in his palace. They had to be strong, healthy, handsome, intelligent, well-informed in all the fields of learning, and cultured enough to be at ease with high officials. And they had to be smart enough to learn the new language and ways of this other country. What high standards!

The king honored Daniel and his friends who were chosen by assigning them a daily portion of the same rich food that he ate and the wine that he drank. They were to be trained for three years, when they would stand before the king to see whether or not they were fit for the king's company.

But Daniel had been brought up with his own family's high standards according to the law of God, and they were not the same as this king's. What would he do? Turn to the Book of Daniel, chapter 1, verse 8. Evidently the chief reason for refusing the king's meat was that it had been consecrated by a heathen rite, which would have made the eating of it idol worship for him. It took courage to do what Daniel did. It could have resulted in "off with his head." But God was a living God to Daniel; He took care of those who obeyed Him.

Jim and Sue, read the conversation between Daniel and the king's assistant in verses 10-13. That's often a good approach to a problem: Try us and see.

What was the result in 14-16? The Jewish youths passed the first test with flying colors!

Then there was the problem of the new language. In verse 17 what did God give Daniel in addition to wisdom? Later he impressed the king with his under-standing of visions and dreams.

Finish that chapter to find out how the language test came out. Not just better than any of the young men of the country, but ten times better!

The Lord's Discipline—Hebrews 12:5-11

The Bible is very realistic about our human nature. How do we usually feel about controlling our natural impulses? Look at Hebrews 12:11. We don't go running to meet our disciplines, saying, "What fun!" But if we are sensible and not foolish, we'll ask ourselves, "Am I content to be a weakling, or do I really want to be strong?" It helps me to think of the long process that is required to refine raw nuggets into gold, the hot pressure that is needed to make fine steel, the polishing to make a sparkling diamond, the molding to make a strong man of God.

Therefore how should we take the discipline of the Lord? Look at the verses that preceded verse 12, beginning with 5. I'll never forget a teen saying to me, "My parents didn't care what became of me. They didn't love me, they didn't punish me. I just did anything I wanted to, and soon I didn't want anything. Nothing mattered. I had nothing to live for, nothing to strive for, nothing to become. *Until* I met Jesus Christ." God cares enough about His children to mold them into His likeness with the family resemblance.

Verse 10 gives a serious warning to us parents. When parents get angry, it's easy to punish children to make themselves feel better. Proverbs 23:13 tells us not to withhold discipline from our children, but to do it with love and your good in mind.

Disciplining Ourselves

When the Lord sets up a situation for us as He did for Daniel, will we rebel against Him or will we cooperate with Him? Far away from home in a foreign land Daniel could have forgotten all about the ways of the Lord, whom his family had worshiped. If he had, he would have been just another forgotten person, instead of becoming a top man in the foreign king's government.

There is one time when it is healthy for us to act like two persons. Our better, higher self can take our lower self by the shoulders and talk turkey to it. We can say, "Now you don't feel like grinding away at this, but we've got to do it, so just grit your teeth and pitch in."

In what part of our lives are we well disciplined? In which part is discipline weakest? For me personally it's escaping into my workshop to putter around instead of doing something I don't feel like doing. What should we tackle boldly this week? To what do we need to say "I will" or "I will not"? If we put our will on the Lord's will and team up with Him, He will carry a lot of the load, for His yoke is easy and His burden is light. Discipline is difficult in our times because in general this is a lawless age, with many people kicking over all the traces.

What are we ready to say to the Lord about discipline? Maybe we aren't all ready to say the same thing, but we may as well be honest, since He reads our thoughts.

Being Responsible

TED TOLD Mr. Aldrich next door that he would mow his lawn in the afternoon. He was eager to earn all the money he could because he was saving for a new bicycle. When he was just about ready to start mowing, his friend Matt and his father stopped by in the car to ask if Ted wanted to go with them to the ball game in the city. Yes, Ted wanted to go to the game, he was always ready to go to a game, but he had promised Mr. Aldrich to cut his lawn. It would be too late to do it when he got back. He wanted to go to the game and he wanted the money, but he had promised. What would he do?

Isn't it frustrating when we get in situations like this, when we don't like either decision we have to make! Ted didn't want to miss the game and the money, and he didn't want to let his neighbor down. Which would be worse? If he missed the game, what would happen? If he broke his promise, what would happen? Would Mr. Aldrich be the only person who would lose out? No, both Ted and his family would lose. Why? Ted would lose his self-respect, he wouldn't like himself, and what is worse than that, for a person has to live with himself. And his family could no longer say, "Ted is a dependable person." Would you want to be a person whom people can't rely on?

Responsibility is the ability to respond as a mature person, a person with honor and honesty and integrity according to principles—in our case according to the Lord's principles.

Solomon's Irresponsibility and Sin—1 Kings 3—11

The young man Solomon seemed to have everything going for him. He was the favorite son of good King David, was loved by both his father and mother. He grew up in the palace with both spiritual and material advantages. What was his attitude toward the Lord when he was made king? See 1 Kings 3:3. What is the implication of that word *only?* God told His people to destroy the high places where the heathen worshiped their idols.

When God told Solomon to ask for any gift he wanted, Solomon was intelligent enough to realize that as a young man he needed wisdom to govern his great nation. God was pleased with this request, and even gave him what he didn't ask for. Read 1 Kings 3:13, 14. Three times God said to Solomon—*If* you will obey Me, I will prosper you (also 6:12 and 9:4).

Solomon did prosper, but later what also happened to him? 11:9-11. Even with so many advantages and with the Lord's warnings, God had to tear the kingdom away from him.

Let's see if we can discover the reasons for Solomon's irresponsibility and sin. Probably the first reason we'll find in 11:1-4. Nothing is so important as what we love. When Solomon disobeyed the Lord, was it because he didn't know God's commands? No, he had been brought up to know the Lord's will. But which is easier—to know His ways or to do them? How many wives did he have? Read 11:4, Sue.

And in verses 7, 8 what did he even build for his wives?

Of course, when he married women from other countries instead of one from his own land, it made it easier for him to get along with the kings of those countries. He had peace instead of war with the other nations, which enabled him to spend time enriching his own kingdom.

As Jim reads 10:14-25, find another reason for Solomon's lack of responsibility. Though the Lord gave him riches, he was never satisfied; he always wanted more, and more. In a word, what was his trouble? Selfishness, or we might say pride.

In order to get all the luxuries he wanted, what did he force his own people to do? Sue, read 5:13-18. He made his people work very hard and pay heavy taxes so that he could live at ease with everything he wanted.

Growing in Dependability

Solomon can help us check ourselves, to see if we are becoming more dependable. What might we get so interested in that we would love it more than the Lord? Adults could even love their Christian service more than the Lord. What person or activity are you most involved with? How much do you love him, her, or it? Could you get along all right without it? How is it related to the Lord? Is He in it with you, or do you love it instead of Him?

So often these other things are such strong influences on us, just as Solomon's wives influenced him to build high places for them. What is the strongest influence on our family now? Is it a healthy influence, or does it tend to take us away from the Lord?

Then there are all the luxuries that Solomon wanted: gold and silver and horses and chariots and ivory and peacocks! It's easy to set our heart on getting things until we're never satisfied. Are there any material things that we feel we just must have? If the Lord doesn't give it to us, it's probably best that we don't have it.

Finally Solomon seemed to be doing so well that he didn't need the Lord. The person who feels like that is headed for a fall. We're usually in a more dangerous position when we're strong than when we're weak.

Can we be trusted with prosperity? Are we occupied with God's gifts or the Giver? Which of Solomon's weaknesses would most likely keep us from being dependable?

"Lord, keep us responsible, dependable. Give us the ability to respond to Your best, higher ways."

Feeling Proud

ONE OF Sue's friends was not very popular with the gang, for she was always either up or down. She acted either as a princess who should be the center of attention or she acted like a worm crawling in the dust. The girls didn't like her in either role. They didn't feel that she was real in either one. The reason for this behavior was that her father treated her as if she were the only important person on earth and gave her all kinds of presents, while her mother—maybe to counteract the father—was always putting her down and making her feel she was no good. The poor girl had a hard time.

How do you feel about a TV star who acts proud, as if he is better than anyone else? About the baseball pitcher who acts as if he won the game by himself? Or about the student who won't let anyone else answer questions? God feels the same as we do about these people. The Bible says, "God opposes the proud, but gives grace to the humble" (James 4:6 RSV). Some people think that pride is the root of all sin. Why would that be? If we're proud of ourselves, we won't believe the Lord when He says that we can't save ourselves, that we have to come humbly to Him for forgiveness of our sins.

Suppose you're in a group having a good time with congenial friends when a proud person joins you. What would happen? He would want to boss things and do them his way. How would the others in the group react? They'd get disgusted with him and perhaps break up or do something else.

What makes a person feel proud? He sees himself as the center of everything, with everything good due to him. What's wrong with this?

The Example of Joseph—Genesis 41—45

In the Old Testament is an example of a person who had more right than most people to be proud. When his older brothers came to Egypt to buy food because of the famine in their own land, they bowed to the ground before the mighty governor, who was in fact their own younger brother (42:6). When Joseph recognized them, how might he have felt? What could he have accused them of doing?

His family had not helped him a bit to gain his high position. How had he gained it? Look at Genesis 39:2-6. How many times in those verses does it say that the Lord was with Joseph or the Lord blessed him? Joseph was made overseer of all that his master had after being sold as a slave to him.

When Joseph was cast into prison because he wouldn't sin with his master's wife, how did the Lord help him there? 41:25. Then the king set Joseph over the whole land of Egypt! Because of him there was food in Egypt even during the famine.

When his brothers came to Egypt the second time for food, how many people would have treated them as Joseph did? Would you have used your high position to put them in their place when you had the chance? What did Joseph say to his brothers in 45:5-8? How could he say that "it was not you who sent me here, but God," in 8 RSV? To them he was still younger brother rather than proud governor.

The Example of Jesus—Philippians 2:3-11

In the New Testament God speaks very clearly about pride also. Look at Philippians 2:3. What in this verse shows that Christianity is supernatural? We don't naturally think of others as better than ourselves.

And what don't we naturally do in the next verse?

Verse 5 gives the only way we can do these hard things. Have the very mind of Christ.

Though the Lord is the only One who can rightly be proud, instead of that how did Jesus humble Himself? 8. It's hard for us to imagine what a comedown these were for Him! It was no more humbling than it would be for us to take the form of a worm and let the worms eat us.

Because Jesus was obedient even to death on the cruel cross, what happened next? Mother, read 9-11.

Peter tells us that that is the only way we too shall be exalted (1 Peter 5:6). He says, "Humble yourselves . . . under the mighty hand of God, that He may exalt you in due time."

True Humility

If a person is not to feel proud of himself and what he can do, how should he feel about himself? Should he feel that he is no good? What would be the result of that attitude? Then why try? What is true humility? It's related to honesty. If we are honest, and we do something well, won't we acknowledge the fact? What will keep us from feeling proud?

Let's mention one thing that each member of our family can do well, and ask ourselves these questions about that ability:

How much work and practice did it take to achieve that ability?
How much success was due to ability that the person was born with?
How much was due to help that other people gave?
How much was due to gifts that other people gave?

For example let's take Sue's ability to play the piano. She has done her part in practicing even when she would rather do something else. She does have musical ability, more than the others in our family. Her teacher helps her every week, and Mother also helps her remember to practice and exempts her from other duties. And Sue couldn't practice if we didn't own a piano. So if Sue is honest and humble, how will she describe her ability to play? I do my part, but I can't be proud because the Lord, my family, and my teacher all have a part in it.

True humility is saying yes, I can do things, I am strong in certain ways, and I am weak in certain ways. I have nothing to be proud of, for I am merely developing my God-given abilities with the help of other people.

Feeling Inferior

THE CHALLENGES of life are so great that most of us feel inferior at times. In our distressed world the call to excellence and leadership and expertise are always with us. So it's natural for us to feel inferior. The Lord's standards, the accomplishments of others, and our own expectations all make us feel inferior.

Why do the Lord's standards make us feel inferior? He says to us, ". . . go on to maturity" (Hebrews 6:1 RSV), ". . . the people who know their God shall stand firm and take action" (Daniel 11:32 RSV), and ". . . be holy, because I the LORD your God am holy" (Leviticus 20:7 NEB). These are such high goals that we never completely reach them in this life.

Why do the accomplishments of others make us feel inferior? For everything you do well, see if you can't think of someone else who does that better. This is life, this is normal, but it doesn't make us feel high. The question comes to us, "Shouldn't I be best in something?" There aren't enough skills in the world for everyone to be best.

I suppose most of us use our imaginations to dream of what we could be. This is healthy if we are moving in that direction, because we need to visualize ourselves reaching our goals, doing things we've never done before. But what happens if we feel that we are no good? Probably we won't be, for we won't bother to try. That is as bad as being proud. Why is it sinful to have a poor self-image?

Moses' Response to God's Call—Exodus 3:1—4:16

The man Moses is an example of the sad effects of inferiority feelings. Alice, what was important about Moses when he was a baby? Where did he grow up? Do you remember why he left the palace and fled to the desert? As he took care of sheep, what strange sight did he see one day?

From the burning bush God speaks to him. He is concerned about His people who have been working very hard as slaves in Egypt. What does God say in Exodus 3:10?

In the several conversations between the Lord and Moses, Jim, read what the Lord says and Sue what Moses says. After each conversation let's pause to discuss it.

We often feel like Moses when he says, "Who am I, that I should do this important thing that sounds scary?" (*See* 3:11.) How would you feel if the Lord answered as He did in verse 12? Would it be enough for you if He promised to be with you and showed you just where you would come out?

This promise is not enough for Moses. What is his question in 13? God gives him a long full answer. Jim, read the beginning and end of it, 14, 15 and 20-22.

But this assurance is not enough for Moses. What is his difficulty in 4:1, Sue? So the Lord patiently shows him miracles that he can perform if he needs to. Read these, Jim, 2-9.

Still Moses gives another complaint in 10, Sue. How will you read the Lord's answer in 11, 12, Jim? He is not so patient as before. Why not? Moses should know what He tells him.

What is Moses doing in 13? When the Lord answers all his excuses, Moses simply says, "Lord, I don't want to go. I don't want to obey You."

What is the Lord's answer this time in 14? The almighty Creator is angry with Moses. I wouldn't want the Lord to be angry with me! But He gives Moses his brother to speak for him. Moses shows us how painful it is when we don't trust ourselves.

God's Viewpoint—Isaiah 40:28-31

How does God expect us to feel about ourselves? Turn to Isaiah 40:28. The first step is to see who the Person is who is in charge of this universe including myself. He never gets tired of helping us and He understands everything about us, everything.

What does He expect to do in 29, 30? Since He is ready to give us power and strength, even to strong young men, how should we feel?

Verse 31 tells our part. Those who appropriate the Lord's strength not only walk and run but even soar like eagles! That's what He expects of us! When we get God's perspective on ourselves, we feel humble but not inferior.

Dealing with Inferiority Feelings

It is legitimate for each of us honestly to acknowledge what we don't have, but we should also acknowledge what we do have going for us. If we don't contradict the Lord as Moses did, we have to admit that we have many pluses as well as minuses. What should keep us from feeling inferior?

First, we see that we don't have to count on our own strength or ability. The Lord knows that we alone don't have what it takes. So that doesn't bother us.

Secondly, God has a particular purpose for each of us to fulfill in life, and when we were born He gave us everything we need to accomplish that goal. So we never need to feel that we're missing something basic or essential.

Thirdly, what He asks of us is not something we can't do. What does He ask? That we give ourselves wholly to Him and obey Him. When does He get angry with us? When we rebel against His best.

Now do you have any reason left for feeling bad about yourself? If you do, let's talk and pray about it. What do you want to thank God for?

Isaiah 40:29-31 is a good passage to memorize.

Priorities

I'M GIVING each of you ten slips of paper and a pencil. I will read a list of twenty-five of the most important values in life. Of these twenty-five you will choose and write on your papers the ten you think should be put first. Almost all of them are excellent qualities; all are things that some people strive for and put first. So it won't be easy to leave out some of them, but remember that we are selecting ten out of twenty-five.

Here is the list. I'll read them slowly enough for us to write the ones we choose as the first ten. Knowledge, honesty, wealth, love, pleasure, physical health, emotional well-being, self-respect, food, clothing, shelter, fellowship, Christlikeness, loyalty, service, justice, peace, success, self-control, power, beauty, skill, new experiences, morality, fame.

Have you written ten of these? I'll read them again. If you wish to revise any of them, you can write a second word on the back of a paper. Do we each have our first ten or nine or eleven?

Now arrange these words in an order that shows what you were most concerned about last week. To which of these on your list did you give most time and attention? Last week these were our priorities, the things we put first. How would the Lord arrange these for us?

Scriptural Priorities—Matthew 6:19-21, 25-34

Let's see if Matthew 6 can help us get the Lord's perspectives on our values. Look first at the 19-21 paragraph. This value presents a serious problem to some people. The more earthly treasure they have, the more they want, until they are never satisfied. Rich people always have to worry about thieves. Do any of us love things? What do you consider your greatest treasure? How much would that be worth to others? How much treasure have we already laid up in heaven? In other words, how much have we given the Lord to use for His purposes? Yes, what we've given for the church and for missions is part of our treasure in heaven. Do any of us have wealth as one of our first ten values?

Have any of us been anxious about anything this week? When are people anxious about the needs mentioned in verse 25? Yes, when they've been victims of war or floods or earthquakes or tornadoes or mine cave-ins. Then the food, clothing and shelter necessary to live are first concerns. How does this passage help God's people to trust Him for these needs? Read 26-31, Sue. They can ask Him to provide in unusual ways if not in the usual ways. But what about the people who aren't trusting the Lord for anything? They just have to fend for themselves unless they cry to Him in their hour of need.

Have we ever lacked any of the material necessities of life? Let's thank God this minute for all His material provisions and ask Him for our brothers and sisters in Christ who lack them this day.

Why does our family have the necessities of life? Look at 32. Our heavenly Father knows we need them. How do we know He cares for an individual family like us? He says that He sees even a sparrow fall and knows how many hairs are on our heads (Matthew 10:29, 30)!

We have trusted Him to supply and have done our part. So now we are free from the essentials of physical life to do what He asks in 6:33. How do we seek first His kingdom?

Let's turn to the two great commandments in Matthew 22:37-39 and read them together.

Rearranging Our Priorities

If we obey these first commandments, which of our ten values will we put first? I don't think it matters whether we put love or Christlikeness first. If we love Him, we'll grow like Him, into the family likeness. Yes, probably knowledge should be included near the top of the list since we can't love God without knowing Him, and we need to know so many other things in order to relate properly to them. If we love our neighbor as ourself, which values will come next? Probably service, fellowship, perhaps morality. We will share ourselves with others, serve them, and do right by them.

Which values might come next? Can we eliminate any of them? Which won't we need in the first ten? Not wealth or pleasure or fame. Does that mean we won't have good times? We'll have more good times, but they will result from our love and fellowship and serving; we won't have to seek pleasure.

If we love God and our neighbor, which of these other values will follow in their wake? Yes, we'll be honest because He is honest, His life pulsing through our veins keeps us healthy, He keeps our feelings in tune as we let Him take control, He gives us an exciting place in His plans with great self-respect, etc. If we seek God first, what kind of power will we have? Spiritual power. And that will also bring spiritual beauty and new experiences as we serve.

After these top priorities let's be individual in what we select for the others. When we put God first, He doesn't mold us all alike. Here's paste to stick your slips of paper in your order onto these cards I'm giving you. Keep your list on your dresser where you'll often see it.

Of course it's one thing to make our list and quite another to carry it out. So let's ask the Lord to enable us by His Spirit to put first things first.

Choosing the Best

DECISIONS! DECISIONS! Decisions! Which brand of toothpaste will you buy? Which TV channel turn on? Which magazine read? Which candidate vote for? How spend your leisure time? When write that letter? Life is just one decision after another. We are today what we are because of the decisions we've been making.

Think back over the decisions you've made lately. Think of one you're glad you made. One you're sorry you made. One you were sure of. One you were not sure of. One that was hard to make. One easy to make.

What decisions will be coming up for you in the future? How important are they? What will be involved? Very often we ourselves aren't the only ones affected. Can you think of someone else's decision that affected you either positively or negatively? None of us lives to ourself.

What are the biggest decisions that most people have to make throughout their whole lives? Yes, saying yes or no to the Lord, how they'll spend their time and energies, how they will prepare for their vocation, and whom they will marry. Which is the most important, on which the others depend?

The Lord says:

> I call heaven and earth to witness against you this day,
> that I have set before you life and death, blessing and curse;
> therefore choose life . . . .
>
> Deuteronomy 30:19 RSV

Ruth's Big Decision—Ruth 1:1-18

What should we consider in making our decisions? The decision of Ruth in the Bible should help us. In a time of famine the family of Elimelech of Bethlehem moved to the land of Moab where there was food. There Elimelech died, leaving his wife Naomi with two sons, both of whom married girls of Moab. After ten years the two sons died, leaving poor Naomi with two young daughters-in-law.

When Naomi heard that there was again food in Israel, she had a big decision to make. What reasons would she have for staying in Moab? What reasons for returning to her own land? The two young women also had decisions to make. They had learned to love Naomi, for she was a very gracious person. They had also learned great respect for the God of Israel, whom Naomi loved. We infer their decision from Ruth 1:7. They started back with her.

But Naomi could visualize better than the girls the uncertainties that the future might hold for them. She had no home now in Israel, they had no man among them to take care of them, they couldn't predict what would happen. So what did Naomi say to the girls in verses 8, 9? She trusted the Lord to provide for them in their own land. It was a sad moment, for their lives had become interwoven with each other.

How did the girls reply, in 10? Now they couldn't think of living without her, she had added so much to them, even if they had lost their husbands.

Thinking that it would be too much for them to venture into the unknown with her, how did Naomi try to persuade them? Read verses 11-13, Sue.

How did the girls take this reasoning, in 47? So Orpah decided to return home.

Verse 15 notes that Orpah went home to her people and to what else? Also her gods.

The sentences in 16, 17 have become well-known and famous. Read them the way Ruth must have said them, Mother. What do those words tell us about Naomi? She must have been a most winsome, strong character who truly reflected the Lord. And what do those words tell us about Ruth?

Naomi's hard life must have helped her to get through to faith in the Lord for herself. The Lord Himself took care of these two women who went back to Israel. Do you know what happened to Ruth in that land? She married an outstanding well-to-do man who was a relative of her husband, and became one of the ancestors of the Lord Jesus!

Will we like Ruth choose the best, and make our lives count for eternity? Turn to Jeremiah 9:23, 24. Let's each read one of these phrases, starting with Sue reading about the wise man, then Ted reading about the mighty man, Alice the rich man, Jim the man who chooses the best, and then Mother, the description of the Lord.

What to Consider in Our Decisions

What then would be the first thing to do when we have a decision to make? Ask the Lord to reveal His best to us. What else should we think about? Let's each think specifically about a decision we will be making. Next let's probe the underlying motive, our chief purpose. Is the reason selfish or for the sake of the Lord or other people? For the good of the two young women Naomi thought they might better stay home though she didn't like the thought of going to Israel alone.

Then we'll consider what the decision will cost in money, time, effort, tension, relationships. It cost Ruth all her home ties to go with Naomi to a strange land. Often I'd like to do something exciting, but it wouldn't be worth the price I'd have to pay.

Also what will be the results? Whom will it benefit? Whom will it hurt? Since I may not be the only person involved, I think about the others too.

Sometimes timing is very important. What might be disastrous this week might be all right next week. When I'm away at a conference, you at home might not do things that you would while I'm here.

In our prayer let's ask the Lord specifically about the decisions we will be making.

Achieving Goals

IN THE daily newspaper one evening were two death notices. One described a missionary to Brazil who had started six churches, taught in two schools, written two books on missions, and aided the government with a description of two tribes that he had worked with. The other notice gave the bare facts of the birth, marriage and death of a man who apparently had just lived. Nothing he had done was worthy of mention.

Two boys in the same family grew up very differently. Very early in life one became interested in rocks and rock formations. Wherever he went he collected rocks and noticed the various layers and the way they ran in cutaway hillsides. He read all he could on the subject, went to illustrated lectures, and in high school received an award for a paper he wrote on the subject. He got a scholarship to college and knew just what he wanted to major in. When his brother was asked what he was interested in, he replied "Everything," and said he just wanted to be happy. So he went from one thing to another, collected a few records, a few stamps, a few coins. After high school he didn't know what to do. He had no goals. Which boy was happier?

When a member of Sue's class in school had to go to the hospital and was worrying about how he would pay the bill, some of his friends decided to help him out. Do you think they would get more if they said to their classmates, "Let's put together some money to help Tony," or if they said, "Let's raise twenty-five dollars to meet Tony's expenses"? Why? What is involved in setting and achieving goals?

God's Overall Plan for the Ages

Can you help me tell the story of God's overall plan for our world? Chip in whenever you have the facts.

In the beginning God wanted to share Himself and His fulness of eternal life with human beings who would love and fellowship with Him. But He didn't want response that was forced, so He gave them wills of their own that they might love Him spontaneously of their own accord. He put Adam and Eve in a beautiful garden without weeds. When there was only one thing they were forbidden to do, they did that one thing. Look at Romans 5:12. Sue, read it aloud.

As more people were born, what kind of people were they? Jim, read Genesis 6:5-8. Alice, how did the Lord punish these wicked people? But Noah walked with God.

Not long after that God called Abram and gave him a special promise. Read to yourself Genesis 12:1-3.

Abram's son was Isaac, one of Isaac's sons was Jacob, one of Jacob's sons was Joseph, who was sold into Egypt. Joseph became governor of Egypt because he saved food during the famine. But when a new king didn't know Joseph, how did he oppress God's people, who were very many by this time? Whom did God choose to lead His people out of Egypt? What did the Lord have to do before the king of Egypt would let them go? After the miracle of the Red Sea, He gave His people laws that would make them a strong nation. They experienced many trials and wanderings before they finally reached the land that God had promised them.

What kind of people lived in that land? Because they were such wicked heathen, the Lord told His people to destroy them so that they would not be corrupted. When they didn't do it completely, what took place? Mother, read Judges 2:11-16.

But God's people wanted a king like the nations around them. Who was the man they chose, who looked like a king? But when Saul sinned, the Lord chose a man after His own heart. Yes, David, who extended the kingdom and had a glorious reign because he mostly obeyed God. His son Solomon started well but ended poorly. A rival of his son got the ten northern tribes away from his son, leaving him only the two southern tribes.

All the kings of the northern kingdom sinned against the Lord until the powerful Assyrian king carried them away captive. The southern kingdom had good kings as well as bad, but finally they too were so corrupt that the Babylonian king burned their city and temple and took them away.

After four hundred years when God was silent, angels announced to shepherds the greatest event in history. Ted, read the angels' glory song in Luke 2:14. God's own Son was sent to do what the law could not do because human nature is too weak to keep it. Jesus showed our world what God is like and took our punishment on the cross so that we can now come directly to the Father. He is our risen Saviour-Lord!

Today the Lord is building His church composed of all the believers. What did Jesus say about His church in Matthew 16:18? When it is completed, the Lord will return, rule a thousand years on the earth, destroy His last enemies, and create new heavens and earth. Jim, read Peter's description of the end time in 2 Peter 3:9-13.

God started with a goal and He will achieve this goal. Human beings have frustrated His plans because they have wills of their own and can say no as well as yes, but they can't keep Him from achieving His goal. He keeps right on moving toward it.

Achieving Our Goals

The Lord will help us achieve our goals if they are part of His plan which glorifies Him. What are the steps in reaching them? 1. How will we select a goal? Yes, it should be in the Lord's will and accord with our interest and ability. We can explore possibilities until we discover what our gifts and abilities are. 2. What can we visualize doing? We probably won't do something that we can't imagine doing. 3. How can we prepare? What information will give us greater confidence? What skills will make us more comfortable? How can we break the whole into manageable parts? 4. Are we ready to launch out, trust the Lord and take a risk? Since we can't be sure what will happen, are we secure enough to make a mistake or two in order to learn? 5. Will we persist until we finish? Do we care enough to overcome obstacles and keep trying when the going gets rough?

Let's each decide on a personal goal for this next week. What do you want to have done by a week from now? Are you ready to do your part to achieve it? What shall we say to the Lord about it?

Establishing Good Habits

AT CAMP Nick was not very popular. He always seemed to be at loose ends. When it was swimming hour, he had started to do something else, then wanted to swim later. When his cabin was ready to set out for an overnight, Nick didn't have his food ready. He could never find his clothes because he left them wherever he took them off. When he was in the mood, he was a good ball player, but sometimes he didn't feel like playing. Sometimes the boys found that he told the truth, but sometimes he didn't.

The boy who emerged as the natural leader of Nick's cabin was Jerry. Jerry always seemed to be in command of the situation. One day Nick asked Jerry, "How come you're always with it, and I never am? Why are we so different?" That evening all the cabin mates were talking very personally about themselves. The counselor asked them about their habits at home. Nick said that at home nobody knew or cared whether he came or went, when he ate, when he slept, what he did, so it was always hit or miss. Jerry said that his home was just the opposite, organized and orderly, with meals at certain hours, and habits that all the family agreed on, and responsibilities for each one.

One of the best things we can do for ourselves is establish good habits. What is so important about habits? What did Jerry's habits do for him? What did Nick's do for him?

When we are forming a habit, we have to think about it each time. Can you remember when you first learned to brush your teeth? If we don't have habits, we have to think each time we do or don't do something. But if we form habits, we don't have to think about them. We are free to put our minds on the important things in life. Do our good habits free us as Jerry's did him, or leave us hanging as Nick's did him?

Some Scriptural Habits—Proverbs

Like a young colt we all naturally want to run wild, do what we want to do when we want to do it. The civilizing process is one of taming ourselves to fit into society, to turn our energies in the direction of our goals. To accomplish this, we have to say no to ourselves as well as yes. Let's read Proverbs 12:1 from our various versions.

Now let's each take another verse from Proverbs, study it silently for a minute, and then share with the rest of us what it means to us personally:

I'll take two that go together: 14:12 and 3:5, 6. It is so natural for us to trust ourselves, to think that what looks best to me is surely best. But often I can't see all sides of the picture. The Lord sees everything from beginning to end from a higher perspective. I have to check myself to see if I'm acknowledging Him in all my ways, and trusting Him with all my heart.

Mother: 4:23. Are we inclined to pay more attention to our outer being or our inner being? This word of the Lord tells us which is more important. So much depends on our motives, why we act as we do. If our heart is right, we can cope with the rest of life.

Jim: 3:29. What will we do when evil thoughts, temptations, come to our mind? We can't keep them from coming, but we don't need to let them stay in our minds. We can dismiss them immediately. When the easy, natural thing comes to mind, we can say scat!

Sue: 18:9. Nobody likes a slacker, one who cuts corners, does as little as possible to get by. What is the opposite of lazy? How thorough are we in all our work, in all our habits?

Ted: 12:17. When is it difficult for us to tell the truth? How can we be always ready to tell the truth? If all our habits are good, we have no reason to lie. If they are not, we are always getting into trouble.

Alice: 11:13. This verse is talking about a talebearer, a tattler, a gossip, who is always talking about other people. Have we formed the habit of telling on other people or talking about them when it's not our business?

Improving Our Habits

What good habits has our family established? Can you think of some that are partly established—sometimes we practice them and sometimes not? Which ones do we need to work on seriously? Select for yourself one that is important. Probably we should work on one at a time until we can be sure of that one.

Since "out of the heart are the issues of life" (4:23), let's be honest about our motives. Do we really want to make a good habit our own, do we care enough to stick to it until we don't have to think about it? How shall we practically get started? Each morning we can think ahead to the times in the day when we'll need this habit, and ask the Lord to help us be consistent in it. Then at night we can check ourselves, to see when we succeeded and when we failed. This habit should then become easier and more regular each day.

Would we like to have a family chart on which each of us records our progress each day? We might put a plus if we did well that day, a minus if we did poorly, and a zero if it was so-so. If one of us should have trouble with a habit, the rest of us could concentrate on it with that person.

Being Organized

WHAT DOES your room look like just now? Your desk, if you have one? Are you inclined to be an organizer, or not? Most people enjoy a good mess at times, but most people don't like to live in a mess. A few people efficiently organize themselves into a breakdown, but most of us need to work at organization.

How organized is this universe of ours? What if we couldn't depend on the relationships of the heavenly bodies in space, on regular seasons, on day and night each twenty-four hours? Our God is a God of order, system, organization, not confusion. When nature does not operate smoothly, what happens? Why do you think the Creator allows floods, earthquakes, tornadoes, plagues? If all of nature operated harmoniously without incident, people would forget God more than they do now. When something occurs that mortals cannot control, at least some of them think about Him, to curse Him if not to pray to Him.

Can you think of examples of organization in Scripture? Yes, first God dealt with His people in an old covenant and when Christ came, in a new. When Christ fed the multitudes, He asked them to sit on the hillside in groups of 100s and 50s. He sent His disciples out two by two. Paul warned the disorderly Corinthians to do everything decently and in order (1 Corinthians 14:40). Paul appointed overseers in the new churches that he started (Acts 14:23). When Moses' father-in-law saw that Moses did not have time to judge all the people who came to him, he advised him to delegate responsibility to trustworthy men over thousands, hundreds, fifties and tens, so that Moses would be free for the greatest matters (Exodus 18:13-27).

Why does this universe need to be organized? What happens when our lives are not organized? We waste precious time and energy and money. Has our family had any sad experiences when we weren't organized? The Old Testament tabernacle is an example of God's attitude toward organization.

The Arrangement of the Old Testament Tabernacle—Exodus 25—31

As God's people journeyed through the wilderness on their way to the land that God had promised them, they needed a center of worship. The tabernacle was evidence of God's holy presence among them. In several chapters in the Book of Exodus He told them exactly how to build the kind of holy place that they could carry with them as they journeyed. He gifted people especially for the fine work on it, and when it was finished God's divine glory hovered above it in a cloud.

The very center of the tabernacle was the holy of holies, where only the high priest went, only once a year. Look at Exodus 25:10-15 to see how the Lord told the people to make the ark that contained the tables of His law.

In 17, 18 what was on top of the ark? When the atoning blood for sin was sprinkled on the mercy seat, God communed there with Moses, representing His people. In the holy place were a table of showbread, a lampstand, and an altar of incense, all covered with gold.

In 26:1 what was to enclose the tabernacle?

In 31-33 what separated the holy place from the most holy?

In 27:1 what was outside the covered holy place? This was the place for public acts of worship where animals were sacrificed to the Lord.

The people were also organized as well as the place. In 28:1 what were Aaron and his sons chosen especially to do? Special clothing was made for them. The tribe of Levi was separated to care for and carry the tabernacle.

In 30:17-19 what was made for the cleansing of the priests?

When the people were in camp, three tribes were assigned to each side of the tabernacle, so that they completely surrounded it (Numbers 2).

Organizing Our Daily Lives

What part of our family life is well organized? Of course that means organized flexibly, not rigidly. What happens if a schedule is too tight? We can't keep it, for there's no room for the unexpected. Some of the greatest things in life come unexpectedly, and we need leeway for them. But what is the result of family life being haphazard, hit-or-miss? We don't form good habits that free us for the important matters, and we're never sure whether or not we have carried out our responsibilities. Does each of us know what the other members expect of us? Do we agree with them on what they should expect?

Because certain arrangements have worked well in the past doesn't mean that they are appropriate now, for situations are continually changing. Every time conditions change, we should evaluate our schedule again, or conflicts will result. Do we at present have the most sensible arrangements for conditions as they are now? Let's evaluate our rules for meal hours, getting-up time, quiet at night, use of the TV and car, etc. Are they the best for all concerned? Are any of them unnecessary at the moment?

Home is the one place where members of a family should feel as free as possible to be themselves with their own natural life-style. This isn't wholly possible because even in a close-knit family natures differ. But we should make every effort to respect each member's preferences. There is usually some viable solution if we ask how Sue's desire for quiet study can be reconciled with Jim's guitar practice. If each of us is ready for unselfish give-and-take, all of us should be able to relax and be at home here.

"Dear Lord, we're thankful that we can depend on the organization of Your world. Help each of us to organize our life sensibly, flexibly in relation to the rest of us, so that no one feels he is being imposed upon."

New Experiences

DO YOU like new experiences, or do you tend to shun them? There are both kinds of people. Some who feel that their daily lives are humdrum and monotonous are eager for the newness of adventure and excitement. Others want to remain as they are, they feel comfortable now, they want to be left alone without change.

What kind of people crave the new? Usually those who feel secure, sure of themselves, who have had plenty of support in the past. What kind of people avoid the new? Those who have been frightened by the new, who dread the unknown. In general older people find it harder to change, yet many young people are afraid of new experiences. For instance, a musician will practice over and over his old pieces rather than go on to a new one.

God lets some of His people go along very smoothly through life, while others He seems to upset and uproot with many changes. Since we believe that nothing happens to God's children merely by chance, God has a purpose in all that He directs and allows. What could be the reason why He keeps changing some people so often? Probably He is preparing them for a ministry that requires them to be flexible, ready for anything.

How can we be ready for the changes that God orders for us?

David's Varied Experiences—1—2 Samuel

Though the David in the Bible sinned and was very human, he was in many ways a model of the man after God's own heart. David shows us what kinds of experiences we can expect when we set our heart in God's direction. How often God's people through the centuries have been blessed by the psalms of David because he experienced so many of the joys and sorrows that we experience. He helps us express and deal with them.

Let's highlight some of the new experiences that David had, put them in their setting, and share with each other how we would naturally feel if we were doing the things he did for the first time. This will help us to understand each other.

1 Samuel 17:17. If you were asked to take some food to your older brothers in an army, would you be eager to have that experience? What would your attitude depend on?

17:32, 37. When none of the soldiers of Israel were brave enough to engage a giant of a man, would you say what David said? What was he depending on? The Lord and his own past experience with bears and lions. We can't start with the great challenges, but we can take them one at a time, each greater than the last.

18:10, 11. Because Saul was not the Lord's man for the throne, what happened to him? How did David try to help him? Would you like the thrill of trying to keep the king's sword from pinning you to the wall? How alert David must have been!

20:17. Have you loved anyone as much as Jonathan loved David, even though David was going to be the next king instead of him? How important is it to love deeply?

2 Samuel 5:3. At last David was king over the two southern tribes, then over

all Israel. How would you feel if you were chosen top man over many others? How do you feel when chosen over a few others? It's a satisfying feeling, and yet what concerns us about being number one? It's a great responsibility to be a leader, for a leader must look out for the welfare of all the others. Some people enjoy tackling big problems, while others are overwhelmed by them.

The end of 8:14. David led his armies in many battles. Why could God give him victory wherever he went? He was in the Lord's will, obeying Him.

12:13, 14. But with all his good qualities, how did David sin against the brave Uriah? Not only did the child die that he had by Uriah's wife, but he had other troubles with his family. Though God forgave, punishment and scars remained.

15:6. What did one of David's sons do, a very handsome man? When he conspired against his father, the whole household had to flee from the palace.

But David never rebelled against the Lord. Jim, read Psalm 51:1, 2. David was always genuinely heartbroken over his sin.

How Prepare for Change

New experiences can be both plus and minus. The people who are afraid of them miss some sorrow but also much joy. How can we have the joy without the sorrow? By obeying the Lord. The people who miss everything are unsure of too much.

What change does our family anticipate in the near future? How shall we get ready for it? First, we must see the need for it, its advantages, the Lord's purpose in it. If there isn't a good reason, why change? If there is a good reason, what's the good of complaining, pouting, feeling bitter? What do these feelings do to us? They poison our systems. We can't help negative thoughts from coming to us, but we can get rid of them quickly instead of nursing them.

Often the problem is that we feel we will lose something by the change, that something will die. If we list as honestly as we can what we will lose and what we will gain, we can see if we actually will gain more.

What we often fear is the vagueness of the unknown. How can we find out more about our new situation? Even when we don't know what is ahead, what can we say to God?

> . . . he knows the way that I take;
> when he has tried me, I shall come forth as gold.
> > Job 23:10 RSV

> . . . he knows me in action or at rest;
> when he tests me, I prove to be gold.
> > Job 23:10 NEB

> [He says]
> I will teach you, and guide you in the way you should go.
> I will keep you under my eye.
> > Psalm 32:8 NEB

What We Should Experience

CHRISTIAN YOUNG people sometimes feel cheated because they can't describe how the Lord delivered them from awful sins as can some of their friends who had very poor starts in life. They sometimes feel that their lives are tame compared with those who have had adventures with the devil. Sometimes they ask, "How can we know what our friends are talking about if we've never tried drugs or drinking or sex? How can we identify with these kids when we have so little in common?"

Knowing by experience is an essential idea in Scripture. We are not just to talk about the Lord or know about Him, we are to experience Him. We are not just to hope for eternal life in the future; we are to experience it now. The Book of James says, ". . . to him that knoweth to do good, and doeth it not, to him it is sin" (4:17). God doesn't plan for any of His children to lead ordinary humdrum lives. He wants us to go adventuring with Him just as soon as He can trust us with responsibility.

What can we expect life to be like if we accept God's authority and plans? And what can we expect if we don't?

Scheming Jacob—Genesis 25—45

God called out a people for His name beginning with Abraham, Isaac and Jacob. Do you remember how Jacob was different from his brother Esau? When their father grew old and blind, what did he ask Esau to do? But their mother, remembering that God had said that the younger son would serve the older, instead of waiting for the Lord's way of bringing this about, took it into her own hands. What did she tell Jacob to do? So he received the blessing instead of Esau. What was the result? Jacob had to flee from the anger of his brother.

When Jacob lay down alone at night on his way to his uncle's house, what did the Lord promise him when he saw a ladder from earth to heaven, with angels coming and going? Jacob made a covenant with the Lord. At his uncle's house when his beautiful daughter Rachel came to the well to water her sheep, what did Jacob do? How did Jacob bargain with his uncle for the hand of Rachel in marriage? Why was he given Leah first? When he outwitted his uncle in stockbreeding and got many of his uncle's flocks and herds away from him, how did his uncle feel toward him? Jacob secretly started home with his family and herds, but his uncle found out about it, pursued and overtook him. Finally they settled their relationship by making a treaty.

Next Jacob had to plan to meet Esau, who might have been as angry as he had been when Jacob left. Mother, read how Jacob approached Esau and his prayer to God, in 32:4-12. Jacob the schemer was always in hot water. An angel of the Lord wrestled with him all that night. When he saw that he could not throw Jacob, he knocked his hip out of joint. Though Jacob was used to conniving to get his own way, yet he wanted God's blessing.

How did God answer Jacob's prayer? His impulsive twin brother forgot the injuries of the past and the brothers wept together as a relief from their tension.

Is this the kind of excitement that you want? Deceiving and being deceived, afraid of your own brother, having to leave home and go out into the unknown, at odds with your relatives, your hip put out of joint?

Noble Joseph—Genesis 37—50

Jacob's son Joseph is an example of the kind of life we can expect if we work with the Lord. His life wasn't tame by any means. What made it exciting? Can you contribute most of the highlights in his life? Why were Joseph's older brothers jealous of him? Both because of the special coat his father gave him and his dreams in which his family was bowing down to him. So what did his brothers do to him? Wasn't it plenty of adventure for him to be riding to Egypt in a caravan of merchants!

In Egypt he was sold in the slave market to one of Pharaoh's officers. Because Joseph was so keen and responsible, what was he soon trusted with? All the affairs of the household were placed under his administration.

When Joseph refused to sin with his master's wife and she lied about him, when he said no when he should have said no, what did his master do to him? Even in prison Joseph was such a natural leader that he was put in charge of the whole prison. What brought him out of prison? He was the only person able to interpret Pharaoh's dreams. His reward was being put in charge of the whole country's food supplies. What happened when his brothers came to Egypt to buy food? Jim, read Genesis 41:37-45.

When Joseph revealed himself to his brothers, what place did he give God in all the events of his exciting life? Sue, read what he said to his brothers in 45:4-15. Wouldn't you say there was plenty of excitement in Joseph's life? What made his life exciting? In his youth he sounded cocky, but the rest of the time it was because he was so capable and mature in obedience to God.

The Troubles of Sin—Isaiah 57:20, 21

Use your imagination to construct as vivid a picture as possible when I read two verses from Isaiah (57:20, 21). Let's hear it in a couple of other versions. Adventures in sin make us feel like a storm-tossed sea that stirs up dirt and filth. It poisons our lives and leaves scars that may be forgiven but are never erased. Jacob seldom had inner peace and rest; Joseph lived in continual peace even when he was in prison.

"Lord, we want the adventures of our lives to overcome sin, not be overcome by sin. Thank You for preparing opportunities for us to make this world a better place with You, not a worse place, because we have lived."

Becoming a Leader

THINK OF the leaders that you've had in groups of which you've been a member. Have they all been the best kind of leaders? Do you feel at the moment that it is hard or easy to be a good leader? God needs human leaders to work with Him, and often He picks up young people with a Christian background for positions of leadership. When Christ is the head of His body the church, and the Head gives directions and power to carry them out, what is the role of a human leader? He performs the human tasks that Christ directs and empowers. What would be his most essential qualification? Yes, his own life in Christ, the example and model that he is, for what he is is more important than what he does.

Think of the Christian leader as extending one arm up to the Lord and the other arm down to people. What happens if he doesn't keep close to the Lord? Everything will go awry if he makes decisions and works in the energy of his lower nature. What happens if the leader doesn't keep close to people? He doesn't lead them, they don't follow, he doesn't understand their feelings and problems, he goes ahead without them.

Are you more inclined to be task-oriented or people-oriented? Those who see a goal and like to concentrate until they reach it, may work better alone than with others. Leaders need both to have a clear vision of possible goals and be able to work skillfully with people to reach those goals. This kind of expertise requires careful training. What kind of training can we expect the Lord to give His leaders?

God's Training of Moses—Acts 7:24-29, Exodus 3:10, 11

God carefully trained Moses for forty years in Egypt, for forty years in the desert, with only forty years left for him to serve. What kind of home did he come from? A godly Israelite home in the land of Egypt. How did his parents keep him from being killed when a baby, Alice? Even as a baby God was protecting Moses. Highly educated in the court of Egypt with princes of other countries that were subject to Egypt, he became a powerful speaker as well as a man of action.

As a young man Moses made a very important decision. Turn to Hebrews 11:24. It would have been a great temptation for him to enjoy the pleasures of sin as the son of Pharaoh's daughter.

Until he was forty he was identified with the Egyptians. When it occurred to him to look into the conditions of his own people, what kind of experience did he have? Look at Acts 7:24, 25. How did he feel toward his people, and how did they feel toward him? Probably at this time he felt very good about himself, was full of self-confidence.

In 26, how would you judge his actions as a leader? He had the best of intentions.

But how did the Israelites respond to his overtures? 27, 28. His people did not identify with him. To them he was one of their Egyptian taskmasters, who worked them unmercifully.

So in 29 what did Moses do? What a contrast between forty years in the splendid court of Egypt and the next forty years in the back side of the desert!

What did the Lord need to teach him when they were alone together that he hadn't learned in the company of sophisticated nobles? In Egypt he learned to trust himself; in the desert he learned to trust God. In the desert he found favor with a priest, whose daughter he married and whose sheep he tended. This was the very place where he would later lead the great nation of Israel on its way to the promised land.

After forty more years when he learned who he was and who his God was, he was ready to lead God's people. How did God call him? In the bush that burned without being consumed. What did God say to Moses in Exodus 3:10?

How did Moses answer the Lord, in 11? Where was his self-confidence now? Now his trust would be in the Lord.

Our Preparation for Leadership

Is it going to take us eighty years to learn both the wisdom of this world and the wisdom of God? Is it going to take us forty years to learn to trust God and not ourselves? We have to be good followers before we can be leaders. When God calls us to lead, what will we answer?

Let's list here on the board the good qualities of leaders that we have already experienced, and the qualities in leaders that we don't appreciate. What do we want leaders to be and do? Yes, first to lead, and that means to lead the group, not dictate to it. Some leaders feel that in order to be a real leader they must dominate the group. What is the leader's relation to his group? He is there to help the group do what it wants to do, steer where it wants to go. He is a pace-setter, a moderator who sees that all the members' ideas are heard and fairly considered, that all sides of a question are included.

What don't we want leaders to do? We don't want them to be bossy, to insist on their own ideas, and try to push them through. They shouldn't be partial to anyone, but try to get all the members involved in the conversation or activities. They help the group focus on the basic issues and come to decisions about them.

Are we taking the opportunities that the Lord gives us to practice leading? Are we becoming skilled both in achieving goals and in relating to people? Do we like responsibility, are we challenged by problems rather than shrinking from them? Do we try to change things that can be changed and accept what cannot be changed? Are we sensitive to the Lord's timing? Can we organize problems that are complex, not simple? Do we really like people, all kinds of people, and try to understand those who feel different from us?

"Dear Lord, we thank You that You leave essential ministries for us humans. Grant that each of us may find the place where You can use us fully, and guide us even this year in getting ready for that place."

6 GROWING IN LOVE

Loving the Lord

JIM DIDN'T go out much with girls until he met Janice. She attracted him from the start. He liked the way she looked, the way she talked, the way she acted. They seemed to hit it off together. The more he got to know her, the better he liked her. She was in his thoughts most of the time, and he was with her whenever he could be. He bought all kinds of gifts for her. There was nobody like Janice, until one day he discovered that she had lied to him. Then he was all broken up. He didn't know whether he still loved her or whether he now hated her. He was churning inside.

All of us have Someone who is wooing us, courting us, seeking to win us. He loved us even before we were born. He has been giving us all kinds of gifts including laying down His own life for us. Like Jim, the Lord loved us first; our love is a response to Him. He wants to be with us just as Jim wanted to be with Jan. But what is different about the Lord's love for us and Jim's love for Jan? Did the Lord choose us and call us to Himself because He liked us better than other people? No, but because He has a purpose for us, a purpose no one else can fill as well. When we do something that disappoints Him, is He ready to throw us over? No, He loves us just the same, just as much no matter what we do! How can that be? God is love. It's His nature to love. Not much human love is as steady as that.

Have you ever felt love for a person one minute and hate the next? Or seen a person change like that on TV? Why is that possible, when love and hate are opposites? Real love goes deep. It opens us to being hurt by the one we love. If he rejects the love that we offer, we may react just the opposite.

The First Commandment—Matthew 22:37

Some people act as if the first and great commandment is to know the Bible or know about the Lord. What is it, in Matthew 22:37? Is love something that can be commanded? How is it that the Lord can command love? Because it's an ungrateful wretch who will not respond to the greatest self-giving love that we can imagine. Then the Lord tells us just what our response should be. Why isn't halfhearted love enough? Martin Luther said, "Whatever man loves, that is his god; nothing else counts if it isn't in love." If we don't love the Lord with all that is within us, is He our God?

Mary's Love—John 12:3-8

Mary of Bethany, the sister of Martha and Lazarus whom Jesus raised from the dead, was a person who loved Jesus with all her heart. When Jesus stopped at their house, she didn't care what they had to eat. While Martha bustled about preparing a fine meal for their guest, Mary seated herself at Jesus' feet and stayed there listening to His words. She just wanted to be with Him and hear Him talk about the Father (Luke 10:39).

What could she do to show Him how much she loved Him? Near the end of

His life on earth when a supper was given in His honor and Martha served, what did Mary bring with her? Look at John 12:3. A pound of very costly perfume or ointment, which was worth what a working man would earn in a whole year! What did she do with it?

In verses 4 and 5, how did Judas feel about Mary's gift? Verse 6 explains why. We can see here what Judas' heart was like, even if he was numbered among the disciples.

In 7 how did Jesus answer that? Even then what was Jesus looking forward to? He knew that He would be giving His life for the sins of the world. It was customary in those days to anoint dead bodies for burial. Jesus recognized what Mary did as the act of devotion that it was. I doubt that Mary cared what Judas thought as long as Jesus accepted her gift of love.

Loving the Unseen

Many people who know about Jesus and talk about Jesus have never loved Jesus. Why would that be? They think of Him as a fact perhaps, or an historical character like George Washington or Napoleon. They have never loved a person they haven't seen. Since He is a real Person with all the qualities of a person, we treat Him as a person even if we can't see Him.

How do we learn to love the people we see? Like Mary, we like to be with them, listen to them, talk to them, do things with them, give them things they like, do special things for them. This last week did we enjoy being in the presence of the Lord when there were just the two of us?

After Father, Mother and young Joan had knelt and prayed one evening, Father and Mother rose to leave, but Joan still remained on her knees. So Father and Mother waited quietly until she got up. "What were you doing?" asked Mother. "I just waited to love Jesus," answered Joan, "and then He loved me."

People who love each other like to get as close to each other as possible because love is warm and very personal. Do you listen to the Lord when you're alone as well as talk to Him? Do you do things together? Can you think of something special you'd like to do because you love Him?

When love grows cool, it is usually because people haven't taken time to be together or something has come between them to separate them. If there is anything between us and the Lord, let's remove it right now. If we love Him, let's tell Him how much.

Loving Ourselves

GOD SAYS to each of us, ". . . love your neighbor as yourself" (Matthew 22:39 RSV). How then will we feel about ourselves? What kind of self-love is this? It certainly is not pride, conceit, egotism, for Scripture condemns these. This second commandment comes after the first, which is loving God with all our heart, putting Him in the center of life, not ourselves. What is healthy self-love?

Maybe we can discover its meaning by asking first what happens to the person who hates himself? There are many people who do. They feel they are nobody, trash, junk. How does Scripture dash that idea? Yes, each of us was created in the image of God to take our place in the body of Christ and make our own unique contribution. If I consider myself a zero or a minus, I have nothing to give to Christ or anyone else. If I hate myself, my neighbor is in trouble, for I will hate him, too. We project onto others our own self-contempt. If we cannot accept Christ's love, we cannot extend it to our neighbors. People who don't accept themselves usually try to gain satisfaction by means that never really satisfy—by gaining money, power, fame, pleasure, etc.

What Self-Love Is

What then does it mean to love ourselves as the Lord uses that idea? Look first at Matthew 5:13. How important is salt in our diet? How bland and taste-less would our food be without salt! Then in 14 what other comparison does Jesus make? Without light what would our world be? And verse 16 gives God's purpose for His people.

Then look at Matthew 10:29-31 for another comparison. Verse 30 is difficult for us mortals to comprehend, it is so tremendous!

John 17:23 is another revelation of God that is hard for us to take in. That God the Father loves us as much as He loves His own Son, the Saviour, who is perfect! If God loves us this much, how should we feel about ourselves?

Ephesians 1:6 also expresses how the Lord feels about us. In your version what words stand out to you? "Accepted in the Beloved, freely bestowed on us in the Beloved, taken into His favor in the person of His beloved Son." Each of us can say to ourselves, "I am somebody." One young man who had a poor self-image wrote the words "Accepted in the Beloved" in large letters and put them over his dresser in his room so that he would often see them. The Jewish child in Jesus' day had no question about his being wanted.

The self-love that Jesus is talking about is a healthy respect for myself as created and accepted by God for a particular purpose. Our lives are to be rooted in love.

A Prerequisite to Self-Denial

The Bible also talks about self-denial. How do these two ideas fit together? Turn to Luke 9:23. What does it mean to deny ourselves? Give up all right to ourselves, say no to ourselves. What would be our cross that we are to take up day-by-day? Anything that hinders the life of Christ in us, anything that keeps us from obeying Him and receiving His best.

God has given us wills so that we may have the privilege of giving them back to Him of our own free will out of love. The only thing we really have and can give is ourselves. If we are free to be ourselves, we can then take the next step of giving ourselves. Though the Lord knows that we are sinful, what does He ask us to do in Romans 12:1? He values us as a living sacrifice that He will make holy and acceptable in Christ. How does that make you feel about yourself?

Healthy Self-Love

Let's see if we feel about ourselves as the Lord does. Can you affirm, say *yes,* to these statements that the Lord makes about you:

1. Can you truly say *yes,* the Lord made me just the way He wanted me to be to fulfill a particular purpose in His great plan for the ages? Can you visualize yourself doing something significant with Him?

2. Do you listen to everything that all parts of you are saying; are you aware of all that your complex being is saying to you? That includes your body, your mind, your will, your feelings, your spirit. Are all these parts of you pulling together, without one going off in another direction? Too often our body and feelings run counter to our spirit and mind and will. Our spirit, mind and will decide that something hard is best to do, even if it is hard. But our body and feelings prefer a soft life, and may keep us from carrying out our decision. Do we love our real inner self enough to grit our teeth and pull body and feelings into line?

3. Have we enough self-respect to evaluate honestly what we have and don't have? Can we say, "Yes, I'm thankful that I am a good thinker, but I need to be more organized? I know how I am strong and how I am weak, but most important is what I receive from the Lord, which will always be sufficient."

4. Do I get my values from the Lord, not from myself or from other people? Other people's values may differ widely from the Lord's. Do I check myself each evening as to how I did on His rating scale?

For what do you thank the Lord in relation to yourself? In what way is it hard for you to see yourself as He sees you? Talk to Him about that.

Loving Others

THE SECOND great commandment after loving God is ". . . love your neighbor as yourself" (Matthew 22:39 RSV). How much love do we feel toward our neighbors right now? How have we been expressing our love? Is it strong enough for them to feel it? Or do our neighbors think that we are indifferent toward them, that we Christians like to be separate from other people?

Today our world is composed of so many huge systems that the individual often feels that he gets lost in the immensity of it all, that no one really knows or cares about him. The ordinary individual has little place in the big corporation, the big institution, the big political party, sometimes even in the big church. He often feels that he is being treated as a thing rather than a person. With life so uncertain he feels that he is being tossed about haphazardly by circumstances, manipulated as a tool, tangled up in its competition, ignored when he is no longer useful. All the time he is yearning to be treated as a person with his own abilities, his own needs, his own concerns. It is likely that some people in our neighborhood feel like this.

Is our Christian love strong enough to reach out to find people like this, who are dying for a bit of genuine love? Who want people to care for them just for themselves, not for any selfish reason? It is natural to love people who love us or who are themselves lovable. We need this kind of love. But how is Christ going to love the unlovable if He can't love them through us? They are the ones who need His love most.

Because love is considered by almost everyone as the strongest force in the universe, through the centuries sweeping statements have been made about love. Petrarch said, "Love is the crowning grace of humanity." William Penn who founded Pennsylvania: "Love is the hardest lesson in Christianity; but, for that reason, it should be most our care to learn it." Daniel A. Poling: "Hate cannot destroy hate, but love can and does."

Loving the Unlovable

What does the Lord expect of His people in whom He has put His Spirit? Turn to Matthew 5:46. How did people feel about tax collectors in Jesus' day? They were hated because they took more than their share from those under them. The Living Bible calls them "scoundrels," and says that even scoundrels love those who love them. The Gentiles in this setting are people who had no connection with the Lord, as the Jewish nation had.

Jesus was criticized for being a friend of tax collectors and sinners, because He loved all kinds of people. Matthew, who wrote the first gospel, was a tax collector before Jesus called him.

Who is another tax collector in the gospels that we are familiar with? Turn to Luke 19. What kind of person was Zacchaeus from verses 2 and 3? I suppose most other important persons would have gone on their way without looking up into that tree.

How did Jesus surprise everyone there? 5. Even go to the house of this man? Many others would have liked Jesus to go to their house.

What a contrast between the way Zacchaeus responded to this and the response of the others in the crowd! 6, 7.

What did the presence of Jesus do to Zacchaeus? 8. When we enter a strange house, what effect does the presence of Jesus in us have on the people there? The record does not tell of any words of condemnation that Jesus spoke. He brought love as well as holiness. Zacchaeus laid down his own penalty.

Won't it be thrilling when our neighbors say about our contacts with them, "Today salvation has come to this house"? We can help them to realize that they were made in the image of God for His own purposes.

Will the one of you who has The Living Bible please read the wording of verse 10? To save such souls as the soul of Zacchaeus, the hated tax collector.

Reflecting Jesus' Love

No one was too sinful for Jesus to love! One day when He was teaching in the temple, the proud Jewish leaders who pretended to be perfect brought to Him a woman caught in the very act of sin. Look at John 8:5. What did Moses in the law say to do to such cases? The leaders were probably more interested in what Jesus would suggest for the woman than about her. 6. What did Jesus do instead of getting caught in their trap?

When they kept demanding an answer, what did He say? 7. How did they react to that? 8, 9. Finally what did Jesus say to the woman? 10, 11. How that woman must have loved Him to her dying day!

It's easy to love people who are clean, pretty, and who do nice things. But those who most need our love may not be clean, pretty, and nice. How is it possible to love them? Only if the Lord gives us His own love, which doesn't depend on what kind of people they are. It's just His nature to love. If we are filled with His Spirit, we too will supernaturally love—all people whoever they are, just for themselves.

Will loving all people mean that we will approve of all that they do? Not at all. "While we were yet sinners, Christ died for us" (Romans 5:8). "God so loved the world" (John 3:16). How can we separate what we love and what we disapprove? We can enjoy with others the things that we both do because we are human beings, but we can show them what good times Christians have when we obey the Lord rather than disobey Him.

Which people we know seem to need love most? Let's ask the Lord to love them through us and show us how to reflect His love. Should this be as a family to another family, or as individuals to other individuals?

Matthew 22:37-39 should be memorized if it hasn't been already.

Loving God's People

IN HUMAN societies there have always been gatherings of large numbers of people. Why do many people come together in one place in our day? Yes, representatives of the people assemble as government officials to make laws for the welfare of everyone. What difficulties do government leaders have in making decisions? It is hard to agree on what is best when special interests pull for their own concerns. People from all over the country come to conventions—sales conventions and teachers' conventions to display the latest methods, political conventions to nominate political candidates. Sometimes there is a great deal of conflict over which political candidate would be best. And yes, crowds gather to watch sports events. In these one person or team usually wins while the others lose. Most of the spectators are cheering or maybe betting on the one they want to win. Some always win while others lose.

When God's people come together, how do we expect their gatherings to be different from other kinds? What should be distinctive about our groups? Often the difference isn't as great as most people expect. Would we expect Christians to agree on everything? No, we are very different kinds of people from all kinds of backgrounds. What else makes us differ? We have different gifts and responsibilities in the body of Christ.

The Test of the Reality of Christ—1 John 4:7-21

The Book of 1 John explains the sign of discipleship, which is love toward each other (John 13:35). Turn to 1 John 4:7, and read to yourself the rest of that chapter, through verse 21. Look for the main idea that John is stressing here.

What is his chief concern in this section? He begins with it and ends with it. Yes, loving one another, and he is speaking of the Christian fellowship here, although of course our love extends to all people.

Now let's work in two groups. Mother and Alice will work together; Jim and Sue and I. (If you have only one child, he can work with one parent while the other parent works alone.) As you read this section again, make two lists: one listing all that it says about God's love, and in a second, what it says that we should do. The two lists will look something like this:

God's love	What we should do
love is of God	love one another (repeated)
God is love	know God
He sent His Son to be punished for our sins	live through Him
	know we abide in Him
God abides in us	confess Jesus as the Son of God
His love is perfected in us	know and believe God's love
He gave us His Spirit	have confidence in judgment
He first loved us	have no fear
He commands: love your brother	

Ted, will you please read your first list, and Sue, your second list. What ideas did you find repeated? Yes, loving one another, God's love, and also abiding in

God. What is the relation among these three ideas? Which comes first? God's love is always first; it's the source of all other love; our love is a response to His. We can love because God Himself lives in us by His Spirit, or abides in us, or dwells in us.

Notice that the best translation of verse 19 is not "We love *him,* because he first loved us," but "we love, because he first loved us" (RSV). We are naturally selfish, not loving unless He lives in us.

We have to know most human people before we love them. What do verses 7 and 16 say about knowing God? Of course we need to know something about God before we love Him, but we won't know much about Him till we love Him. A small child truly loves God before he knows much about Him; that love enables him to learn more and more.

Living Christ's Love

What then should be true of all God's people as we come together? When the unseen Lord of the universe is in our midst, His love should be shed abroad in our hearts so that we love each other, He should be perfecting His love in us, we should have confidence, not fear, because He suffered the penalty of our sins! With all that going for us, what should we expect to happen in meetings of God's people? Compare that with meetings of people who remain on the human level.

What should we expect first? Instead of competing with each other, trying to win over someone else or trying to put it over on someone, we should be showing love, looking out for each other, sacrificing for each other. If one experienced a joy that the Lord had given him, he would share with the others so that all of us could praise Him. If one had a need, all of us could help him meet it. We would be concerned about each other, not merely about ourselves.

What else would we expect among Christians? What would make it easier for us to agree with each other, even if we did have different backgrounds and responsibilities? The same Lord is living in all of us, and we are all listening to His directions. We wouldn't all be doing the same things, but we'd all be working for the same purpose. We'd appreciate what the others were doing, for there would be no cross-purposes.

And we would enjoy being with each other. In fact we would attract each other, for when I see reflections of the Lord's love in you, I am drawn to you. The Apostle John finds it impossible to believe that if we don't love our brother whom we have seen we can really love God whom we have not seen.

Let's just be quiet for a minute, asking the Lord to fill our being with His own divine love, so that it will radiate to all people.

Showing Love

WHEN NEW neighbors moved next door to the Martins, our family wanted very much to show them the love of the Lord. They asked the Lord to help them take advantage of all the natural opportunities they would have to reflect Christ. But they weren't prepared for all that happened.

The high school son asked Jim if he could borrow his tennis racquet and balls. Jim hesitated because he had received a new racquet for his birthday and he had hardly used it himself. But he thought he better not refuse. That evening when he came home late from the library he found his new racquet on the porch with a string broken on it. You know how he felt. Not like showing love. But do we expect people without the Lord to act as we do when the Lord strengthens us? The Martins soon discovered that the boys next door didn't have the kind of upbringing that their family had.

At the school lunch room Sue saw plain Jane sitting alone, so she took her tray over and sat next to her. Did Jane smile and answer her questions? No, she didn't. She turned away from her and didn't speak. How did Sue feel? How must Jane feel about herself to withdraw like that? She must have had very distressing experiences. What can Sue do now to try to get through to her?

Ted had just spent an hour raking the red and gold maple leaves from his front lawn, when one of the boys next door began to jump in the piles and scatter them all over again. He thought that was great sport. But not Ted! Would he show him love?

When things are going smoothly, it is easy to agree with the Lord that we ought to show His love to others, that they won't see it any other way. But when unloving people treat us in a mean way, our feelings are inclined to take over and wish them evil instead of good. Isn't it then that we most need the Lord's help?

Jesus Showing Love to Peter—John 21

Peter had been traveling with Jesus for three years, and had expected that He would become Israel's earthly king. It was alarming to him and very frightening to see Jesus taken by soldiers and brought to trial. In an attempt to protect himself, thinking only of himself, what had he said to people who accused him of being one of Jesus' disciples? Three times he had said he didn't even know Jesus! If you were Jesus, how would you feel about that? But Jesus was not thinking of Himself, He was thinking of Peter, of turning him from a wishy-washy person into a solid follower.

So when some of the disciples went back to fishing and caught nothing, how did the Lord show love to them? When they cast their net on the right side of the boat as He directed, they had the boat full of fish! And there was Jesus on the shore, with fish broiling on a fire and bread ready for them. This was after Jesus' death and resurrection! Imagine how Peter felt. How would most people treat you if you had three times denied that you knew them?

Turn to John 21:15. After breakfast what question did Jesus ask Peter? The New English Bible translates that first question, "Do you love me more than all else?" In verses 15-17, Jim, will you read the words of the Lord in this conversation, and Sue, what Peter says.

Why do you think Jesus asked Peter three times if he loved Him? Probably because Peter had denied Him three times. What tone of voice would Peter probably answer in now? Not in the quick rough-and-ready way he usually did.

What do you think it meant to Peter to have the Lord commission him to feed and tend His sheep and lambs? He had planned to work with Jesus, but after his denial he was afraid that the Lord would be finished with him. But three times Jesus said He wanted Peter to work with Him. That's the way the Lord shows love even after people mistreat Him!

What It Takes to Show Love

If we seriously intend to reflect the love of the Lord, we'll have to be ready for what it takes. What will we have to expect from people?

We won't be upset if people are selfish and careless. Since people are naturally self-centered, they will be thinking of themselves, not us. If we too are thinking of ourselves, the result may be conflict rather than love. But what will impress them? If we do what is supernatural rather than natural, they may begin to question why. It will often require sacrifice and endurance and longsuffering, but the servant is not above his master. People may annoy us, interrupt what we are doing, make us wait for them, be dishonest about us. We don't expect them to be Christlike until He comes to live in them.

There is also the danger that people will reject our love. Why would they do that? They have grown to suspect people's motives because most people are out for themselves. They wonder what we'll get out of this, since they can't imagine our doing something only for them. So it may take a while for them to develop trust in us.

(Role play a real person that one of you wants to contact.) Let's role play a situation in which I act superior and see how you feel. Sue, you be Mrs. Nichols who lives across the street, and I'll be myself. I go to her and say, "Hello, neighbor. I'm starting a Bible class next week for some of you who have no Bible background. The Bible is the most important book. Will you be able to come?" "No, you probably can't understand the Bible yourself, but I'll explain it. Don't you have questions about the Lord and His ways for us?" "He says very practical things about training children in the home."

How do you feel about me as Mrs. Nichols, Sue? If you were this neighbor, how would you like to have me start to show you love? Show us by taking the role of a Christian, and I'll respond as Mrs. Nichols.

Loving the Unlovely and the Lonely

ONE OF the problems in Christian homes is neighbor children wanting to be there too much because their own homes are unpleasant places. What kind of person would you likely be if you were never sure whether or not your parents would be at home, whether a meal would be ready or not, whether or not you'd have clothes ready to wear, what was expected of you, whether your parents would be kind or cross? If you found a home with a loving atmosphere where people appreciated each other, enjoyed doing things together, and had interesting materials to work with, what would you do? You would naturally spend as much time there as possible. A child is naturally drawn to this home.

But how do the members of the family feel about the child? Because he has not been brought up as they have, he is probably very annoying. What bothers them? He uses bad language that they don't like to hear, he is selfish and unkind because he hasn't been trained to think of others, and he isn't careful of the family's property. How will they treat him? Will they say, "We are happier without him," and send him home? What should be their attitude toward him?

God's Love in Us

How do these parts of God's Word help us establish our attitude toward this kind of person:

1. Matthew 22:39. Loving our neighbor isn't a question for us to decide; it is a command of God. If the tables were turned and we were that other person, wouldn't we want the home to share with us? We have had advantages that he has not had.

2. Romans 5:8. How does this verse speak to our problem? Christ didn't die for us because we were such good people, but because He loved us just as we were. He chose us and drew us to Himself or we would be unlovely and alone.

3. Romans 5:5. Maybe in ourselves we would never feel love toward people who are selfish and hateful. But Christ loves them and His love in us is great enough for the worst of people.

4. Matthew 5:43-48. Verse 43 tells how people naturally feel toward their enemies. But Jesus reverses natural ideas. How will people know that we belong to our heavenly Father if we don't resemble Him? Doesn't verse 46 ask penetrating questions! Even scoundrels love those who love them! Start 47 with the words, "If you are friendly," instead of other wordings. Since Matthew was speaking to Jewish people, who were the Gentiles to them? They were heathen who had no relation to God. Verse 48 is very helpful in The New English Bible: "You must therefore be all goodness, just as your heavenly Father is all good."

5. Ephesians 4:2. If God's love is shed abroad in our hearts and our goodness knows no bounds, how will we be able to treat the unlovely person?

6. Romans 15:1-3. When a person seems to require too much forbearance in love, what can we say to ourselves? "I am not pleasing myself, but my neighbor for his good, to edify him, just as Christ did not please Himself. I am acting like a child of my Father."

7. Colossians 4:5, 6. If we actually demonstrate the love of Christ to the unlovely person, what can we ask the Lord to do? This is the best way of drawing

him to the Lord so that He can change him into a lovely person. When he exasperates us, it may finally get through to him that we are kind and gracious whereas most people respond with biting hostility. We are then witnessing in our own home without having to go outside to reach people.

Who Needs Our Love?

In the light of these words from Scripture, what shall we do about the unlovely neighbor who likes to stay at our house? By our love and patience we'll try to help him see that he needs the Lord, to see what the Lord can do for him. We are much concerned about him. We want our home to be an attractive place where we like to be and others like to come.

Is there any limit to what we will allow at our house? Is it fair for others to come in and disrupt our family life? What could be the limits of what we will allow outsiders to do? Can't we say firmly that an outsider can come at certain hours or go just so far in his abuse of our time and our property? We could lovingly say to him, "I don't want to hear anymore of that foul language," or "You can't continue to destroy our property like that." When he is at our house, we can insist that he try to fit in with us. We can explain to him what we are working for and why, so that he understands. He won't always be able to live up to the Lord's high standards, but it should be evident that he is trying.

What about other kinds of lonely people who don't have warm family relationships? Yes, we think of children who don't live nearby, and single men and women and people whose husbands or wives have died. How could we share our family with them sometimes? We could invite them here, to go places with us, and perhaps to sit with us in church, so that they will feel that they belong to God's great family. Are there any new people in our community who might feel lonely? These people would come only when asked, but they would probably be very grateful for any invitation.

"Lord, as we thank You for our family, we don't want to be selfish. Show us which unlovely people and which lonely people we should share with. Help them see Your love and grace through us."

7 DEALING WITH SIN

The Separation of Sin

THE GREATEST thing in life, what counts most of all, what means most to us as human beings is right relationships—being rightly related to God, to ourselves, and to others. How do we feel when these relationships are broken?

Let's take ourselves first. Suppose that all day we've looked forward to playing tennis when the day's work was done. Then Mother asks us if we will please go to the grocery for eggs that she needs. Our spirit, mind, and will want to go for Mother, but our feelings want to play tennis. Our feelings are separated from the rest of us, and we don't feel good.

When was the last time you experienced a break in your relationship with the Lord? What was the cause of it? How did you react? How did you reestablish the right relationship? Are you as sensitive to the way He is feeling as you are to other people?

Only those who live superficially go along smoothly without disruptions in their relations with other people. Which people are the easiest for you to get along with? Which are hardest? Why do you have trouble with these people? What do they do that annoys you? What do you do that annoys them? How do you get back on a good footing?

How do you tend to react when a relationship is broken? Different temperaments react differently. Some tend to withdraw, clam up, get away. Others strike out, fight, challenge. When people feel separated, they erect barriers to keep others away, they build fences, and society puts in jail behind bars the ones of whom we are most afraid.

Separation from God—Isaiah 59:1-13

What is the root cause of feelings of separation? The people in Isaiah's day were saying, "Why doesn't the Lord deliver us, why doesn't He answer our prayers?" Turn to Isaiah 59:1, 2. Because Isaiah is still in communion with the Lord, he knows the reason. What easier word means the same as "iniquity"? Yes, *sin*. When people sin, Scripture often says that the Lord hides His face or turns His face away; in other words, pays no attention.

Then God faces the people with their specific sins. Are people today still doing the things He points out in verse 3? On the board I'll list these sins in a word or two. First is murder and lying.

What is added to lying in verse 4? Injustice, which many are complaining about today.

Verse 5 and the first part of 6 give two illustrations: what the people are doing is like hatching eggs that are poisonous and weaving cloth that is too sleazy for clothing. What word in 6 is a very common sin today? Violence.

Verse 7 refers to another part of the body that the people are using for evil. How many parts of the body have already been mentioned? Hands, fingers, lips, tongue. And after feet is what? People outwardly do evil because their thoughts within are first evil.

Read the way The Living Bible expresses 6 and 7, Ted. What do you think of when the Revised Standard Version translates the end of 7, "desolation and destruction are in their highways"? I think of all the accidents on our highways, due largely to people who are drunk.

In 8 what is it that everybody wants, yet these people do not enjoy? Peace. Therefore they are not experiencing justice or right or light, but rather deep gloom. 9.

The next two verses make four comparisons: these sinners are like four what? They grope along like blind men, they do nothing like dead men, they growl like bears, they moan like doves. Isn't that expressive! How can they expect justice and salvation from the Lord?

Do we feel like the people in verses 12 and 13 when we have sinned? Do we know our guilt? Do we realize that we have broken faith with the Lord? Will we ask forgiveness and be restored?

Separation from People

Sin acts just the opposite of love. Love draws people close together, while sin separates them. We all long to stay close to the people who are important to us. The more important they are to us, the deeper the hurt when sin separates.

Since we have our closest relationships in the family, if family connections are strained, other relationships will suffer too. Have you ever gone to school or to work in the morning feeling at odds with someone? How did that day go for you? Not too well, I bet.

Therefore I am much concerned that we keep our relationship in this house right. Are we as a family honest enough and mature enough to discuss openly the things that tend to separate us from each other? I'd like to ask each of you, "When am I inclined to drive you away from me?" It may be that because the Lord has set me here as the head of this house, you may sometimes feel that I am unjust. I am responsible before the Lord to make what I think are the best decisions with His guidance. I want you to know why I do things, and I want to keep in touch with what each of you is thinking and feeling, for I respect your opinions and your viewpoint. It's easy to misunderstand. What do I do that makes it hard for you to do right and feel right toward me?

Would anyone else like to ask this same question of the others?

How can we prevent misunderstandings? When we can't see any good reason for someone's actions, we can ask politely for an explanation. Wonderfully soothing words are "I'm sorry," which we can use instead of always defending whatever we did just because we did it.

"Lord, help us develop trust relationships, which are difficult to develop, but easy to break."

Self-Will

THIS WEEK each person in the Martin family had a problem with the same root cause. I did not like the decision that the president of our company made because now my work is harder. Mother had to go on a diet that cut out many of the foods that she likes best. Jim was required to take a high-school course he saw no need for, which left no time for a course he did want to take. Sue's church choir chose a new style of choir gown that she considered old-fashioned. Ted was grumpy when rain made his team postpone their Saturday game. Alice was sad because Mother wouldn't let her buy for school a dress that wasn't practical or appropriate.

What was the root of all these difficulties? We all naturally want our own way, what seems good and beneficial to us, not what someone else wants. This is the major cause of the conflict and tension in our world. How can we have peace among nations, in our own country, or in our family when each of us wants his own way?

Jonah's Self-Will

God said to Jonah His prophet, " 'Go to the great city of Nineveh . . . and denounce it, for its wickedness stares me in the face' " (Jonah 1:2 NEB). But Jonah set off in the opposite direction to get out of the reach of the Lord. Why didn't Jonah want what the Lord wanted? Why wasn't he delighted to pronounce the doom of this capital city of the enemy? He also knew the mercy of the Lord toward sinners.

The Lord has His own humorous creative ways of teaching His children. What did He send to teach Jonah, Alice? Jonah was honest in his self-will; he told the sailors that he was running away from the Lord and that they should throw him overboard. When he didn't learn from this experience, what next did the Lord do?

Inside the whale, read the last of his prayer, in Jonah 2:7-9. Since he finally was learning, what did the Lord do? 2:10—3:2.

How did Jonah respond this time? 3, 4.

And how did the people of Nineveh respond? 5. When the king heard the message, what did even he in his high position do? 6-9.

So what did God do, in 10?

How would you think a prophet of God would feel when the people of a great city turned from their evil ways? But look at 4:1. What is the gist of all those words of Jonah in verse 2? This book is full of "buts." Jonah is always opposing the will of God. It was just as he expected! How could he be so bigoted!

In 3 he goes still further, and the Lord questions him to get him to see how self-centered he is.

In 5 how did he sulk until he would see what would happen to the city?

How childish was Jonah! How very human are the events in the Bible? After Jonah had been very angry in 4:1 because the city of Nineveh had been spared, what was he very glad for in verse 6? The Lord is still merciful to him in his pouting just as He was to the city.

In 7 and 8 how did God try to show Jonah the differences between the important things of life and the unimportant? Jonah doesn't want to live if his shade is taken away from him!

In 9 and 10 what kind of person is Jonah showing himself to be? Stubborn and willful.

How would you say in your own words the Lord's implications in 10 and 11? Jonah is much concerned about a plant that lasts for a night, but can't understand how God feels about the eternal souls of 120,000 people in the city! Probably Jonah was of no further use to the Lord. That's self-will. What a miserable life!

Putting Christ on the Throne of Our Lives

What is the answer to self-will, self-centeredness? If we each do our own thing, we ourselves will always be in turmoil and we'll always be in conflict with others.

On the board I'm drawing a circle with all the little self-wills trying to get their own way. How would it be possible for all of them to go the same way, work in the same direction, supporting each other rather than fighting each other? Yes, only if Christ were the center of each life and they all tried to please Him.

What would this mean for each of us? We'd each give our will to Christ, who would develop us fully and use us fully. Why do we hesitate to do this? Are we afraid we wouldn't like what He likes? Why are we afraid His will wouldn't be best? Don't we know Him well enough to trust that His way is best, that He wants only the best for us?

Then we would take everything that comes as from Him. Whether it seemed good or bad to us, we'd know He either sent it or allowed it. And we'd do everything unto Him, everything gladly because we love Him.

If we individuals try to manage our own lives, think of the tremendous forces in our world that could overwhelm us! But we're in the best hands when we give ourselves to the Ruler of the universe. He lets people go just so far and then says, "Enough"! He is in control of the whole.

"Lord, We thank You that You love us enough to want to sit on the throne of our lives. Grant that we won't have to go through the kinds of experiences that Jonah went through before we learn how inadequate are our own selfish ways."

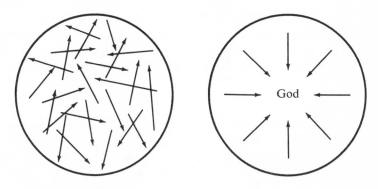

Real Guilt

HOW WOULD you answer this high-school girl who became pregnant? This is the way she says she feels: "I'm sorry my parents are upset. Yes, I'll have to change my plans, but we all make mistakes. The only way to keep from making mistakes is to do nothing. We're always guilty of something. Why is this so much worse than other things? We all have to fulfill ourselves even if things sometimes turn out badly."

Yes, we surely can forgive her because God will forgive her if she does what? But what is the difference between a mistake and sin? We make mistakes when we try to do right, but sin is doing what we know is wrong. Read James 4:17, Sue. Does this girl sound as if she knew what was wrong? Woe unto us if we take sin lightly, for God does not take it lightly. What shows how seriously God takes it? He had to send His own Son to make the greatest of all sacrifices to atone for our sin. That's how serious it is to Him. We better take it seriously!

When we disobey clear directions in God's Word, we ought to feel guilty. Guilt is one of the deepest problems in life. Some people who should feel guilty don't and some who shouldn't do.

Conscience

God has made provision for us to feel guilty when we should. He has given humans something that animals do not have—a conscience, a built-in judge that weighs right and wrong. When we do right, we feel peace; when wrong, a sense of guilt (Romans 2:15, 9:1).

But it is God's Word that provides the standard of right and wrong. This is why Christian training in the home is so essential: God plans that parents shall teach their children what is right and wrong from His Book. Our conscience is like an umpire in a game; it does not make the rules, but it calls out decisions in the light of the rules. God judges us according to whether we obey or disobey His rules. Therefore both parent-teachers and children are responsible for measuring up to God's standards.

The worst thing is to say *no* instead of *yes* to your conscience until it becomes so hardened against the truth that it no longer speaks to you. It's a wonderful feeling to have "a conscience void of offense toward God, and toward men" (Acts 24:16).

Acknowledging Our Sin—Psalm 32:1-5

David's experience in Psalm 32 reflects the experience of all of us. Turn to that psalm. He begins by saying that the person who doesn't try to deceive himself or anyone else is happy or blessed. Why, in verses 1, 2? Three things have happened to his sin: it has been forgiven, covered or put away, and he is not accounted guilty. In the Old Testament a perfect animal died in the sinner's place; in the New Testament the perfect Son of God!

In verses 3, 4 how do we feel when we do not confess our sin, when we don't admit what God says is so? Haven't you felt like that? When we continually groan and moan inside, what does that do to our physical health? We feel as if we are dying rather than living. Even at night we feel the Lord's hand heavy upon us, guilt pressing us down. What picture do you get in the last part of verse 4? Have you ever felt so dry that you could spit cotton, as if you were in a sweltering hot desert with no water to quench your thirst? This is what guilt does to us.

What can we do to avoid such an experience, in 5? What does the Lord want to do? There are three expressions of our part—we acknowledge our sin, don't hide it, confess it. Is that something that everyone can do? What would keep us from doing this? Usually our pride. We don't like to think of ourselves as wrong.

Learning the Joyous Way—Psalm 32:6-11

We can either learn God's lessons the hard way of wasting away with guilt, or the joyous way that the rest of Psalm 32 describes. He wants to help us prevent the distress of guilt. When should we call upon the Lord for help? Not after we have sinned, but at the very moment when we are tempted, in the moment of anxiety when great floods threaten to overwhelm us. Then the evil cannot touch us. Instead of trying to hide our sin or suppress it as if it weren't there, where can our whole being hide? Then our problem becomes the Lord's problem. What can we count on Him to do? Preserve and deliver us.

When we sin, we feel all alone, because sin separates. Instead of that, how does the Lord want us to feel, in 8? He's right with us to strengthen. He wants the close relationship of Heavenly Father and Teacher.

How would you express the illustration in verse 9? Instead of enjoying the company of our Heavenly Father, will He have to keep yanking us back into line because we dash off in our own way?

In 10 the choice is ours. What are the options?

In 11 what is the spirit of the righteous, the upright?

Have we acknowledged our sin, has it been covered by the blood of Christ? Then we can live in gladness. Let's read verse 11 in our various versions. Then go back and read again verse 1.

Psalm 32:1-5 is a good passage to memorize.

Guilt Feelings

ALL HIS life Fred had told lies. His parents didn't think much about them when he was small, but when he didn't outgrow the habit, they became concerned. Because they realized that there are reasons for all behavior, they tried to figure out why Fred felt the need of lying. They maintained very high standards with him and they thought they were being wise when they punished him whenever he did wrong. But the result was not what they were aiming at. Because Fred felt that he never measured up to what his parents expected and they didn't show their love in a warm way, he never felt forgiven after he did wrong. It seemed to him that his parents were always waiting for the next misstep. He formed the habit of lying to escape what punishment he could, and that made him feel worthless and inferior. The worse he felt about himself, the more he felt he just had to lie to keep in his parents' good graces.

Psychiatrists find that guilt feelings are one of the most common reasons for emotional difficulties. They create barriers between people and deaden our spiritual life. Guilt must either be forgiven or punished. Since all of us sin, God has graciously provided a way of forgiveness that is available to everyone. How would you express that way, Ted? (1 John 1:9) But people who do not know God's way or have trouble accepting God's way often punish themselves to try to get rid of their guilt feelings. Do you feel forgiven after you have confessed your sin?

The Lord's Complete Forgiveness

When David in the Bible had a brave soldier killed in battle so that he could take his wife, would God forgive as dastardly a crime as that—really two crimes? Did God still love him? In Psalm 51 we have David's prayer for forgiveness and what he expected God to do. Look first at the way David felt about himself in this situation. In verse 3 did he try to hide his sin or make it seem less than it was? Have you had sins that you felt were ever before you? I have.

In verse 4 David didn't mean that he hadn't sinned also against the soldier and his wife, but that essentially he had sinned most against the Lord, who is holy. What else did he acknowledge in 4 and 5? That God is perfect in His judgments and that the whole human race is sinful.

In what part of us is the Lord most concerned about finding truth and wisdom? 6. Our inner being.

Now go back to the beginning of the psalm and see what David expects the Lord to do after he has frankly confessed his sin. I'll write the key words on the chalkboard; let's see if any of them are repeated.

Because David still counts on God's steadfast love and abundant mercy, what does he ask God first to do? Have mercy, blot out, wash, cleanse. When he says, "Wash me thoroughly from my sin," or "Wash away all my guilt," how complete a job does he expect the Lord to do? How much guilt does he expect to have left?

Since we've already studied verses 3-6, drop down to 7. How does The Living Bible word the first of verse 7, Ted? Yes, here is the idea of washing again. And how clean does David ask the Lord to wash him?

In 8 he has faith enough to ask the Lord to do more than put away his sin, even fill him with joy and gladness. Can we feel happy and guilty at the same time? David even believes that the bones which the Lord has broken can rejoice again!

Because David's sin has touched him deeply, he comes back to the negative in 9. We can say with him, "Lord, don't hide Your face from me, but from my sins." Yes, here is "blot out" repeated again.

In 10 David is asking the Lord to do what He loves to do—create new things. What new things? Do we each have a clean heart and a right spirit?

In 11 he comes back to the negative again. The Lord would have a perfect right to do the worst things David could think of—in 11. How dreadful it would be if He cast us out of His presence and took His Holy Spirit from us when we sinned!

Instead of that, what does He want to do, in 12? He longs to restore us!

How is it that David can expect the Lord to forgive him so completely, and restore his joy? See what God has promised in Psalm 103:12. When you think of the whole universe, how far is the east from the west?

Also look at the last part of Micah 7:19. If all your sins were cast into the depths of the sea, how easy would it be to get them back? Can we trust the Lord then to forgive us completely, totally, unconditionally? When the blood of Christ cleanses from all sin, He will never remember it again! How free that makes us!

Bringing Our Feelings in Line

When this is what God wants to do, will we suffer with guilt, or will we ask Him to forgive immediately and completely? Why do some people have trouble accepting this tremendous offer? Some feel it is too good to be true because they have never experienced such forgiveness on the human level and they don't trust God to be different, to be God. Then some are in the habit of trying to pay for everything, trying to atone for everything themselves, though this is impossible. Others feel guilty because they have never confessed their sin, they won't own up to being wrong, which is often painful. Others are depending on feelings, which are not dependable. When our mind and our will decide what is right, we can insist on feelings coming along and cooperating.

Are we bothered by any of these excuses? If we are, let's deal with them right now. If not, let's thank the Lord that He forgives us completely, totally, unconditionally, with no ifs, ands, and buts.

Forgiveness

TED GOT one truth from the Bible very strongly in his mind: the idea that God forgives sin and that God's people forgive. So he was very ready to say, "I'm sorry, please forgive me." When he was careless in his duty of taking care of the trash, he said, "I'm sorry," and ran off. When he didn't get the facts of a story right, he said, "I'm sorry," without bothering to correct them. When he interrupted people's conversation, he said, "I'm sorry," and kept right on interrupting.

What is wrong with Ted's idea of forgiveness? He was using forgiveness as a magic formula for having his own way. That is not at all God's idea. What is the purpose of God's forgiveness? To keep us from sin, and to keep us from being pressed down by guilt. Suppose Ted says that he will watch the baby next door for a few minutes, then goes off with a friend and the baby gets out into the street? What good would his *I'm sorry* be then?

Sin is very serious for another reason, and forgiveness is very serious for another reason.

The Cost of Forgiveness

Forgiveness is free but it is not cheap. Some people confuse those two. When the charges of sin are against us, the penalty must be paid. Whenever Ted sins, his sin must be punished. If Ted says *I'm sorry* and is not punished, who has to take it instead? How can Ted take it lightly when he is making Christ suffer in his place?

Turn to Hebrews 12:2. We are to keep our eyes fixed on Jesus, for our salvation depends on Him from start to finish. He was willing to make salvation possible because of the joy it would bring to Him. Why would it being Him joy? Isn't it amazing that He really desires our fellowship!

What was He willing to go through in order we bring us to Himself? Death, the cross, shame, agony, disgrace! Where is He now? In the seat of honor at the right hand of the Father. If we get tired and discouraged at the way sinners act, we can remember what opposition, what hostility He endured. When He was here on earth teaching the truth and helping people, how did they treat Him? What did they do to Him at the end? They betrayed Him, arrested Him, false witnesses lied about Him, put a crown of thorns of His head, mocked Him, and crucified Him. That's what He suffered for you and me.

Philippians 2:5-8 gives the ways in which Jesus humbled Himself in order to save us from sin. First, what is Christ's real nature? He is God, in the form of God, equal with God. How did He feel about this high position? He did not demand and cling to His rights as God.

In verse 7 what did He do? He emptied Himself of what? Of his glory, majesty, dominion in order to come down here to earth. The kind of comedown it would be for a human to go down into the depths of the ocean to become a fish—a real comedown. He made Himself nothing, a slave, bound by the things of earth instead of the mighty sovereign Lord He really is.

How humbling it was for the Supreme Ruler of the universe to be born in a bed of hay, to grow like other humans, and to be treated with scorn by the

Jewish rulers. But He was obedient to His Father even to the point of death when that was needed. Yes, even the cruelest, most shameful kind of death!

When you think of all that Jesus suffered for your sake, how do you feel toward Him? What do you want to say to Him right now? Forgiveness is free, but it is not cheap.

Results of Forgiveness

When Ted realized what it cost the King of glory to forgive him, how do you think his behavior changed? He no longer said "I'm sorry" casually. He began to feel a very special way about the Lord, very close and very warm. He often thanked the Lord for doing so much to save him.

And how did he now feel about his sin? It hurt him now because he knew it hurt the Lord, and so he began to dislike the things he used to enjoy, like telling little fibs and getting out of home duties. His next step in becoming a stronger person was that he was no longer tempted to do wrong. When his conscience said, "No, you don't want to do that," his feelings also said, "No, let's not." His third step was eliminating the words *I'm sorry,* because he didn't need to use them much any more. He wasn't doing things that he was sorry for. People noticed the changes in Ted. One of his father's friends remarked, "My, but that boy Ted is growing up. I bet you're proud of Him." And Father was, in the right way.

How does the Lord's prayer ask God to forgive us? "As we forgive our debtors." Forgiveness is one of the tests of a Christian. Jesus told a story of a servant who owed a king a crushing debt. When the kind king completely forgave his big debt, the debtor would not forgive a fellow servant a small debt (Matthew 18:23-35). When the king heard this, he insisted that his debtor pay the full amount.

"Lord, we can never fully thank You for forgiving our sins. But may the thought of it keep us from sin and help us to forgive others."

Mistakes to Learn On

TODAY WE'RE talking about mistakes, and we're distinguishing mistakes from sin. How might we describe the difference? We're using sin as deliberate disobedience to what we know is right. When our heart is set in the direction of obedience but we don't make it, we'll call that a mistake.

How do you feel when you make a mistake? Some people take it too seriously, and some not seriously enough. Since none of us is yet perfect, we will all make mistakes. What happens when we get upset over mistakes, get depressed, mope around because of them? We're in no condition to do our best with the next opportunity that comes. We can do our best without feeling "I've got to succeed." No, you haven't. The only thing you've got to do is love and obey the Lord. If we concentrate on doing that, we won't make too many mistakes.

What happens if we don't take mistakes seriously enough? If we're too casual about them, we keep making the same ones over and over, without profiting from our experience.

Do you realize that our private Tutor plans spiritual lessons for us every day, lessons that are just as important or more important than the lessons we learn at school or in business? As soon as we learn one lesson, He is ready with the next as fast as we are ready to go. We don't want to repeat a grade in our spiritual education. Sometimes we don't know exactly what His aim is in all the experiences that come to us, but eventually we discover His purpose. He teaches us in the way that He chooses, not just the way we expect (Psalm 25:12).

How does the Lord view our mistakes?

Reshaping the Potter's Vessel—Jeremiah 18:1-8, 12

Turn to Jeremiah 18:1, 2. What did the Lord tell Jeremiah the prophet to do? From verse 3 do you think Jeremiah was used to obeying the Lord? Yes,

when most people in his day were not. Have you seen a potter working at his wheel? When the potter pedals the wheel with his foot, the upper part of the machine rotates so that he can shape the pot or jar as it turns.

In 4 what did Jeremiah see happen? What might spoil a clay pot on the wheel? Some foreign material might be in the clay, or a bubble that causes it to crack, or part of it might be too dry. So what would the potter do when he saw that it wasn't turning out the way he wanted it? He would knead it into a solid lump and start again to create what he had in mind.

In verses 5 and 6, what does the Lord say this scene illustrates?

In 7 and 8, what has been happening to the nation of Israel? Things foreign to God had kept Him from shaping the nation according to His purpose. What would He like to happen? He would like to shape it again in the best way. But clay must be ready to be molded.

When the people say what is expressed in verse 12, what will be the result? The divine Potter will not be able to make something beautiful. He will have to throw away the clay as useless!

Preventing Mistakes

Will we let the master Potter shape us for His own use without having to remold us again and again? How can we prevent mistakes?

1. Look first at 1 Corinthians 11:31, 32. How would this work out in our daily lives? As I am undressing at the end of a day, I like to think back over the day, and recall what I have learned. I'm always glad when I learn positively—do what turns out well. Sometimes I have to learn negatively, from things that turn out badly. But if I don't do that bad thing again, I haven't been a slow learner. It's when the same thing occurs over and over that I have to judge myself harshly.

2. Hebrews 5:13. Paul is here talking about adults who have not learned the lessons that the Lord gave them. When they've lived long enough to eat solid food and be teachers, they still need spiritual milk like a child. Those last words in 13 are important: how can we train our faculties to distinguish good from evil? By practice. We can sharpen our judgment by wisely sizing up the whole situation, all aspects of it, and then evaluate our decisions. If we have hard judgments to make, we can discuss them here as a family.

3. Matthew 22:29. Some Jewish leaders tried to catch Jesus with a tricky question. We often make mistakes for the same reasons that they did. Many of our problems are neatly solved by knowing the Scriptures. And the Scriptures tell us how we may have the power of God. Many of us who know what the Lord says fail because we try to please Him without His power.

4. Proverbs 10:17. Why doesn't this good advice keep us from making mistakes? Who likes to be reproved, corrected, criticized? It takes strength of character to acknowledge, "Yes, though I like my own way, the other way is better." Then this person becomes stronger still.

Shall we each ask the Lord about one of these ways of preventing mistakes: judging ourselves, discerning good and evil, knowing the Scriptures, appropriating the power of God, and accepting correction? Alice, will you thank God that He cares enough about us to be our Teacher every day?

Anger and Resentment

ALL OF us get angry. Recall the last time you were angry. How do you express your feelings of anger? Maybe "That's not right, not fair, that hurts, that's hateful, how dare you do that!"

Is it wrong to be angry? No, the Lord Himself gets angry. What makes Him angry? God was angry with Solomon because his heart turned away from Him (1 Kings 11:9), at Moses when he didn't respond to His call (Exodus 4:14), with Israel because they did so much evil (2 Kings 17:18), etc. Jesus was angry when the disciples tried to keep children away from Him (Mark 10:14), and at the hardness of heart of the Jewish religious leaders (Mark 3:5). Does this kind of evil make us angry? We are as big as the things that make us mad.

Though anger itself is not wrong, it often leads us to do wrong. If our feelings are badly stirred up, we may lash back immediately without being able to control our feelings, and afterward feel sorry for what we said and did.

Turn to Proverbs 14:29. How can we be slow to anger when we're upset? We can shut our mouth and clench our fists until we calm down a bit, get control of ourselves. Before we do anything else, we can ask the Lord to keep us from doing anything rash.

Look also at Proverbs 29:11. It may make us feel better at the moment to give full vent to our anger, but later we'll realize that we have been foolish. When we let someone or something outside ourselves have this much control of us, we are actually making ourselves a slave to that person or thing.

Psychiatrists stress the harm that is done to us when we suppress powerful emotions like anger. They say that when we keep feelings hidden inside without an outlet, they poison our system, making us tense and anxious. It's like a fire smoldering inside, keeping us from feeling free and relaxed. All of us have experienced this, haven't we? If there's danger in giving vent to our anger and danger in keeping it inside, what shall we do when we're angry?

Preventing Bitterness—Ephesians 4:5-32

Paul tells the Christians at Ephesus how to prevent actions that they'll be sorry for afterward. Turn to Ephesians 4:25. What is one of the chief causes of anger? How much easier this world would be if there were no lying, dishonesty, deceit! De we ever stretch the truth just a little for our own benefit?

In 26 the sense is: When you are angry, don't sin. How can we keep from it? How can we get rid of it? It won't go away by wishing it away. If we nurse the grudge, it will stay with us. We'll just have to bring it out in the open and tackle the difficult situation. How could we approach a person with some hope of getting together with him? Certainly we won't if we attack and threaten him. But he might respond favorably if we began, "Friend, I am really upset about what you did. May I hear from your perspective why you did what you did? Then I'd like to show you the way it looks to me."

In 27 how will we give a foothold or a loophole to the devil if we don't make up our differences? He can get between us and poison the attitudes of both of us.

Then Paul mentions in 28, 29 two more problems that cause anger. Doesn't it disturb you when some people on a team don't do their part? Do any of your acquaintances use bad language that makes you cringe when you hear it? Or tell dirty jokes? Do you keep still rather than talk when you don't have anything profitable to say?

When we are angry, how does that hurt the Lord Himself? The Holy Spirit is our mark for the final deliverance from sin.

Then in 31, 32 Paul summarizes what we are not to have in our hearts and what we are to do with anger. Hebrews 12:15 also warns against letting any root of bitterness spring up and cause trouble to many. The wording of 31 in the various versions is interesting.

If we find it hard to forgive others, how does this verse help us? When we think how freely God in Christ has forgiven our many sins, surely we can forgive others. If we can't feel forgiving, we can ask the Lord to forgive in us. Often if we do something special for a person even if we feel cross toward him, our feelings will improve.

Being Reconciled—Matthew 5:23, 24

Anytime we approach the Lord to praise Him and pray to Him and remember that we are angry toward anyone, what does He tell us to do first, in Matthew 5:23, 24? For us this would mean that when we come together for family devotions, if we feel angry at any member of the family, we ought to straighten out that problem before we expect Him to give us new truth. And who does He say should make the first move? Normally the one who feels wronged goes to the other person; here the Lord says the one whose brother has something against him.

Love Covering—1 Peter 4:8

The last word to be said about anger is in 1 Peter 4:8. How does love cover a multitude of sins? If we truly love others, we won't see or notice many little slights and failings. They don't make us angry because we understand how the other person feels and why he has problems. We're loving with the love of Christ.

"Dear Lord, we thank You for your longsuffering with us. Give us Your love for frail human creatures, and keep us from sinning when we get angry."

Punishment

NOBODY, JUST nobody likes the idea of punishment or penalty for the wrongs we do, yet what would our world be without it? If we each had our own way, if each of us were a law unto himself, this world would be in chaos, would no doubt destroy itself. There must be order in the universe. Our God is a God of order, system, law, organization.

What would happen if car drivers ran red lights whenever they were in a hurry without getting tickets? If they didn't have the penalty of a fine, they themselves or someone else might pay the penalty with their lives. What if no one were punished for failing to pay his taxes? No one would want to pay them, and we would have no schools, no roads, no police. What makes our society safe to live in?

The trouble is that some people appreciate some of the laws, the ones that protect them, while others approve of others that benefit them. What rules or laws do you appreciate? Let's name as many as we can.

How does the Lord feel about people He has to punish, and how should we feel about punishment?

David's Punishment—2 Samuel 24

When David was king, the devil incited him (1 Chronicles 21:1) to order the commanders of his army to go through all the tribes of Israel and number all the people. Turn to 2 Samuel 24:3 to see what Joab, his captain, thought of that idea. It was a selfish idea prompted by pride and lack of trust, all that time and effort to show David how many people he was ruling over!

In verse 10 after the census had been taken, what happened? Why is it that we humans so often see the light after we have sinned rather than before? At least when David got the Lord's perspective, he was ready to confess his sin and ask forgiveness. He never had a stubborn, rebellious spirit.

In 11-13 how would you like to choose among the three kinds of punishment offered to David? What would be the result of three years af famine in the land? Fleeing before the enemy for three months? Three days' pestilence or plague that quickly kills people? If you had to choose, which would it be for you? What a predicament! And when the sinner is a leader, not only does he himself suffer but also his people as well!

In 14 what was David's choice? Why? What did he mean by falling into the hand of the Lord? The plague was the one penalty that was administered directly by the Lord Himself.

So what was the result in 15? Seventy thousand men lost their lives! I'm glad we're told that they had also sinned, for the anger of the Lord was kindled against them too (24:1).

How does 16 reveal the mercy of the Lord? He cut short the plague before the three days.

How would you state 17 in your own words? Here David showed his concern for his people. "Punish me, not them," he said.

So God told David to build an altar on the threshing floor where the plague was stopped. When the man who owned this property saw the king of the land

and his courtiers coming toward him, what did he do and what did he say? 20, 21.

In 22 this man wanted to *give* the king his floor and what else for a sacrifice? The middle part of 24 is a famous sentence, a good one for all of us to use: I will not offer the Lord what costs me nothing—after all He's done for me.

Finish the story in 25. The plague was stopped, but oh, the suffering before it stopped!

Preventing or Suffering?

As for me, I'd like to work at preventing rather than suffering punishment. I'd like to consider the consequences before I sin rather than afterward. Too often others have to suffer with us—our family, our friends, our country. And we give unbelievers a chance to say, "See those Christians, they aren't better than anyone else." The Lord suffers too when His people disobey Him—the ones who should be reflecting His holiness. Even if the Lord mercifully gives us less punishment than we deserve, the pain of our guilt isn't easy to get rid of. Mother, read the first and last of Psalm 38, which shows how deeply David felt the weight of his sin (1-8, 21, 22).

What else could keep us from committing sin? We could examine our motives. David should have realized why he wanted to number his people. Are we selfishly planning to do something that will make us feel or look good? What will it do to others? It's easy to be dishonest with ourselves, to deceive ourselves into thinking that our motive is a worthy one.

Sometimes we kid ourselves into thinking we're brave and persistent when instead we are stubborn and rebellious. A good test is: Am I clearly obeying the Lord? If we aren't sure, we better find out. If we don't feel like obeying, if we feel edgy and ornery, what is likely to be the reason? Maybe our love is growing cold, maybe we aren't as close to the Lord as we should be, maybe we're out of touch with Him. If we love Him, we want to please Him.

"Lord, keep us so sensitive to sin and so sorry for sin that we'll prevent rather than suffer punishment. Don't let us hurt You, others and ourselves by doing foolish things."

Overcoming Evil with Good

AT THE moment do you think of anyone who has wronged you? How do you feel toward that person?

Ted felt hurt when his friend Phil didn't ask him to go to the out-of-town ball game. He had gone several times with Phil and his father, but this time he wasn't asked. The next day when the family was planning a picnic, Mother asked if they would like to invite any of their friends to go with them. "We won't ask Phil," spoke up Ted.

What would happen if Ted kept trying to get even with Phil? Then how would Phil naturally react? They might end up doing worse and worse things to each other until one was really wounded in some way. And how did the hard feelings all start? Ted didn't know why he wasn't asked to the game. What good reasons might Phil and his father have had? Often we don't know people's inner motives. But Ted let Phil's action poison his spirit. How can the vicious cycle of getting even, paying back evil for evil, be broken?

David Sparing Saul—1 Samuel 26

When David was anointed as the future king of God's people, Saul the first king was jealous and was tormented by an evil spirit. Saul felt better when David was playing his harp for him (18:10, 11), but what did his jealousy cause him to do while David was playing? So where did David live for years while Saul was hunting him that he might get rid of him? When David was hiding from Saul in the wilderness of Ziph, how many soldiers did Saul bring with him to get David? Turn to 1 Samuel 26:2.

In verse 6 what did David ask two of his bravest men one night? Would either of these warriors volunteer to go with David?

Visualize the scene in 7. Saul lay asleep in the middle of the encampment of these three hundred soldiers.

In 8 how did Abishai look at this situation? What an opportunity for David to do away with his enemy! In spite of all the sleeping men he would have to go through, he was sure he could get to Saul in the middle.

Did David agree with him? Why not? How would you express the ideas in 9-11 in your own words? Even though David had to wait and wait, be chased by an army, and often narrowly escape, how did he say that Saul would die, in 10? He said, "I will not sin against the Lord because he is. I will not return evil for evil." But what did he do to let Saul know that he had spared his life?

Why didn't one of all those soldiers wake up when David and Abishai walked among them and talked together? 12.

When they had left the camp and got far away on the top of a mountain, what did David do? 13, 14. Abner was Saul's general. Jim, read what David shouted to Abner from the mountain. 15, 16.

From what Saul said in 17, how do you think he felt?

What is the spirit of David's answer in 18-20? Was he angry and bitter, as a person might be in a situation like that? Notice how David related all that he did to the Lord. He didn't talk like a proud would-be king, but likened himself to a small game bird that Saul brought three hundred men out in the hills to catch.

In 21 how did David's humility lead Saul to respond?

Read David's concluding remarks, Jim. 22-24.

So in what spirit did Saul return home? 25.

Returning Good for Evil

Are we strong enough in the Lord to return good for evil instead of evil for evil as we are naturally inclined to do? When something goes wrong or someone wrongs us, what can we do instead of trying to find out who is to blame or how we can get even?

Yes, first we can do what David did—turn the situation over to the Lord instead of trying to settle it ourselves. Can we say to our enemy what David said, "The LORD rewards every man for his righteousness and his faithfulness. . . . As your life was precious this day in my sight, so may my life be precious in the sight of the LORD, and may He deliver me out of all tribulation" (26:23, 24 RSV)?

Do we believe that the Lord is just? That He treats each of us fairly according to what we truly deserve? He knows people's thoughts which we don't know; often when we mean good, it looks bad to others. He will punish evil exactly as it deserves. Who are we to punish others—we who don't know the whole situation! Can we trust the Lord to vindicate us, to give us justice?

What else can we do when we are wronged? We can pray for the other party. If we don't feel like praying, we can ask for God's love and wisdom.

Is there anyone who has wronged our family? If so, let's plan what we can do in love for that person. Would you like us to pray for any of your individual relationships?

Destroying Evil

AT THE same time that the Lord tells us to love people, He tells us to destroy evil. And He tells us very forcefully. Again and again in the Old Testament when He was getting His people ready to go into their own land, He repeated to them— You shall purge the evil from the midst of you . . . you shall rid yourselves of wickedness . . . take all evil away from you (Deuteronomy 17:7, 19:19, 21:21, 24:7). He said, "You shall destroy all the places where the heathen nations served their idols on the high mountains, on the hills, and under every green tree. Tear down their altars, dash in pieces their pillars, burn their idols" (*see* 12:2, 3). But time after time Scripture records that kings did not do this. Some obeyed the Lord in other ways *only* the high places were not removed and the people continued to worship the idols. The high places became snares, temptations.

The New Testament too uses strong language about evil: ". . . hate what is evil, hold fast to what is good" (Romans 12:9 RSV), "loathing evil and clinging to the good" (NEB).

Some problems in life are like shades of gray, a complex mixture of black and white, when it's hard to separate the good from the evil. But there are also things that are either right or wrong, black or white. The white light of God's holiness condemns the black to destruction, for either we destroy it or it destroys us. What does a rotten apple do to the whole basket?

It's the same with our old natures that are basically selfish. The Lord doesn't say, "Serve Me and gradually you'll get better and better." He says, "Get rid of the old; I'll give you a new one created in Christ Jesus unto righteousness and holiness."

How does the Lord want us to deal with evil?

The Golden Calf—Exodus 32:19, 20

After God had wondrously redeemed His people out of slavery in Egypt, had led them supernaturally by His cloud and fire, fed them with manna from heaven and refreshed them by water from a rock, He called Moses to come up to the mountain to give His people His essential laws. While Moses was there communing with the Almighty, the people got tired waiting for him. They said to his brother, "Up, make us gods to go before us. We don't know what has become of Moses" (*see* 32:1). God's people so soon forsook Him to worship idols like the heathen nations!

When Moses came down the mountain with the two tables of the law that God Himself had written and heard the noise of dancing, turn to Exodus 32:19 to see what he did. Was his anger justified? God had called him to lead this people to Himself, and there they were so soon worshiping a golden calf that they had made!

What did Moses do with the calf? Any worship that is not worship of God is to be destroyed entirely!

The Bonfire at Ephesus—Acts 19:18-20

In the New Testament when a team of traveling Jewish magicians saw the miracles that Paul performed and saw him casting out demons in the name of Jesus, they decided to use the name of Jesus to cast out evil spirits. An evil spirit answered them, "Jesus I know, and Paul I know; but who are you?" (Acts 19:15 RSV). The man with the evil spirit then leaped on them and beat them up so violently that they fled out of that house naked and wounded. The whole city was amazed at this and gained great respect for the name of Jesus.

Turn to Acts 19:18. What did many of the believers do who had been secretly practicing magic? They openly confessed their sin.

What did they do with their books of magic? 19. As they tossed book after book into a huge bonfire, what did the unbelievers no doubt say as they saw all those expensive books going up in smoke? They probably would have liked to have them themselves. To them this was a great waste, to God's people it was good riddance.

In 20 what was the result of that destruction of evil? The Christian community then had more power.

What We Should Destroy

What are the evils in our day that should be destroyed as drastically as the golden calf and the books of magic? Yes, we can think of many of them—harmful drugs, liquor, cigarettes, dirty jokes, filthy language, books and pictures that lead to wrongdoing. What usually happens if we say, "I know something is bad, but I'll just try a little to see what it's like. I'll just experiment a bit so that I'll know what the people who like it are talking about." That experimenter is usually sucked in to become one of the addicts.

What are the idols that people worship today instead of God? Some worship sports or business or education or fame or pleasure or just themselves. These things may be good in themselves, but they are bad if they are worshiped.

Some of the worst evils to be destroyed are inside us rather than outside. What kind of thoughts should not be allowed to remain one minute in our minds? Thoughts of disobeying God, blaming people, getting even, getting something in improper ways, etc. Will we let evil songs go 'round and 'round in our minds without banishing them quickly? "Be gone!" we can order them, and ask God to keep them out.

"Dear Lord, help us to call evil what You call evil and to destroy it utterly so that we can be free to walk with You in light."

8 COMMUNICATING WITH EACH OTHER

Listening

WHEN WE think who the Lord God is and who we human creatures are, isn't it amazing how much of the time we expect Him to listen to us! Just anytime we expect He will concentrate on what we're saying. We can't expect anyone else to do that! How does He listen? We feel His presence with us, we are assured of His concern, we are aware that He is responding to us though we can't see Him.

Can you recall a time when it meant a great deal for some human to listen to you? How good are we as listeners? One of the very best ways of helping people is to listen to them. Is anyone saying, "How can that help? Listening isn't doing anything." Is listening doing anything? Real listening is doing a lot—it's active, it's alive, alert, responding.

For instance, suppose something exciting happens in school that you are bursting to tell someone. You come home and I am reading the newspaper. You say, "Dad, got something to tell you!" I grunt, "Yeh?" You start telling me, I keep on reading, saying only, "Uh-huh." When you protest, I reply, "I heard you. I can read and listen at the same time." How do you feel? But if I put down my paper, concentrate on what you're saying, feel right along with you all that happened, and show my excitement too, how do you feel? Sharing with me makes the experience all the more interesting to you.

Many conversations have no give and take in them. I just keep quiet so that when you finish, I can talk. What I say doesn't relate to what you say. Neither of us is listening.

Listening to the Lord

Alice, do you remember how the boy Samuel in the Bible came to live at the house of the Lord? When his mother had no children, she promised the Lord that if He would give her a son, she would give the boy back to Him for His service. So even as a boy Samuel helped the priest care for the house of God. Not many people in those days were listening to the Lord.

Turn to 1 Samuel 3:4. Let's take parts reading this conversation through verse 19. Jim, be Eli the priest, Ted be Samuel, and Sue, read what the Lord says. I'll read the connecting narrative. What does this incident say to us today? Yes, the Lord speaks to children, we shouldn't expect Him to speak to us if we are living in sin, and because Samuel listened to the Lord people listened to him.

Look also at Isaiah 50:4. The first part of the verse deals with teachers who know how to talk so that they can help people. In the last part of the verse, what does a person need to do before he is ready to talk wisely? How sharp is our hearing? Do we listen more or talk more?

In verse 5 what expression is used for this same idea? How do we listen to the Lord? Yes, we read His Word and listen as well as talk to Him in prayer. Let's ask Him right now to sharpen our hearing and open our ears to hear and understand all He wants to say to us. Even though our Bible was written for all people through the centuries, He wants to speak a personal word to each of us each day through it.

Becoming a Good Listener

It takes real skill to become a good listener. Right now listen to your own inner being. What is it saying to you? Are all parts of you saying the same thing, or are several voices trying to get your attention? One voice could be wanting to do something outside the house at this particular time. Can you still the voices you don't want to hear?

Turn to Job 13:4. Job suddenly lost his family, his possessions, his health in a severe test that God was putting him through. Three friends came to comfort him. When they saw how deeply he was suffering, they just sat with him for seven days (2:11-13). Would it be a comfort to him to have them sit with him like that? It surely would. It showed that they cared. And what was there to say actually?

Then they began to talk. They talked and talked. They thought Job must have sinned to have this misfortune come upon him. How did that help him? He couldn't think what he had done wrong. Look at Job 13:5 and 6. What did Job wish they would do? It's so much easier for most of us to talk than to listen.

Especially when a person feels bad, how can we listen most helpfully? Yes, we'll concentrate on him and what he is trying to communicate. How can we listen more deeply than his words? We can try to grasp his world from the inside, feel how it feels to him, sense the hard things he can't put into words, not assume that he looks at the problem just as we do. We'll watch for ideas that he repeats again and again, as being most significant. We'll watch also for what he carefully avoids saying. We can show by our very attitude and posture that we're trying to understand him rather than judge him. He will likely judge himself if he doesn't need to defend himself against us.

"Lord, we thank You that You are always ready to listen to us. Help us to have sharp, open ears to hear what You want to tell us and to be good listeners to other people's problems."

Let's all be quiet for two minutes, listening to whatever the Lord wants to say to each of us personally.

Being Open and Honest

JUST AS an X-ray machine can make a picture of the bones inside our bodies, if a machine could penetrate our inner thoughts, motives and feelings right now, would you be pleased to have them brought to light, or would you be afraid of them? Would you know exactly what was inside, or would you wonder what would be revealed? Are you always sure how you will respond in different situations, or do you sometimes surprise yourself?

How many roles does each of us take in a week or so? I am husband, father, employee, friend, church member, and Bible study leader. Am I a different person in these various roles, or do I act just about the same wherever I am? To please the people we're with or come up to their expectations, we sometimes put on different masks, different appearances. Do Mother and I see you children as your school teachers see you? In which situation do you feel most free to be your real self, with no pretenses? In which are you least free?

We really don't know ourselves until we find out how people respond to us, until they give us feedback. They may surprise us when they say, "When I first met you, I thought you were proud and boastful." It may be that we really don't feel proud, or it may be that they were seeing something we didn't see but should see. Since we don't want to be proud or appear proud, we'll make some change in ourself.

The Dishonesty of Elisha's Servant—2 Kings 5:15-27

Alice, do you remember the Bible story of Naaman, the mighty Syrian commander who had the dreadful disease of leprosy? Who told him about the man of God, Elisha? A young girl captured from Israel. How was Naaman healed of his leprosy?

Turn to 2 Kings 5:15. What did Naaman do to show his thanks for being healed?

How did the prophet Elisha answer him? 16. Let's skip verses 17 and 18.

His servant didn't approve his master's decision. What was his thinking? 19, 20.

So what did he do, in 22? A talent of silver was $2,000. What does his action tell us about this servant? He was both greedy and dishonest. He no doubt thought, "After Elisha said he didn't want any reward, what story could sound sensible that he changed his mind?"

How did Naaman respond to that request? 23. It probably made him feel good to say thank you in this way.

When the men came to the hill where Elisha lived, what did the servant do before he went back to Elisha? 24. He made it look as if he hadn't been out of the house.

When Elisha asked him where he had been, what did he answer? 25. After all the amazing things that the man of God knew and did, wouldn't you think this servant would realize that he couldn't deceive Elisha!

How did Elisha deal with his faithless servant? 26, 27. Was being a leper for the rest of his life too severe a punishment for greed and lying? What would this deceit do to Naaman? It kept him from seeing the pure grace of God, that God loves and heals without pay. The servant now had Naaman's disease for a reason.

Being Open with Each Other

The family should be the closest, warmest social unit, where each of us is perfectly free to be ourselves without any need for deceit. In the family whenever we have a need, it is healthy for us to bare ourselves with each other and be sure we understand each other so that we have nothing to hide. Let's take time to do that now. I'd like to start by telling you about the kind of day I had today. I want to tell you for what I thank God because of what I enjoyed, the ways in which I know I failed and why, and I want to ask you to pray for me where I need help. I want you to know very personally what kind of person I am and what I am striving for. Then we'd like to hear the same from the rest of you.

It is often beneficial to tell each other what we have appreciated about them during the day, but when it comes to confessing faults, it's better to confess our own. If we began by telling what we don't appreciate in the others, we'd try to defend ourselves, for it's easier to see other people's faults than our own. We'd soon be arguing and fighting. But when we begin with our own shortcomings, that opens the conversation. It's a wonderful feeling to have a conscience void of offense toward God and toward men (Acts 24:16).

Let's thank God that He has been so open and honest with us in His Book, and ask Him to keep us free to be our real selves without any pretending.

Respecting People

CAN YOU think of times when people have made you feel small, inferior, no good? What did they do that made you feel like this? Yes, they didn't listen to you, made sarcastic or slighting remarks, left you out of things, said you couldn't do something, rejected your opinion, etc. Then how did you feel toward these people?

Now putting ourselves on the other side of the fence, are we aware when we don't respect others? Many times we aren't even aware that others feel slighted. When have we made others feel small? Maybe we've wondered why people have reacted as they did, when the real reason was that they didn't feel we respected them.

Why should we respect every human being, no matter who he is? Each one has been made in the image of God for His particular purpose. What about people who are obvious sinners, who don't even seem to have respect for themselves? How did the father of the prodigal son treat the boy when he returned home after sinking very low—Bring quickly the best robe, put a ring on his hand and shoes on his feet. Kill a fatted calf so that we may rejoice (Luke 15:22-24). When the sinner returns to the Lord, the divine Potter can put him on His wheel again and remake him.

Sometimes people don't respect children as important people in their own right, as if they aren't somebody yet until they are full-grown. The Lord respects children as people.

Rehoboam's Lack of Respect—2 Chronicles 9—10

Because God gave David's son, King Solomon, both wisdom and wealth, he was richer and wiser than any other king in all the earth. Jim, read how magnificent he made his rule, in 2 Chronicles 9:15-26.

When Solomon died, the leaders of Israel came to his young son Rehoboam, and what did they say in the next chapter, 10:4? How does that verse tell us that Solomon treated his people in order to get and make all the splendid trappings of his kingdom? What was his motive for making them slave so hard? Not for their benefit as much as his benefit! His throne and his reputation were famous.

Instead of answering the people immediately, what did Rehoboam reply, in 5?

Whose advice did he ask first? 6. Was that a sensible thing to do? Yes, for the older men had had years of experience.

What was the answer of the older men? 7. Was that a good answer?

But because he didn't like that answer, he didn't want to do that, what did he do to confirm his own ideas? 8, 9.

Now look at the advice of the young men his own age, in 10, 11. Jim, read their answer in the tone of voice that is implied in their words. What does that language say about Rehoboam's respect for his people and for the older men? So that's what Rehoboam did in verses 12-15.

God had promised David that if his successors obeyed Him, Israel would always have a king from his line on the throne. When the people heard this unreasonable decision of Rehoboam, what did they do, in 16? And 17 says that Rehoboam ruled only over the cities of Judah.

In 18 when Rehoboam sent the taskmaster over the forced labor, what did the people do to him? Verse 30 says that that was the beginning of the division of the kingdom of Israel. The ten northern tribes left Rehoboam and established another nation, which was often at war with their own people to the south of them. The last straw in the dividing of the kingdom was Rehoboam's lack of respect for his people.

Showing Respect

Have we in our family been showing respect first for ourselves and then for all others? Have you felt that all of us respect your viewpoints, your abilities, your interests, even when they are different from the rest of us? It is natural that while we all have the same basic values on which we're building our lives, our different ages, experiences and feelings give us different perspectives. Which of our viewpoints have you found it hardest to understand?

What does it take to have genuine respect for others? Since we are naturally centered in ourselves, it takes real effort to get out of ourselves and put ourselves in the place of others. We all live in our own world and see things in our own way. Do we care enough to put on the glasses of the other fellow? The results will be to our own benefit, as they would have been for Rehoboam, but the motive is not selfish.

If we truly respect others, we'll be more ready to comment on the positive than the negative. If people have good feelings toward us, they want to please us. Let's each of us mention one thing we like about each other person here, and then let's mention the things we don't like to the Lord and ask Him to correct them if they are wrong.

Is there anyone that our family finds especially difficult to respect? Can we visualize being in that person's circumstances? Probably if we were walking in his shoes, we would act the way he acts. Therefore let's pray for him and for the times right here at home when we find it hard to feel and show respect.

Being Unselfish

KAREN WAS brought up to get everything she could for herself. Because her parents were both working, neither of them spent much time with her. She had to fend for herself and supply all of her own needs that she could. She soon learned from experience that she had to take care of herself, get what she could since no one else was looking out for her. As a result she was always pushing to be first in line, rushing for the best seat, grabbing the quality materials, protesting that it was her turn.

Sue, on the other hand, had a family that supported her and were continually on the lookout for her welfare. She expected other people to be kind to her and she often went to their aid, to rescue anyone who was not getting a fair deal. She would sometimes team up with Karen to help her. One day Karen said to Sue, "You're the greatest! You never push ahead, yet you seem to get more than I do. How do you do it?"

What happens in the gangland wars? People with the same interests band together to further their goals. But very often we read of them popping off each other. What is the reason for this? Christ said:

> give, and it will be given to you;
> good measure, pressed down, shaken together,
> running over, will be put into your lap.
> For the measure you give will be the measure you get back.
> Luke 6:38 RSV

Think of a person you know who seems unselfish. Does he seem to be lacking anything because he is always giving? For what unselfish acts have you been thankful this last week? How often last week were you, was I, unselfish?

Abram's Unselfishness—Genesis 13—14

Way back near the beginning of our world Abram journeyed to the land that God had promised him, where God wanted to make him a blessing to all peoples. Abram was very rich not only in gold and silver but also—very important in those days—in flocks and herds of cattle. His nephew Lot also had many flocks and herds, and tents for the servants who tended them. What became their problem in Genesis 13:5-7? There were too many animals for the amount of pastureland available. Why was it dangerous for the two relatives to quarrel when there were other tribes in the land?

What did Abram suggest in verses 8 and 9? What does this tell us about the character of the man Abram? Though he was the older of the two, he was willing to give Lot the choice of the land, either to the right or the left. Read those two verses in The Living Bible, Jim.

In 10 and 11 how did Lot make his choice? Whom was he thinking about? Only about himself, to get the best for himself.

What do 12 and 13 imply about the temptations that Lot's selfish choice led him into? While Abram stayed out in the pasture lands, Lot lived among the cities in the plain and settled near the city of Sodom, which was notoriously wicked!

Mother, finish reading to us the rest of that chapter that tells what the Lord promised Abram.

Now look at the next chapter, 14, verses 11, 12. What happened to Lot? Abram had to muster forces to rescue Lot and his goods. Even when God destroyed the city of Sodom, Lot didn't want to leave the comforts of the city. Hiding in a cave, he and his daughters disgraced themselves.

That's what happened to a selfish man even though his righteous soul was daily vexed with the lawless deeds of the people of wicked Sodom (2 Peter 2:8).

Growing Out of Self-Centeredness

Sometimes like the psalmist we look at the people who are prospering in their selfishness and we wonder whether or not it pays to be unselfish. Let's take turns reading the first seven verses of Psalm 37, which expresses this idea.

Are you ever afraid that you'll get left if you look out for the other fellow? How can we discharge our responsibilities if we are unselfish? That is a very practical question. What suggestions can you think of for this problem? Just as we don't put self at the center of our lives, neither do we put others at the center. The Lord helps us with our priorities, what to put first. Sometimes it is duty first. Or maybe a duty can wait if someone needs our help. We can plan leeway in our lives for the unexpected need that comes up.

Let's each check ourselves this next week to see how often we are unselfish and report next week on the experience that gave us most personal satisfaction.

Instead of planning as a family something we'd enjoy doing from our own viewpoint, let's start with a need of someone else. What family project could we undertake that is purely unselfish? Think of someone who doesn't seem to be very happy. How could we make him smile?

"Lord, we thank You that You look out for us and the members of our family look out for each other. Because You have given us so much, show us how best to be unselfish with others, whom You want to help through us."

Communicating Effectively

WILL EACH of you please elucidate your philosophy of the transmission of meaning? You are not responding to me. I'll repeat those words more clearly this time (repeat slowly and distinctly). You say you don't know what I mean? Why not? Didn't I speak the words very clearly so that you heard them?

This demonstrates what is so often our problem in communication. Why didn't you get my meaning when you heard my words? Because meaning isn't in words only; it's essentially in you, in people. But we assume that it's in words. The greatest obstacle in communication is assuming that it has taken place when it hasn't. If you are going to understand my words, what must be true of you? The words must mean the same to you as to me. Why is this often not the case? Because our experiences have been very different. Maybe you love the name of Madge because you knew a fine person by that name, but I don't like it because my associations with it have been very poor. When I communicate, I have to ask myself, "What will the other person put into my words? What will they mean to him?"

When did you last experience an error in communication? Maybe you and a friend agreed to meet at a certain place. You got there and waited and waited. He came too, but he was waiting at another place that he visualized when you talked about it.

No doubt the most difficult idea for us mortals to grasp is the idea of the divine world. The great Creator-Redeemer had to communicate this eternal realm to us in such a way that we would get a true, not a distorted, picture of it. How did He do it?

Communicating the Divine Life

What is the material object that God uses to communicate Himself, that we can see and touch? His Book, the Bible. How is this Book different from any other book that was ever written? God supervised each writer so that he wrote what the Lord wanted him to, and included what He wanted. Though God used many people to do this, their material all fits together to focus on our Saviour-Lord!

But even this extraordinary Book is not all of God's plan for revealing Himself. Being, of course, the number one Communicator, He knows just how much to expect of human nature. It still is difficult for us to comprehend the heavenly world and God as a spirit, but how did He show us in the very best way what He is like?

Turn to John 1:18. It helps us so much to see things we're trying to understand, but how long will it be before we will see the Lord? Not until we leave this world and meet Him face-to-face in heaven. Why is Christ able to show us what the Father is like? Because He is "nearest to the Father's heart" (NEB), or ". . . he is the companion of the Father" (LB).

In that same chapter look at verse 14. What was the greatest comedown of all time? Even in heaven I wonder if we'll ever be able to fully appreciate what it meant for the divine Son of God to come into this sinful world! Here are three of the most wonderful words in any language—glory, grace, and truth! Close your eyes and try to imagine Christ seated at the right hand of God in His glory, grace, and truth.

But it wouldn't even be enough to have the words of the Bible and the Saviour outside us, we need something inside us if we are to comprehend the unseen world. What do John 16:13, 14 say that the Holy Spirit will do to communicate Christ to us? We even have the divine Interpreter inside us, who will guide us into all the truth!

What does the Spirit do in John 6:63? The Spirit takes the words of Scripture and makes them spirit and life in us. They come alive to us and they kindle life in us. This is supercommunication that outsiders know nothing about!

Overcoming Barriers to Communication

If we want people to understand what we say and respond as we expect them to, how can we overcome the very natural barriers to communication? It's fun to check people's responses. When they don't respond as you expect, see if you can figure out why not.

1. What is our most common difficulty in communicating? So our first principle will be: Adapt what we say to the receiver's experience and words. If I say something the way I would most naturally, what would those words mean to him? I won't talk to the kindergartner next door just the way I talk to Grandmother. Before I speak, I'll try to visualize the other fellow's world and how my words will appear to him.

2. What other barriers are there to communication? Yes, we have to feel out people's depth level. Does the other person just want to be friendly on a superficial level, or would he really like to know me as a person, what I am like inside? I'll keep going a little deeper until I see what he is interested in.

3. I'll keep checking to see how he responds to what I say. If I'm not sure, I'll ask questions or I'll put what I think he means in my own words. I'll read his facial and bodily expressions as well as his words. I can tell a lot by them, and by what he doesn't say.

4. I'll respect him as a person with his own values and opinions. I won't expect him to be like me or anyone else. I'll try to get to know him without getting any benefit for myself or manipulating him according to my desires.

Aren't we thankful that the Lord has provided such remarkable ways of communicating His divine life to us on this earth! Let's ask Him to help us to really understand the various kinds of people we meet.

Identifying with Others

THE VERY nature of the gospel is change, from selfishness to Christlikeness. God is engaged in the business of change, and He wants us to work with Him. Think of a person you'd like to help change toward the Lord. How eager is he to change his ways? What do you think it may take to accomplish the change? What is the best way to begin?

The most natural approach would be: "I've got something that you ought to have." How does this make the other fellow feel? "So you think you're better than I am, that I'm no good, that you don't like me as I am!" What kind of start is that? What is the other person ready to do? Defend himself against us, tell us why he is as he is, give more reasons than he had thought of before, become more entrenched in his position than he was before. We've made it harder for him to change rather than easier.

How can we start in such a way that the other person will feel that we are with him, not against him?

Being All Things to All Men—1 Corinthians 9:19-27

A passage in the New Testament gives a very clear answer to this question. Turn to 1 Corinthians 9:19. What attitude was Paul willing to take in order to win more people to Christ? Instead of being the superior one, he was ready to become the unbeliever's slave or servant. That's going pretty far, isn't it? When most people prize their freedom above all else?

How does he mean "become a slave"? Next he mentions three kinds of people and how he related to them. First his own people, the Jews. How would he become as a Jew? Since they tried to live under the law of God, when he was with them, he kept the law with them. How might we today limit ourselves as do the friends we are trying to reach? When we're with them, we can listen to the same TV programs and records that they do even though we prefer something else.

Right here in our family we often have to shift gears because of our different ages. When we are relating to the other members, can we put ourselves in their place, feel as they feel, think as they think? When we're talking to Alice, can we understand how a seven year old looks at life? Can we feel with Mother, who is the only one who stays at home most of the day getting food and clothes and the house ready for the rest of us? We naturally assume that the other fellow is responding just as we are, but he isn't. His temperament, background, needs and abilities are all different. Can we identify with people who are different from us?

In 21 what other group of people did Paul relate to? In his case these were Gentiles. Today some people don't seem to appreciate any law, want what we call license to do just anything. This is the way many young people seem to the older generation, and it frightens them dreadfully. Can we identify with both these kinds of people? What would be our problem? We're not going to disobey the Lord; there would be no profit in that, for it wouldn't help them come to the Lord. But we can like them as people and do things that both of us enjoy.

In 22 what was the third class of people that Paul identified with? How can we become weak without hurting ourselves? It may seem like wasting time when we try to make friends with some people or talk about the trivial things that they are interested in, or we may have to say the same things over and over because they don't get the ideas. But we may have to begin there, wherever it is that they are. The last part of 22 summarizes Paul's important principle in working with people. Let's read it from our various versions.

In 23 we have the only motive that is powerful enough to get us humans to forget ourselves and focus upon others. Only the love of Christ prompts this. On the board I am drawing a simple diagram. We here at this circle cannot hope to reach people on our human level unless we are also continually related to the divine. So I am drawing lines both to the side and above. The Lord wants us to make this connection. While we keep in touch with both, in answer to our prayer He works directly also with the unbelievers, so I'm drawing an arrow from the top to the person at the side.

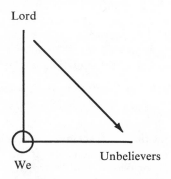

In 24, 25 what does it take to win a person to Christ that is comparable to winning an athletic prize? If runners exercise and discipline themselves for the sake of a trophy that is worthless in itself, how much more should we exercise and discipline ourselves for the sake of a precious human soul who will praise the Lord for all eternity!

Though it may take many contacts before an unbeliever comes through to Christ, let's not grow weary before he does. In 27 what is Paul even ready to do to win that goal? Read the way The Living Bible expresses 27, Ted.

One of the greatest compliments an unbeliever can give us is to say, "Yes, you understand how I feel." That may not be the way we feel, but his life is open the minute he realizes that someone understands him, when most people don't bother to take time to understand. That gives him hope that maybe God —if there is a God—can understand him too. And he's ready to move in that direction.

Is there any action of any person in our family that you don't understand? Let's pray for that and for the people that all of us are seeking to reach for Christ.

Witnessing

SUPPOSE THAT among your acquaintances was a member of Jehovah's Witnesses who was trying to make converts. Every chance he got he zealously pressed upon people the need of accepting his religion. If he got a chance to talk to you, he'd tell you how much you're missing because you don't believe as he does. How would you react to this kind of witnessing? You'd feel that you were being treated as a thing rather than as a person.

Suppose you happened to find out that another acquaintance was a Seventh Day Adventist, but you never heard him say a word about his religion or reveal in any way that he had one. How would you feel about his religion?

Again suppose you knew that another person was a strong Catholic. He went to church a lot, he stayed with his own little group of Catholics, and related only casually and superficially with other kinds of people. How would you feel about him? He seemed to be content to live in his own private world.

Would you be attracted to the religion of any of these three kinds of people? How would the person act who would attract you to what he had spiritually? The Lord has left His people in this world to show forth the wonderful deeds of Him who called us out of darkness into His marvellous light (1 Peter 2:9).

The Christian Community—Acts 2:42-47

The Catholic above is right in that the Christian community is very important. Turn to Acts 2:42. After the day of Pentecost when the Lord poured His Spirit upon His disciples, how did the believers relate to each other? In our Christian groups are we devoting ourselves to instruction in the Word, in fellowship with other members of the body of Christ, and to worship together? Why are these group activities so essential? The body needs the contribution of every one of its members for its total working. Look also at verse 46.

What else were these early believers known for? Do we expect the Lord to do signs and wonders today? Why not? He is still in the business of healing bodies and souls and spirits. If we haven't experienced the supernatural in our groups, we better get together and pray in faith to see the Lord work in our midst.

What did the believers do if any member of their group had a need? 44, 45. Do we know what are the personal needs of the members of our groups? How ready are we to share what we have?

With people like that, what were the results? 47. The Lord was able to do so much for them that they were high on Him, full of praise and overflowing joy. With so much tension and anxiety in our world, what attracts more than a buoyant spirit!

How is the outsiders' reaction expressed here? What were the implications of the believers' having "favour with all the people"? No one was antagonized by their high spirits, no one questioned their motives, everyone appreciated their excitement.

Then what was the result of this praise and favor? How do you visualize people being saved and daily added to their number? They would naturally inquire about the Christians' happiness, and when they discovered that salvation was the free gift of God, that they too were eligible for it, they joined the enlivened group.

Do the people we contact feel this way about us? Are we supported and strengthened by our fellow believers until our radiance attracts others?

Time for Others—Acts 9:36-42

Some of us may be wondering how we can expect to impress others without the miraculous kinds of healings that the disciples performed in the Book of Acts. Does our witness depend on miracles like that? Turn to Acts 9:36. Here was a woman who had a strong witness for Christ without the so-called miraculous. What was she known for? She filled her days with acts of kindness and love, the ordinary kind of good deeds.

What happened to Dorcas in 37, 38? What kinds of people that she had witnessed to were now distressed without her? What had they brought with them to show how much she had done for them?

Mother, finish reading this incident in the rest of the chapter. Many believed in the Lord not only because she was raised from the dead, but first because she was just plain kind. Are our days self-centered, or do we have time to do deeds of kindness for those we normally contact?

The Essence of the Gospel—1 Corinthians 15:3, 4

When our natural contacts have been attracted to the life of Christ in us, they may ask what makes us so happy and so strong. When they are ready to hear, what shall we tell them is the essence of the gospel? What is the good news of Christ? It is very clearly expressed in 1 Corinthians 15:3, 4; turn to those verses. How would you say that in the fewest possible words? Christ died for our sins and rose again. Why did He have to die? Because He has a best plan for each of us, but we cannot approach Him or work with Him while we are sinners and He is holy. So Christ took the punishment that we deserve, and rose again to be our living Saviour. Now He prays for us and gives us His resurrection power when we work with Him on His great purposes.

After we are saved, the most thrilling experience is to lead others to Christ. How do we need to be strengthened in order to be better prepared to do this? What should we work on as a family in our family contacts? And what individually in the opportunities that the Lord gives us?

Worldliness

ONE OF the controversial questions among Christians through the years has been the question of worldliness, with many different ideas on the subject. Romans 12:2 RSV commands, "Do not be conformed to this world but be . . . transformed by the renewal of your mind." We also read, "Love not the world, neither the things that are in the world" (1 John 2:15). This is an important question because a worldly person is contrasted with a spiritual person; the person who considers himself spiritual looks down on the person he considers worldly.

Do we think of any Christians as worldly? If so, why? What is our basis for judgment? Usually people's attitudes toward worldliness depend on their background and the customs of those in their surroundings. These differ greatly in different parts of the country and in different periods of history. Often dress and habits and practices that are frowned upon have had immoral associations. As fashions in our fast-changing world change, so do our standards. The length of women's skirts is a clear example. Try to imagine how dresses above the knee would have looked to the era when skirts were close to the ground.

How did this world and all that is in it come to be? Our loving heavenly Father created all things, and saw that they were good. Nothing is bad in itself. But it can be used harmfully. Grain is a necessary staple as well as being used for liquor, and alcohol is a medicine too. Drugs heal disease as well as hurt people. What else can be used wrongly as well as helpfully? We can even burn our skin if we expose it too long to the beneficent sun that is absolutely necessary to warm and brighten the earth.

What then is worldliness?

What We Love

The answer is found in 1 John 2:15. What is the key word here? It's a question of what we love. How is love for the world contrasted with love for the Father? Since every good gift and every perfect gift is from the Father above, the things He has given us ought to direct our love to Him. But people love the things He gives instead of Him.

In 16 are listed the three kinds of temptation that entice us away from the Father. How does your version word the first one? Lust of the flesh is anything that our lower nature loves that is opposed to our higher nature. This includes illegitimate sex, overeating, and gossip. Secondly, what entices our eyes that makes us covet what we don't have? Our stores are full of attractive things that we'd like to buy. Is there anything that we feel we just must have? Thirdly, what kinds of success could make us proud? We could be proud of gaining a promotion, baking a prize-winning cake, being chosen as cheerleader, or earning top school grades. When we gain success, how should we feel about it?

In 17 what is the reason for loving the Father rather than the world that He made?

Turn to 2 Corinthians 3:5 to see why the Christian can't be proud. We thank the Lord who enabled us rather than loving the glamour that success brings us.

In verse 6 how is the new covenant that we are living under different from the old covenant in the Old Testament? Read this verse in your various versions. The old covenant had very definite rules: Do this and this and this; don't do that and that. But not the new covenant. Why? Human nature could never keep all those laws. What does the Spirit do for us? He helps us discern the Lord's will and empowers us to do it. When we don't know whether or not something is worldly as opposed to the Lord's best, what question can we ask the Lord? Our decision depends on our own inner attitude and whether or not it would hurt someone else.

Our Relation to Sinners

The Bible says that Jesus was both a friend of sinners (Matthew 11:19) and separate from sinners (Hebrews 7:26). How can we too be both friend and separate? Look at the paragraph beginning with 2 Corinthians 6:14. How were these Christian believers related to unbelievers? They were marrying them! So in 17 what did Paul command them to do? We are to touch nothing unclean in God's sight, nothing that would defile us.

Now turn to 1 Corinthians 5:9-11. If we were to have no association with sinners, what would we have to do? We'd have to go out of this world. But the church can isolate Christians in order to get them to repent of their own sins.

In John 17:15 how did Jesus pray for His followers?

In the next verse the question for us is: in the very core of our being do we feel tied to the world or to the Lord? People who are tied to neither of them feel at loose ends.

In 17 what did Jesus ask the Father to do for us? If we are sanctified in the truth, our Christian values are clearly distinguished from the world's values, which are centered in self rather than in Christ.

In 18 what is the purpose of our being sanctified in the truth? The Lord doesn't want us isolated in our ghetto, but He sends us into the world to show what He is like and what He wants to give everyone.

Therefore let's check our own relation to the world. Are we strong enough in the truth to associate with the world in order to demonstrate Christ without loving it and becoming tied to it? Is there anything in the world that we love more than Christ?

"Lord, we thank You for all the possibilities of using this world aright. Don't let us use anything harmfully, but be free to relate to unbelievers without accepting their values."

1 John 2:15-17 is a good passage to memorize.

9 TRUSTING GOD

What Trust Is

USE YOUR imagination to picture a situation in which you'd be inclined to panic. What would be the cause of it? Would you feel that you'd lose yourself, feel so insecure that you'd perish? Was there nothing in the situation you could trust to help you?

Let's make two lists on the board: one of people or things we can usually trust, and one that we can't. How many of the ones we can usually trust can we always trust? One of the reasons people commit suicide is that they find there isn't anything or anyone they can really trust, and so they feel they can't live any longer.

Let's mention one quality in each of us that we as a family feel we can trust. What do we feel we can truly trust about Mother? Etc.

Next to love, the second quality of a Christian is trust, and some people say it is the most important. Why is trust so important?

Asa's Trust and Distrust—2 Chronicles 14—16

While some of the kings of Judah disobeyed the Lord, we are so glad to read that King Asa did what was right in the sight of the Lord. In what two main ways did he obey the Lord, in 2 Chronicles 14:3-5? He demolished all the heathen idols that the people worshiped instead of the Lord, and he ordered them to seek the Lord and keep His laws.

When an Ethiopian general came against him with an army of a million men, what did Asa cry to the Lord, in 11?

Because Asa was trusting Him, how did the Lord answer in the rest of the chapter? What stands out to you in this section? God's people even carried away much booty, for the fear of the Lord was upon the enemy.

As Asa was returning home, the Spirit of God came upon a prophet, who spoke to him God's words that are as appropriate for our nation as it was then for his, 15:2-7. The words in verse 2 after the salutation are good ones to remember; because they are almost the same in the various Bible versions, let's read them aloud together, beginning with "The Lord is with you." Let's try that again.

Read verses 3-7, Jim.

Then Asa did take courage. He gathered the people together at Jerusalem and truly pleased the Lord, for what did they all do, in 12-15? Sue, in that section read all the phrases that use the words "all" and "whole." The response to the Lord was wholehearted, not halfhearted. Asa led his whole realm in trusting the Lord. So the Lord gave the land peace for many years.

After this covenant what would you expect to happen when the king of Israel declared war on Asa and built a fortress to control the road to his realm? Read 16:2, 3. Whom did Asa call on for help? Not the Lord, who had given him such a great victory before, but the king of Syria! What did he have to give this foreign king to get him to break his alliance with the king of Israel? Instead of giving anything to the Lord when He helped him win, what did he get?

Then the Lord sent another prophet to Asa. Read to yourself verse 7, and Mother, read 8, 9.

Verse 9 is another outstanding verse. Read that in the various versions. From then on Asa had wars instead of peace.

Instead of appreciating the prophet who had given him God's words, what did Asa do, in 10?

What do these two battles tell us about human nature? Because we trust once doesn't imply that we always will.

What It Means to Trust

What did Asa actually do when he trusted the Lord? What did he do when he didn't trust God? What does it mean for us to trust Him? How can we trust a Person we've never seen? What difference does it really make?

Yes, let's organize all the ideas that you've mentioned under three steps of faith:

1. What is the relation of the word of the Lord to trust? First we acknowledge that the Lord is the real Person He says He is and that He has revealed Himself truly to us. We don't expect to know everything about God or He wouldn't be God, yet what we have is true knowledge.

2. We respect His Word enough to give ourselves to Him as the supreme unseen Reality. This allows us to grow to know and experience Him personally.

3. Intimate personal relations with Him give us the assurance that He will be to us all that He has promised, that He will not let us down. As we keep exercising the risk of faith, we develop more and more trust.

Do you have any trouble with any of these ideas or experiences? If so, let's discuss it.

"Lord, we thank You that You are wholly trustworthy. Therefore help us to respond by wholly trusting You. Keep us trusting You more each day so that we may experience exciting victories."

Do you feel like singing with me "Trusting Jesus" (or another familiar song of trust)?

When to Trust

WHEN ALL is going smoothly and the Lord is supplying our needs, it's very easy to say, "Yes, we must wholly trust the Lord," and sing merrily "Trust and Obey." But that isn't trusting, that's just talk, just an idea. What is actual trust? We trust when we don't see how our problem is coming out, how our need will be met, how the right is winning—at least from our perspective.

What experiences has our family had in really trusting, when we didn't see God's answer? The more experiences we've had in the past, the easier it is to trust for the future.

When we can't visualize how things can work out in a way that seems right to us, what do we mortals do? We may get out of God's will and do something else. That is serious. Or we may feel that we have to solve the problem ourselves. Or we may sink into the slough of despond, not doing anything but grieving.

But if we trust, what will we do? We'll say, "Now won't it be interesting to see how the Lord works out this situation." Suppose one of the three boys in a family has a bad bout with pneumonia, which leaves him with such weak lungs that he'll never be husky physically. That's hard. Is it hopeless? Will the family be depressed and blame the Lord? Though they may not see it now, how could the Lord work that out for good? That boy could become a writer or mathematician or something that requires quiet concentration.

Habakkuk's Trust

A whole small book in the Old Testament deals with this problem of trust—the book of Habakkuk. We won't read it all, but we'll get the gist of the whole. Let's try to put the prophet's poetical expressions into our own words.

In 1:2-4 what is Habakkuk's problem? The Lord isn't answering him when he calls. The land is full of oppression and lawlessness and injustice, and God does nothing about it.

In 5-7 the Lord answers Habakkuk in a way he never expects. How will He punish the wicked? By raising up a cruel nation that will march across the world and conquer it!

Why doesn't this seem right to the prophet? "These fierce people are more wicked than our nation! Will You let these people destroy those who are better than they?" (*See* 12, 13.)

In 2:1 Habakkuk is so sensible. He does what we so often fail to do when we'd like an answer from the Lord. We ask Him but don't wait long enough and aren't quiet enough to hear His answer.

How does the Lord reply? "My answer may seem slow to you, but be patient, it will come. My timing is very important." (*See* 2:3.)

What does verse 8 say will be the fate of the fierce conquerors? Other nations will ruin them.

Who still is in control of all the nations on earth? 2:20. No man knows better than the sovereign Creator; no man can suggest to Him what to do.

How does Habakkuk respond to this in 3:2? He remembers the wondrous works of old and takes courage to ask the Lord to do them again.

After Habakkuk has recounted how the Lord saved His people from Egypt, how does he feel now, in 16?

When the enemy come to punish the wicked, they will devastate the land, crops and flocks will suffer, *but* after this conversation with the Lord, what is the condition of Habakkuk's faith? Verses 17-19 give us one of the finest pieces of poetry in the Old Testament. Let's read it in our various versions. Habakkuk's doubt is gone; he has seen the Lord's viewpoint.

Trusting Together

As a family let's trust together for something that each of us is concerned about. For each of the requests that we mention let's check to see that it would be in the Lord's will according to His Word, that it would be good from our human perspective, and that each of us is doing his or her part to bring it about.

I'm trusting the Lord to help me to reflect Christ to the fellow who works at the desk next to mine in the office. I want him to really see the Lord in me. I'm sure the Lord wants to save this man, and I'm doing my best to let the Lord work and talk in me to him. Mother, for what do you want to trust the Lord? Etc.

Said the Robin to the Sparrow:
"I should really like to know
Why these anxious human beings
Rush about and worry so."

Said the Sparrow to the Robin:
"Friend, I think that it must be
That they have no heavenly Father
Such as cares for you and me."
ELIZABETH CHENEY

"Dear Lord, we're glad that You see the whole picture, the end from the beginning, and all that's involved in these requests. Help us to trust when we don't see and be ready to accept Your answer though it may not be what we expect."

Believing God's Word

IF OUR family didn't have any Bible, what difference would it make to us? We would no doubt be different people, for our whole life is centered in Scripture. It's through Scripture that we come to know our Lord and His ways for us. To some people the Bible makes no difference, for they pay no attention to it.

Through the centuries people have always had contrasting opinions of the Bible. How do those who disregard it feel about it? They consider it just another book, on the same level as any other book. Some read it, but do not believe that God wrote it. Why then do they refer to it? They may think of it as excellent literature, with high moral principles and forceful illustrations. Others believe that it contains the Word of God when God speaks through the writing to individuals.

How do evangelical Christians like us feel about the Bible? The Lord God Himself superintended the writers so that they wrote what He wanted mankind through the years to know. The words of the Bible are God's words. He has revealed to us true knowledge of Himself and His ways that we could never discover by ourselves. None of us would have spiritual life if we didn't have the Bible!

Some people say they believe the Bible, but I wonder if they really do. What is the test of whether or not a person believes it?

The Official's Belief—John 4:46-53

We'll find an example of the answer to this question in John 4, beginning with verse 46. What had this official in the court of the king probably heard about Jesus? How He turned water into wine in his village of Cana. He must have thought, "If Jesus could do that, maybe He could heal my very sick son."

So what did he do in 47? He traveled the twenty miles to the village of Capernaum to see Jesus. How did he make his request? What does that tell us about the man? He must have loved his son dearly, and he believed that Jesus had the power to heal if He would only come to his house where the child was.

What did Jesus mean by what He said? "Do you come to Me only when all else fails, only to get something you want for yourself? Won't you believe without seeing a miracle?" (*See* 48.)

What was the man's response to that question in 49? Say it in your own words. It might be, "Sir, my child is dying! Won't You please come with me? If You'd only come, I believe that You could heal him."

In 50 instead of saying "I will come with you," what did Jesus surprise the father by saying? What did Jesus show the man by this? Did the man learn this? What was the test of his belief? Would you have started on your twenty-mile trip home without Jesus, merely because He spoke the word? That's genuine belief!

Because the official believed Jesus without seeing his son, what happened when he got halfway home? 51. If we believe, we will see. We can imagine how joyous were all the men as they finished their journey!

What question did the official ask his servants? 52.

What did their answer do for him? 53. How do you think this belief at the end of the incident was different from his belief at the beginning? It was probably stronger and deeper, for he was now more sure that Jesus was no ordinary person. No wonder the whole household believed when they saw the dying boy well and lively. What if the nobleman had not believed Jesus sufficiently first to come and then to go!

Using God's Word

Therefore no matter what we say about the Bible, what is the test of whether or not we believe it? Whether or not we act on it, do what it says to us. The official believed and started home. If we believe, what are we doing today?

How would you answer the skeptic who says that the Bible was written for the long ago, not for today? What has God given in Scripture that are as much in force today as two thousand years ago? He has given us eternal principles that don't change. Through these principles God speaks personally to us when we converse intimately with Him. What is the focus of the whole Bible? The Person of our Saviour-Lord. The Old Testament looked forward to Him, the gospels tell His life on earth, the New Testament letters look back to Him. And we look at our situation today in His light.

At the other extreme is the believer who takes any promise out of the Bible and expects to claim it for himself today. What is the error in this practice? We have to keep each promise in its context, to see whether or not it relates to the particular culture of that day or to all times. The Holy Spirit will guide us as to which is which if we ask Him.

What promise do we need to claim right now? Do we truly believe this word of the Lord? Are we ready to act on it? Are we doing our part, doing what we can? If the answer doesn't come as we expect it, we'll know the Lord has something better for us.

When We Don't Trust

THINK OF a person you find easy to trust. What kind of person is he? Think of one you don't trust.

Even though people are not perfect, we still trust them. We can't always be sure they won't let us down. So wouldn't you think we would wholly trust the only One who is wholly true, wholly trustworthy! But we don't, do we? Why not? Suppose a man moved next door to us who was known in his old neighborhood as a most upright noble person. No matter how much other people thought of him, would we trust him right away? No, why not? We have to know a person before we will trust him. Many people don't know the Lord well enough to trust Him. Trust is a personal relationship. That's why we have to keep up with the Lord each day. If we don't, it's human nature to drift away on our own. And we have to risk a little if we are to experience trust. We can expect it only if we open our heart and mind to receive from the Lord. The more we trust, the more solid ground we have on which to base further trust, greater trust.

What happens to the dear children whose parents are so inconsistent that they never learn to trust them? They find it very difficult to trust anyone, for they have nothing to build on. They are always suspicious that people are going to hurt them. What do we have to expect when we don't trust?

When Israel Doubted—Numbers 13:1—14:24

After the people of Israel left Egypt, they walked through the wilderness till they came near the southern border of the promised land. Turn to Numbers 13:1, 2. What did the Lord tell their leader Moses to do?

In the paragraph beginning with verse 17 what directions did Moses give the spies? They needed to find out what kind of land they were going to have, and how strong were the people they would have to conquer.

What does verse 23 tell us about the land? A single cluster of grapes had to be carried by two men on a pole!

In 27, 28 what was the report of the spies? The descendants of Anak were giants! Ted, read what the man Caleb suggested in 30.

And Jim, what the others concluded, in 31-33. Read those same verses in The Living Bible, Sue. So Caleb kept the negative report from being unanimous.

In chapter 14 how did the whole congregation receive this report? Mother, read verses 1-4 expressing the feelings of the people.

How would you like to try to lead a people who had this kind of trust? Poor Moses and Aaron! What did they do in 5?

In 6 what did Caleb and Joshua do and say? What was their line of reasoning, through 9? These two men were not relying on themselves, as the others seemed to be. The others apparently forgot the Lord's deliverance out of Egypt and His promise to give them the new land.

How did the congregation respond to their reasoning? 10.

Suddenly the people saw the glory of the Lord appear at the tent of meeting! Mother, read how the Lord in His holiness reacted to this distrust. 11, 12.

Moses answered by pleading for mercy. He said: "The other nations will think that You are not powerful enough to bring Your people into this land.

Forgive the sin of this people according to Your unconditional love." (*See* 13, 14.)

Did the Lord forgive? 20. But what was His judgment against this generation that rebelled against Him? 21-23. How many times had they disobeyed Him? The adults who had not trusted Him would never see the good land flowing with milk and honey.

In 24 what did He promise Caleb, who followed Him wholly?

What to Expect When We Do Trust

Trust isn't trust if we can see how things are going to work out. So what can we expect if we are going to trust when we can't see? Yes, things will look impossible, overwhelming, so that our lower nature will likely murmur and weep. What will help our higher nature get the upper hand? We'll remember the Lord's great deliverances in the past.

What else can we expect if we trust? What we do may not seem sensible from a human standpoint. Who are we to face the giants in the land? We aren't adequate, but we're not depending on ourselves. And people are likely to oppose us. But I'd rather have people against me than the Lord against me. He can fight against us as well as for us.

And we can expect the Lord to work, to drive out the enemy whoever they are.

On the board I am drawing the relationship between God's promises and our lives. Above are God and His unseen realities. Below are the realities of our lives. If we are open to God in faith, He converts His promises into events that we can see. It's faith that bridges the gap between the unseen and the seen, the promise and the fact.

God, unseen realities

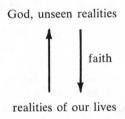

faith

realities of our lives

"Dear Lord, we thank You that You want so much for us, Your people. Don't let us fail to enter into Your promises because of unbelief. Help us to know You better so that we can trust You more."

Trusting in Man

WHEN THIS last week did you trust the Lord most wholeheartedly? When you didn't know how something would work out, but you depended upon the Lord to do what was best? Can you think of times when you trusted other people instead of the Lord? When you trusted yourself? When are you most likely to trust yourself? Probably at times when you feel you are strong. How do you put together the two ideas: that the Lord wants His people to be strong, and yet to trust Him? Why do we need to trust Him when we are strong? Pride goes before a fall. Self-centered man uses his strength for destruction. We need His wisdom to use our strength and His power to become stronger still.

When the Martin family moved, they traveled far to another part of the country without knowing where they would live when they got there. If they truly trusted God, what would they say to Him about their new home? What would they be trusting if they were worried and anxious as they traveled across new country instead of enjoying the new experiences they were having? Their cousins in the new city said they would look for houses that would be possible for them. Suppose the relatives found nothing that they considered suitable. What would the Martins say to that if they were trusting the Lord?

What can we expect when we put our trust in human people?

Jehoshaphat's Alliance—2 Chronicles 18

Jehoshaphat started out very well as king of Judah. He removed the false gods and the high places where the people had been worshiping them. He sent his princes and priests throughout all the land to teach the people the law of the Lord. Because God blessed him, the fear of the Lord fell upon all the surrounding kings and none of them made war on him (2 Chronicles 17:1-10).

Turn to 2 Chronicles 18:1. What was Jehoshaphat's reputation at that time? Though the Lord had given him these great riches and honor, how did he disobey the Lord in his association with King Ahab of Israel, who sold himself to do all kinds of evil, prompted by his wicked wife Jezebel? It was disastrous for him to allow his son to marry Ahab's daughter.

In verse 2 when Ahab threw a party for him, what did Ahab ask Jehoshaphat to do with him? And what did Jehoshaphat answer in 3?

In 4 what did Jehoshaphat suggest that they do first?

So when Ahab called together four hundred men who pretended to be prophets of the Lord, and asked them, what was their reply? 5.

In 6 how did Jehoshaphat feel about these 400? He wasn't satisfied with them. Was there any other prophet in this kingdom? Why didn't Ahab like him?

Read 8, 9 for the setting of this event.

In 10, 11 how did the four hundred reinforce their prediction?

In these next conversations, Jim, read what the other prophet Micaiah said. Sue, what the messenger, sent to get him, said in 12. Ted, what King Ahab said in 14, 15, 17, and 25. Mother, be the false prophet Zedekiah in 23. In verse 14 Micaiah was just parroting the other prophets, saying what they wanted him to say, sarcastically.

What should Jehoshaphat have done then? What must he have been trusting?

Probably he thought that the combined armies of the two kings were sufficient. So in 28 the kings led their armies into battle. What does 29 tell us about Ahab?

In 30 whom was the enemy king gunning for? Finish that chapter, Jim, to tell us how that battle went. The Lord saved Jehoshaphat when he cried out to Him, but Ahab was trusting wholly in himself.

Forming Habits of Trust

Most Christians mean to trust the Lord but they've never formed habits of trust. It can become natural rather than unnatural for us to look to the Lord constantly, just as we pray without ceasing (1 Thessalonians 5:17). Let's hear Proverbs 3:5-8 read in two or three versions. As we listen to these verses, let's think how this works out in our daily lives.

If we want to be directed in all we do, our efforts crowned with success, be given renewed health and vitality, if we want our path to be smooth and straight, we'll acknowledge the Lord in all our ways. How will this work out practically? Yes, in the morning we'll get in tune with the Almighty, we'll give ourselves to Him for the day, and ask Him to direct everything we think and feel and do. Then can we forget Him the rest of the day? No, just as many Christian families regularly say grace before meals, we can form the habit of looking to Him at the beginning of each activity and in the midst of each activity. For me at the office that means every new project I undertake and every part of every project. Mother, what does that mean to you here at home? And to you children in school?

Then whenever a question arises in our work, we ask "What, Lord?" And listen for His answer. There's no need for us to be frustrated and discouraged when we can look to the Lord for help. I try to ask the Lord to guide me whenever I pick up the telephone, because if I make one wrong decision, that may throw others out of kilter.

Let's turn these verses in Proverbs into a prayer. "Lord, help us to trust in You with all our hearts," etc.

Proverbs 3:5-8 is a good passage to memorize.

The Lord's Higher Ways

WHEN WE see a need and try to meet it, what difference does it make that we are Christians? Do we proceed just the same as non-Christians?

In one neighborhood three Christian families had young people who had extra time during the summer months. The youth were wondering what they could do that would really help their community. They tried to think of all the possibilities and asked their parents and friends for suggestions. Nothing they thought of got them excited. Then because they were Christians, it occurred to one of them to ask the Lord what they could do for Him and with Him. They felt that the idea that did appeal to them came from Him. They could clean up an empty lot that was overgrown with weeds, fence it in, and make it into a playground for young children who had no place to play. They felt that this needed to be done and that the Lord was directing them, but it seemed too big an undertaking! Where would they begin? They didn't even know whom the empty lot belonged to. When they found out that it belonged to a grouchy old man who didn't like children, how do you suppose they felt? What would be their next step?

The Lord says to His people, ". . . as the heavens are higher than the earth, so are my ways higher than your ways, and my thoughts than your thoughts" (Isaiah 55:9). Those young people really believed that, so what did they say to the Lord? What shall we say to Him when He directs us to do something hard? Or something that doesn't seem the sensible thing to do?

The Battle of Jericho—Joshua 5:11—6

Even though the good land that God promised His people was already occupied by strong tribes, God told them to go in and take it; that He would be with them. The key to capturing the central hill country was the city of Jericho, a beautiful city of palms, probably the oldest city in the world. Situated by a ford of the Jordan River, it controlled the ancient trade routes. But the city of Jericho had strong walls around it.

As Joshua, the commander of the Lord's people, looked at those walls and wondered how that city could be taken, what did he see and do, in Joshua 5:13? Our enemies can't see the real Captain in our battles.

How did the man answer, in 14? Did Joshua make the right response to this person? He certainly did.

In 15, what was the significance of what this heavenly person asked Joshua to do? He didn't tell Joshua what means to use to capture the city, but he inferred that the Lord was taking charge.

Because the people of Jericho were afraid of the Israelites, how did they try to protect themselves? 6:1.

In verse 2 what did the Lord Himself say to Joshua? "You need not take the city; I *have given* it to you," not "I *will give* it to you."

Then what did the Lord say would be the part of Joshua and the soldiers? 3-5. If you were a commander of an army, how would this strategy strike you? What might Joshua have been thinking? "Am I hearing things? Whose voice do I hear? How ridiculous! The priests carrying the ark of God around and around the city, then shouting, and the wall falling down! How silly can you get!"

Do we read that Joshua went on trying to figure out how he could capture the city by techniques of war? No, Jim, read what happened in 6:21. Try to imagine how the people inside the city felt for those seven days as they saw the procession march 'round and 'round their walls with the priests blowing trumpets. They must have been overcome with mystery and fear as they witnessed such an unheard-of occurrence! Then on the seventh day after the seventh round an earth-shaking SHOUT! How much higher are God's ways than our ways! How many of God's people lost their lives in that victory?

Why did God command that the people of Jericho be utterly destroyed? It was His judgment on a heathen civilization that was so wicked that it was a curse on the face of the earth. If allowed to remain, it would have further contaminated other people.

Working with the Lord

What then are we going to do when a need arises and we don't know what to do? Since Christ is the Head of the body of which we are members, as minute cells in one part of it, we won't make our own decisions. We'll ask the Head both for directions and methods. If He should ask us to march around walls instead of attacking directly, how would we respond? He works in us "to will and to do of His good pleasure" (Philippians 2:13). What difference will it make that we have His Holy Spirit working in us? He sharpens our perceptions and controls our inner thoughts and feelings.

If the young people who were directed by the Lord to prepare a playground seek the Lord's higher ways, what will they do when they find that the empty lot is owned by a grouchy old man? Since the Lord has told them to "take their Jericho," He will also tell them how to do it. What is their part? They need to listen to His voice and obey it. How might the Lord "tumble their walls" of difficulty? He might change the old man's mind, the man might get interested in the project, the man might sell the lot. Or the Lord might do something we could never imagine. That's often our problem—we are not ready to receive the Lord's answer because it is different from what we visualize it must be.

What needs do we as members of this family have just now? Are we assuming that the Lord wants us to do something before He has directed us? Let's ask Him first what He wants us to do. It may not seem the most sensible thing to us. It's natural for us to pray, "Help me do this thing that I want to do." Instead of that, how shall we pray? "Lord, what do You want done as part of Your great plans? What is my part in it?" Then let's ask Him how He wants it done, and listen for His answer to our need.

10 DEALING WITH FRUSTRATION

Giving Up Our Own Way

INSTEAD OF making His human creatures puppets who would move as He wished when He pulled the strings, God made us with wills of our own. Of course this was taking the risk of our saying *no* to Him as well as *yes*. But He wasn't content with beings who were forced to obey Him; He wants us to love and worship Him of our own free will. Then we can genuinely share and fellowship with each other.

We all start out being selfish and self-centered. It is His plan that in a Christian home we shall daily listen to Him and His Word until we gradually turn from being self-centered to being Christ-centered. How will this change come about? If we daily say no to our own self-will and yes to Him, we find it easier and easier to keep turned His way instead of ours. We parents don't want to *break* any child's will, for he will need every bit of the strength of it in making his decisions throughout life. Wills need to be bent, not broken.

Do you often feel a struggle going on between your higher nature that wants God's best and your lower nature that wants its own way? This is a fact that all of us should learn to appreciate. It often helps to face the struggle very openly, even saying to ourselves, "My lower nature is trying to get its own way, but Lord, strengthen my higher nature to win so that I may have Your best way." We may also say, "This course of action seems more sensible to my human nature, but Lord, I trust You to know best."

Our feelings are the part of us hardest to bring into line. How does David in the Bible help us to give up our own way?

David and the Temple—1 Chronicles 17, 28, 29

One day King David had an idea that seemed to him very sensible and glorifying to the Lord. Turn to 1 Chronicles 17:1. When David was then living in his lovely new palace with cedar panels, what did he say to Nathan the prophet? The precious ark of the covenant, the central focus of Jewish worship, was still housed in the tent that was necessary for carrying it as the people journeyed to the promised land. Now they were settled in the land.

In 2 how did Nathan's response show that he felt about the idea? Certainly sounded like a good one.

The Lord was pleased with the idea (2 Chronicles 6:8 RSV), but that same night what did He say to Nathan? 4-6. What did his question in 6 imply? His house was so important that if He had wanted it built before this, He would have said so.

In 11, 12 what were His wishes for the house?

In 16, 17 how did David take this rejection of his idea?

Instead of pouting and thinking how he would be deprived of a great undertaking, what was he thinking about, in 20, 21? When he got his eyes on the Lord, his attitude was one of praise.

Now turn over to chapter 28, verse 3, which gives the reason why not David but his son Solomon was to build the temple. God has reasons for what He does, and specific parts for us all to play. We don't want to take someone else's part.

But God honored David's wish to make a proper place for the center of worship. What did David do for the temple in verses 11 and 19? God gave him the plans for the temple in writing.

And in the first of chapter 29 what else did David do for the temple? Because he consented to the Lord's wishes, he had a part in building the great house of God.

Balancing Determination and Stubbornness

When the Lord says no regarding something that seems good to us, how will we react? If our feelings won't come along with our higher nature, what can we do? Our mind and our will can combine to command our body to obey the Lord; then it is likely that our feelings will gradually if not immediately fall in line.

Sometimes the line between determination and stubbornness isn't very clear. Will power and persistence are strong character traits. When it was God's time for Jesus to accomplish our salvation, He steadfastly set His face to go to the cross (Luke 9:51). When does determination become stubbornness? When we won't change even though change is needed. How can we keep from being stubborn? We can keep checking: "Lord, is this Your best will and way?"

What are you most determined to do this week or month? Are you ready to revise your plans if the Lord spoke to you or the situation changed? Can you forge ahead to a goal and yet keep flexible?

Some people go to the other extreme. They need more persistence in following through an idea. They are too ready to switch to something else, to something new. Are you inclined to go to either extreme?

"Dear Lord, keep us so sensitive to Your still small voice that we are always ready to hear You and to give up our own ideas that seem good when they are not Your best."

Being Discouraged

THE STATEMENT is probably true that discouragement is the devil's best tool. He must chuckle with glee when he is able to get believers depressed. Why would he be so delighted? Yes, we are put out of commission; we don't feel like doing anything but feeling sorry for ourselves. We are actually poisoning ourselves, for it keeps us from loving and trusting. We want people to leave us alone so that we can wallow in our misery. Discouragement distorts our perspective, so that we can't see things as they really are. And it also lowers the morale of those around us.

Try to remember the last time you were depressed. What caused it? How do we get in such a black mood? Probably most often because things don't turn out as we expect them to. We get mad at ourselves when we don't measure up to the picture we have of ourselves. We say to ourselves, "I am this kind of person, and I don't do things like that. Yet I did it." Or other people let us down, don't come through, and spoil all our plans. How can anything remedy a situation like this? Sometimes too we get discouraged because we're under a strain for a long period, and feel that we've had enough.

How does the Lord treat us when we're down? We can learn from Him how to help others.

Elijah's Low Ebb—1 Kings 19:1-18

After the great contest on Mt. Carmel in which the Lord had sent fire to show up the false prophets of Baal, Elijah had run before the king's chariot down the mountain before the rain that ended the drought. Though it had been a great victory, it had been a nervous strain for Elijah, who was now ready for a time of quiet rest. Instead of that, what message did he get from the queen? Turn to 1 Kings 19 and read the first two verses.

He knew she meant business, so he went a long way south to Beer-sheba, left his servant there, and traveled all day into the wilderness, where no one could find him. Sitting down exhausted under a tree, what did he say to the Lord in the last part of verse 4? Did you ever feel like that?

What was the first thing Elijah needed? How understanding the Lord is of all kinds of needs! How did the Lord care for his physical needs in 5-7? If there aren't people nearby to help, He dispatches an angel!

What kind of physique must Elijah have had to do what he did in 8!

When God's choice servant felt so lonely and chased, the Lord Himself became his counselor. When He asked Elijah what he was doing there, how did Elijah answer in 10? Was he the only one left who was true to the Lord? No, he wasn't, but he felt that lonely. And only the wicked queen was seeking his life. In his dark mood he couldn't see things as they really were.

How did the Lord try to get Elijah out of himself? He presented a dramatic spectacular—strong wind, earthquake, fire, but the Lord wasn't in them. How did the Lord reveal Himself? In a light whisper.

Again He asked the same question. How did Elijah answer in 14? Exactly the same as before. He was so low that the physical phenomena and the Lord's own voice didn't bring him out of himself.

Then God told him that while he lived he was to be up and doing. It wouldn't help a bit to nurse his grief. So He told him to anoint a new king of Syria, a new king of Israel, and Elisha the prophet in his place. In 18 how untrue was his statement that he was the only worshiper of God left? He was just seven thousand off!

How Prevent Depression

It's so easy to slide into depression, and so hard to climb up out! Therefore let's think through how we can prevent discouragement. What can we do to prevent physical and emotional exhaustion that get us down? Do we know ourselves well enough to say no when we've had all we can take even if others urge us on? Do we plan periods of rest and recuperation during and after strenuous activities that drain our strength?

What can we do when we ourselves and others don't come up to our expectations? Not that we don't keep our high standards, but we can be realistic about human nature and not expect the ideal or the perfect. When people do come through, we can rejoice, but realize that people will always let us down. And we won't be too proud to acknowledge that we fail.

How can we keep a true perspective when we're inclined to turn in upon ourselves and see a black world through our dark glasses? Instead of hiding in our cave we can talk to the Lord and to others to check our perspective against the realities. How are we inclined to distort the facts?

Finally we can ask the Lord what we should be doing, and get doing something rather than mope. If we obey Him, we can leave the results with Him.

Patience

NONE OF us likes to wait, yet life often demands that we do wait. What happens when we wait impatiently? Yes, we usually get to feeling worse, irritable, ornery, which may lead to sin that we're sorry for later.

When we say that we're waiting for the Lord, the fact is that He is usually waiting for us. We aren't ready to receive what we're asking Him for. We aren't mature enough to use it wisely. Patience is one of the fruits of the Spirit (Galatians 5:22).

The Lord's timing is very important in His plans. An example of timing is the age level for getting a license to drive a car. What young boy or girl wouldn't like to drive a car! But what would happen if they were all allowed to? We have enough accidents on the road as it is.

Sometimes we feel as if we're the only one who has to wait. But think of the people who have to wait for us. And how mankind always makes the Lord wait! First He chose the nation of Israel to show forth His glories. When they failed, He waited and waited to see if they would repent before He carried them away from the good land to which He led them. Now that the Saviour has come and is building His church, He is waiting for it to be completed. But how many Christians are going about their own affairs instead of working for His interests! He waits that He may be gracious (Isaiah 30:18)! How can we wait patiently?

How to Wait Patiently—Lamentations 3:19-33, 40, 41

When the Lord had to destroy the beautiful city of Jerusalem where He had put His name, the Prophet Jeremiah, who probably wrote this book, showed the sorrow of the Lord by weeping and lamenting over the sinful people. Turn to Lamentations 3:19, 20. How does he feel about the experiences he has gone through?

But in 20-24 what gives him hope? If something seems dark and overwhelming to us just now, can we say what Jeremiah is saying, that God's unconditional love is just the same, it doesn't change, it never ceases? Which of His mercies were new to us this morning? Yes, this is where the song "Great Is Thy Faithfulness" comes from. Right out of this book of sighing and lamenting. We are never beyond the Lord's love and care. When we seem to have nothing else, the Lord is our portion.

In 25, 26 to which people is the Lord good? To those who wait quietly, patiently, for Him and seek Him. Usually when we fret and stew and complain, we are seeking our own way, we are turned in upon ourselves. When we seek the Lord, we think of His goodness and His higher ways.

The next four verses speak to young people particularly. The Apostle Peter tells us (1 Peter 4:12) not to think it strange when we have to go through a fiery trial as something out of keeping for the Christian. What is one benefit of it in 28? So often it is hard for young people to get alone with the Lord; they are usually in the midst of a crowd, a gang. What may we even have to endure in 30? Even abuse and humiliation. Even that won't kill us.

Why not, in 31-33? Even in punishment the Lord keeps His steady love. He does not punish unnecessarily; He does not enjoy punishing.

Now drop down to verses 40, 41. How can we bring our waiting to an end and be ready to receive what the Lord has for us? Instead of griping, we can check up on ourselves. What have we been doing that we shouldn't? What not doing that we should? And have we been truly worshiping the Lord with our hearts as well as our lips? Have we been seeing who He is and how He cares enough to develop our characters into Christlikeness?

Testing Our Ways

Let's worship and check our ways right now. First worship Him for His love that was new this morning. (Pause for silent response.) For His holiness that hates sin. (Pause.) For His power that can turn the world upside down if it is for His and our good. (Pause.) For His patience and longsuffering when we learn our lessons so slowly. (Pause.)

Now let's ask Him if we are doing our part, as He sees our situation. Ask Him if there is any sin we should confess. Anything we should do that we aren't doing. Ask Him to give us His own patience to wait quietly for Him and for others.

Wouldn't we like to conclude by singing "Great Is Thy Faithfulness"?

Temptation and Trials

WHEN RECENTLY have you been tempted to sin? Temptation is not sin but a situation in which it is easy to sin, when we're likely to sin if we're weak. Does each of us know when we are weakest, when we most readily fall into sin? What tempts one person may be no problem to another.

When we fall into sin or when our faith is tried, we're inclined to feel very much alone, as if no one else has been in a situation like this, that no one else really understands. But 1 Corinthians 10:13 tells us that others have faced the same difficulty and that God will always show us some escape from the temptation. He never shuts us up in a box with no way out. Therefore He says, "Don't think it strange when you get in a tough situation. I've planned this just for you, just the right degree of difficulty in your present stage of development" (*see* 1 Peter 4:12). He even says, "Count it all joy when you fall into various temptations, for that will produce dependable character" (*see* James 1:2). Though temptation may be an abomination to us, to God it is more precious than gold that perishes because it shows that our faith is genuine, not phony (1 Peter 1:7).

Does that seem like one of the hardest scriptural truths to believe and act on? When a test comes to us, is it possible for us to say, "Hooray! A chance for me to demonstrate that I really trust the Lord! Lord, what is Your way for me out of this situation, or through it"? Maybe as individuals we are not ready for this much trust, but if we bring the temptation to our family, we could all support each other in time of testing. How can we avoid sin when we are tempted?

David's Temptation—1 Samuel 25

David in the Bible got really upset in one of his temptations. When he and his men were living in the wilderness because King Saul was seeking his life, he found a rich farmer shearing his sheep. Turn to 1 Samuel 25:3. How was the farmer Nabal different from his wife?

Because David's men had protected Nabal's flocks, what did David send ten of his young men to do? Read verses 5-8, Jim.

Read Nabal's answer in 10 and 11, Ted.

When this answer was reported to David, what was he ready to do in 13? Those 400 men with their swords weren't just out for fun!

One of Nabal's young men was wise enough to tell Nabal's good wife how angry David was. Read what he said to her in 14-17, Sue.

When she sensed how serious the situation was, what did she hurry to do, in 18, 19?

And what didn't she do? She didn't tell Nabal what she was doing.

As she went along the trail toward David, how must she have felt? Because what was David thinking? 21, 22.

Could Abigail keep David from killing all of her husband's men? If you were as mad as David because you felt insulted, what would it take to calm you down and make you change your mind? Could Abigail do that? How did she try? Mother, read 23-31. What did her posture do for the situation? And saying, "Let me take the blame," though she didn't deserve it? What else impresses us in her speech? She acknowledged the sad truth about her husband. What was her main argument? When David became king, he would not want to regret that he had shed innocent blood or gave vent to his anger.

How did David respond to this? 32-35. He was strong enough to resist the temptation to let out his feelings, to acknowledge Abigail's wisdom, and to thank the Lord for sending her. Nabal soon died and David took good Abigail for his wife.

Avoiding Temptation and Sin

Suppose David had given way to his anger even though Nabal had been in the wrong. What would probably have been the outcome? There's always someone who wants to get back at us when we hurt people. Even though the Lord forgives, sin leaves wounds and scars that we have to live with. Avoiding temptation is always easier than avoiding sin after we are tempted, and avoiding sin is always easier than suffering the penalty for sin. If we're interested in prevention rather than cure, how can we keep out of the way of temptation?

Turn to Proverbs 4:11-15. "When you walk, you won't slip, and when you run, you won't stumble," if you obey verses 11 and 13. (*See* 12.) In our daily lives how do we learn instruction, the way of wisdom, the paths of righteousness? By studying God's Word. That's why we give it priority in our lives, take time for it even though we don't have time for all else we'd like to do.

At the same time what do we steer clear of? 14, 15. The path of the wicked, the way of evil. We have nothing to do with it.

How would you express verses 25-27 in your own words? Our eyes look and our feet go straight ahead.

Do you know how practically to stay out of the way of whatever might tempt you? Or if you are tempted, how to resist it? Suppose the Lord didn't send someone like Abigail to stop you. Are you strong enough to stop by yourself? Our Lord warned, "Watch and pray, that you may not enter into temptation" (Matthew 26:41 RSV). Because the spirit is willing but the flesh is weak, we constantly need to ask the Lord to keep us strong.

Inner Conflicts

WHEN EVERYTHING in us is pulling together and we feel at one with our-selves, we're ready to cope with all kinds of difficulties outside us. We feel strong enough to tackle mental problems that tax our brains and social problems with people. But what happens when a war is going on inside us, when our inner being is in conflict? All our energies are tied up inside. We have to give attention to maintaining our own self. We can't concentrate on anything outside us.

What kind of inner conflict have you had recently? Have you been pulled by two forces, both of them so strong that you wonder which you should give in to? Both seem to have value for you. Maybe part of you wants one thing and part another, like opposing parties in this country of ours. Even our one person is not a simple being. We can feel as torn and broken as a country whose factions are bitterly opposed to each other. When we're in that condition, we don't even enjoy the things that we do do, because we're always wondering whether we should do them or not. Our whole self becomes a big question mark!

If these inner conflicts are not resolved, our thoughts go 'round and 'round, getting nowhere, until they make us sick. What is God's answer to this inner turmoil?

Double-Mindedness in the Book of James—4:1-10

The Book of James says a lot about personal conflicts. What does James say they cause in 4:1? Even Christians fight among themselves.

In 2 what is the root of our fighting? We desire things we can't have or evil things we shouldn't have but are determined to get, or we try to get what other people have. Are these kinds of desires bothering any of us now?

If it's something good that we should have, James says we're trying to get it in the wrong way. How should we get it? Ask God for it.

In 3, when we do ask, why don't we get what we ask for? Our motives are wrong; we are thinking only about our own selfish pleasure, not God's purposes or the welfare of others.

James rebukes his readers. "False, unfaithful creatures!" (*See* verse 4.) Whose love and friendship have they been cultivating instead of God's? Which patterns and values of our present world system are contrary to God's patterns and values?

In 5 this love of the world grieves the Holy Spirit who watches over God's people for our good. When the temptations are strong, what is God ready to give us if we ask Him? All the grace and help we need, if we come to Him on His terms. What are His terms? We come humbly, not in a proud spirit.

Therefore what is God asking us to do in 7? Make a clear-cut decision for Him. How can we get the devil to turn and run? Resist him, stand up to him, don't give in to him.

Then we'll be ready to take the next step, in 8. What will happen if we move toward God? When we see Him in His holiness, we'll realize what sinners we are, and we'll wash our hands and purify our hearts.

As we see sin in His white light, what will happen to our lightheartedness and high spirits?

Finally in 10 what is the only way to have a high position and a good reputation?

Pulling Ourselves Together

What would you say is the main point of this section of James, what is the gist of what he is asking us to do? Yes, come close to God, submit to Him, make a clear-cut decision for Him. How will this help us pull all parts of our being together, get rid of our inner conflicts? Then the Lord will have control of body, mind, will, spirit and feelings. What will become of our selfish desires that benefit only ourselves? He will turn them into everybody's good and His glory.

The Lord says, "Take delight in the LORD, and He will give you the desires of your heart" (Psalm 37:4 RSV). We'll ask and have anything we want because we'll want the best things! Will we ourselves have less because we're asking what God wants and what others want? No, actually we'll have more. How can that be? Luke 6:38 promises: "Give, and it shall be given unto you; good measure, pressed down, and shaken together, and running over." Can we trust God for this, so that our motives will not be selfish?

What will become of our love for the things that the world loves? That will cool as our love for God grows warmer. We will love the people of the world as God loves them, but we won't be satisfied with their values or their pleasures. What will become of the quarrels among Christians? The closer we grow to Christ, the closer we'll grow to each other.

Right now let's do these things that James suggests. I'll pause after each idea for us to pray about it. "Dear Lord, first forgive our sin so that we can come to You with pure hearts. . . . Keep our motives from being selfish. . . . We draw near to You. . . . We humbly submit to You. . . . Help us resist the devil. . . . Help us to pull all parts of ourselves together in one. . . . Establish our desires and our goals. . . . Help us love You with all our hearts. . . . Give us sufficient grace for all our needs. Amen."

Being Jealous

ONE OF the hardest things in some families is sibling rivalry, children being jealous of each other. Parents try very hard to be impartial, to treat each one fairly. But why is this hard? Because each child is different, except identical twins. It was not the parents who made each one different in temperament, interests and abilities. Why wouldn't it be wise for God to make everyone in a family alike? How boring that would be! We'd get so tired of each other! And God has planned different ministries for each of us. Isn't it possible for us to enjoy the fascination of differences without having to have all that others have? Aren't we big enough to see the whole picture and not just our own private viewpoint?

Here are many small triangles of six colors that go well together, as many colors as there are members in our family. Let's work together to make the prettiest design we can with these colors. What kind of design could we make if all the triangles were the same color? What if the light ones insisted that they wanted to be red, and the dark ones that they wanted to be blue? Each color adds its own interest.

How serious is jealousy in the sight of the Lord?

Jealousy in the Wilderness—Numbers 16:1-35, 17:1-11

It wasn't easy for Moses and Aaron to lead the people of Israel through the wilderness to the promised land because the people murmured and complained most of the time. First his own brother and sister were jealous of Moses, who was younger than they. Then Korah and other Levites stirred up 250 leaders of the congregation to rebel against Moses and Aaron. God had appointed all the descendants of Jacob's son Levi to take care of and transport the tabernacle. Turn to Numbers 16:3. What did these Levites say to Moses and Aaron? They wanted to be priests, like Aaron. Why were Moses and Aaron acting as leaders? God had definitely chosen them to lead.

Two other men were also conspiring against their leadership, Dathan and Abiram. In verse 12 when Moses asked them to come to him, what did they answer? In 13, 14 what was their complaint? It was taking longer than they expected to get to the good land and they didn't like the journey.

Would you have felt as Moses did? 15. What did he say to the Lord?

What did he tell Korah to do, in the next verses? 16-18.

How did the Lord manifest His presence? 19. How did He respond? 20, 21.

But Moses felt with these rebels as well as with the Lord, and he interceded for them. 22.

So God told the other people to get away from the tents of the rebels, who stood at the doors of their tents, together with their families. Jim, read Moses' pronouncement in 28-30.

Sue, read what happened to the jealous people, in 31-33. This may have been an earthquake that took place miraculously at the moment when Moses spoke about it.

What did the rest of Israel do? 34.

What was the end of the 250 who had gone along with the rebels? 35. Why do you think the Lord punished them so severely? If this kind of jealousy were allowed to continue, what would have been the result? The leaders who made trouble should have been helping Moses and Aaron with the great problems of the whole nation.

What kind of character did Moses prove himself to be in this situation? You'd think he might be even more ready than the Lord to consume the whole nation.

What then does jealousy do not only to those who are jealous but also to those who are envied? It is damaging to everyone concerned.

Appreciating Differences

Since the Lord chooses some people to be leaders and gives some people special gifts, it is natural for us to be jealous when we see others doing what we would like to do. How can we keep from commiting that sin?

If we blame God for the place He gives us, what are we really doing? We are setting ourselves up as God, inferring that we know better than He does. How can He be just and fair when He distributes the differences? Can we believe that He knows exactly what will be most deeply satisfying for each of us? We will never be happy until we fulfill the purpose for which we were created, fill the one spot designed for us. No one has an insignificant place that doesn't count, not one. Those who have been given most are most responsible; they have to account for the wise use of all their abilities.

Suppose one boy in a family has been given unusual musical talent, which requires instruments, lessons, and travel for its fulfillment. What two ways could the other members of the family feel about the expense involved? If they are glad to sacrifice to help this one, what does that do to them as people? If they give to the Lord as well as to this brother, they will get plenty back, for we can't outgive the Lord. If they are jealous of him, what will it do to them? If they become sour and selfish, they will ruin their own chances to accomplish much.

"Lord, we thank You that You choose wisely the abilities and the place for each of us. Help us to fill it well and live fully so that we'll have inner contentment now and when we finish hear Your 'Well done.' "

Being Misunderstood

AFTER DINNER one evening Jim and his friend Bob got their guitars and were practicing new pieces in the living room. The whole family enjoyed the music for a while, until it was time for the TV program they wanted to see. Then they didn't know what to do. If the boys took their music to another room, it would still interfere with the program, for they didn't play and sing softly. It wasn't like Jim to monopolize the living room all evening, so the rest of the family did other things, but they felt edgy toward him, and hardly spoke to him after Bob went. Jim didn't know what the matter was. Last week he had asked the family if he and Bob could practice on this night, so his conscience was clear, but the rest of the family had forgotten that he asked.

Ted was so disgusted when the eye doctor told him he needed glasses. He and his friends teased the smartest boy in their fifth grade who wore glasses; they called him "student," and Ted didn't want to be called "student." He was afraid that when he wore glasses, he'd have to be careful not to break them, not to be rough, and he liked rough and tumble. He was afraid he would be misunderstood, that other boys wouldn't consider him a real guy any longer.

Have you been misunderstood, or afraid you would be? Do you wonder why some people you know seem to do very weird things, from your point of view? We know some people on such a superficial level that we don't try to understand them. But with the people who matter to us, are we open and honest enough to reveal ourselves and our intentions so that we do understand them? How can we keep from being misunderstood? When we are, how can we get together again?

David Misunderstanding the Lord—1 Chronicles 13, 15

God told His people to make a golden ark of the covenant as a symbol of His presence among them. It was carried with them through the wilderness and into the promised land, was captured by the Philistines, but returned when a plague broke out among them. It stayed in the country in the days of Saul. When David was settled in Jerusalem, what did he say to all his people about the ark? Read the first three verses of 1 Chronicles 13.

How many of the people agreed with him, in 3? So David made the occasion a great holiday for all the land.

Because David wanted to pay the ark the respect it deserved, what did he have it carried on, in 7?

In 8 how was the return of the center of their worship celebrated?

But in 9, 10 came a great shock! What abruptly halted the merrymaking? Note the references to the Lord: "the anger of the Lord" and "Uzzah died before the Lord." Why was the Lord angry, so angry that He killed a man?

In 11 how did David take that? He too was angry. Why? He didn't understand why the Lord had broken up the party. What had the stricken man done? What was written about steadying the ark?

In 12 how did David feel, and what was now his problem? It was surely a good idea to bring the center of worship into the capital city, but how did the Lord want it done?

David left the ark right where it had stopped. In 14 how did the Lord treat the man on whose property it stopped?

I imagine that David didn't rest until he discovered how God said in the law to carry the ark. In chapter 15 he prepared a place for it in the city, and then in verse 2 how did he say it should be carried? He chose Levites as God prescribed and had them sanctify themselves for this spiritual ministry. Look also at 13-15 to see how God had commanded the ark to be transported. The Levites were to carry it on their shoulders with poles, not on a cart, even a new cart. And why weren't other people allowed to touch it? Because it represented the holiness of God, who is approached only on His own terms. What God gives us in His revelation we are responsible for knowing.

Action

Why did David misunderstand the Lord? For the same reason that we often misunderstand—we don't have all the needed information. Not many of us have all the information on all sides of a question, yet we act on the part of it we have and wonder why we don't all agree. Can you remember a time when this bothered our family? Think of the court cases that go on and on as detectives try to ferret out all that is involved. Can we suspend judgment until all the facts are in? Not make snap judgments prematurely?

Surely no person is misunderstood as much as the Lord. It's so difficult for us human creatures to get His point of view. When Jesus was on earth, how often His disciples misunderstood Him! What kind of Messiah did they expect Him to be? An earthly king who would solve their problems politically and economically. Why did He let John the Baptist be beheaded when he was the greatest prophet? Why did He go straight to the cross when He could have summoned legions of angels?

We naturally assume that other people see things as we do. What shall we do when people don't respond as we expect them to? Can we tactfully find out what they are thinking and feeling? How can we do that? We can ask, "Am I understanding you aright? Do you feel so and so?" And let them correct us.

I'll appreciate it if each of you will question me when you don't understand why I do something. Sometimes motives aren't clear on the surface. An action may appear selfish when it isn't at all. It may be that we are looking at a situation from a very different perspective.

Let's try to understand each other so that we won't have to be angry or afraid.

Being Mistreated

RECALL THE last time when you felt that someone mistreated you, didn't give you a fair deal. What do you think was the cause of it? What was the result? Were you pleased with the result?

Some people feel that they have been mistreated so often that they are bitter toward the world, ready to strike back. They have been hurt so often that they try to get others before anyone else has a chance to get them. They expect very little of others. Then some people expect too much. Most of these come from homes which are harmonious and fair, so they expect the rest of the world to be, though often it isn't.

How should we expect to be treated? Since most people are self-centered, why should we expect them to treat us as they want to be treated? It is difficult for Christians to keep Christ the center of life. What would happen if we expected the worst from others? We'd be pessimistic and probably get what we expect. But neither can we hope for the ideal. Since we can't go to either extreme, what can we expect?

When we are mistreated, how shall we respond, in a mature way rather than in a childish way?

Isaac and the Wells—Genesis 26:12-32

God promised Abraham that He would bless him and his children and make them a blessing. Turn to Genesis 26. In 12-14 how did God bless Abraham's son Isaac? Isaac not only had many flocks and herds like his father, but his farming of the land also produced abundantly. How did the Philistines among whom he lived feel about his great wealth?

In 15 how did they mistreat Isaac out of jealousy? Envy is very often the cause of quarrels.

In 16 what did the king of that area advise Isaac to do?

Did Isaac put up a fuss about moving? 17.

In 18 what did Isaac have to do just because of the spite of the Philistines? Why were wells so important to Isaac? He needed many wells for watering all his flocks and herds.

In 19, 20 when Isaac's servants dug in the valley and found an underground spring, what did the Philistine shepherds claim? There is no mention of Isaac or his men fighting over it even though they had found and dug it.

What was the next event, in 21? How would you respond about this time? Would you be angry? We don't read that Isaac or his servants were.

How long did this mistreatment continue? 22. Finally Isaac was left in peace. Would it have been better for him to have quarreled over his rights?

Because Isaac had trusted the Lord to give him what he needed, what did the Lord say to him that night? 24.

What is implied when we are told in 25 that Isaac built an altar? He worshiped the Lord there. And his servants dug another well.

In 26 what did the king do?

In 27 wouldn't you wonder as did Isaac why he would come to him?

In 28, 29 what impression had Isaac made on the king and his staff? What did the king want to do?

So how did they depart from each other in 30, 31?

What provision did the Lord make for Isaac's herds in 32?

Responding to Mistreatment

What would probably have been the result if Isaac had fought for his rights? What are our rights as Christians? Someone has said that our only right is to deserve hell. God has promised His grace and infinite resources, but He doesn't promise us any rights as rights. The people of this world have to be responsible for all that they get, but our God overrules in the lives of His children. He has promised to supply all our needs, and we can leave the rest with Him. Sometimes at the moment we may not see justice, but eventually we will.

How does the example of Isaac help us to respond to mistreatment? Wouldn't it often be best to refuse to fight, as he did? Is it cowardly to refuse to fight, as he did? It is easier and more natural to fight. What is so hard about walking away from injustice? When we don't get a fair deal, our feelings urge us to go ahead and give it to the other fellow.

When people expect us to strike back and we don't, what do they think about us? This is one of the best ways to show the supernatural, that the Lord is with us. The Philistine king said to Isaac, "We see plainly that the LORD is with you" (verse 28). What opportunities may we have this week to show that the Lord is with us?

How can we often prevent quarrels? We can avoid tense situations and keep from antagonizing people. What antagonizes us about other people? Boasting and acting superior bothers most of us. In our efforts to achieve goals, we sometimes plough through without realizing that we are riding over other people.

"Dear Lord, we thank You when people treat us fairly and are sensitive to us as people. Help us to be content with what You do for us and not be crushed when people mistreat us."

Complaining

NONE OF the family liked to see a certain friend of Alice come to their house. As soon as they saw her, they thought, "I wish that child would stay home." Because she was a whiner. She always had something to whine about. At the Martins she often asked for something they didn't want her to have, and complained if she couldn't have it. I wouldn't want people to feel that way about me. Wouldn't you want to be the kind of person that people like to have around? Who would say, "Here comes that cheerful Alice," or "that interesting Ted!"

When we complain, do people feel like giving us what we want? No, quite the opposite. Our natural response is "No, go away." What does complaining imply about the other person? That we don't love him, trust him to give us what is good. It implies that I'm selfishly thinking just about myself, not about the other person or his reasons. Often griping gets to be a habit, a bad habit.

When we see how this attitude appears to others, we decide that we don't want to be this kind of person. How can we keep from complaining?

Israel's Complaining in the Wilderness

After God had powerfully redeemed His people from slavery in Egypt, had plagued the Egyptians until the king let them go, had opened the Red Sea for them to cross on dry land, and destroyed the Egyptians who were chasing them, they celebrated the great victory with a song of praise! They sang, "I will sing to the Lord, for He has triumphed gloriously!" What would we expect their attitude to be after that? But in order to reach the promised land, they had to go through a barren wilderness.

After a three-day journey, what was the first thing they complained about? Turn to Exodus 15:22.

In verse 23 why was the water of Marah disappointing? Instead of murmuring against Moses, what might they have said to the Lord? "Lord, we're trusting You to supply our needs on this journey in which You're leading us. Is there anything we should do to get water?"

When Moses cried to the Lord, what was he told to do? 25.

In 16:2, 3 what was the people's need? Is hunger a real need or a want? How did they ask for food? How insulting were their words to the Lord!

What was the Lord's answer to Moses, in 4, 5? It was no problem for the Lord to rain bread from heaven. But what was He most concerned about? About disciplining them to walk in His law, to reflect His qualities. At the end of verse 8 Moses said, "Your murmurings are not against us, but against the Lord." You remember, don't you, how He gave them manna and quails?

In 17:1 what was the people's problem? Water again. There weren't many oases in the desert. How angry were the people in 4?

How would the Lord provide water when there wasn't a drop in sight? Read verse 6. God made water gush from hard rock, yet the people were questioning, "Is the Lord among us, or not?" 7.

Now turn to Numbers 11:1. When the people complained this time, who got angry, and what was the penalty?

In 12:1, 2 even Moses' sister and brother who shared his leadership found fault with him. What were their two difficulties? Basically they were jealous of Moses, who was younger than they.

How did God vindicate Moses as the number one leader? Sue, read 4-15. Why do you think Miriam was stricken with leprosy, and not Aaron? Probably she took the lead in complaining.

Instead of Complaining

The Lord had good reasons for leading His people through the bare wilderness on the way to the promised land, though they didn't see them. After living in Egypt, they were not ready to fight the enemies in a direct route and live as His chosen race in their own land. In the wilderness He was disciplining them and trying to build them into a strong nation before they were obliged to fight the heathen in the land. His aim is not to make His people's lives easy and comfortable, but to make them like Himself. This takes plenty of doing.

If we profit by Israel's example, what shall we do when we have a need that the Lord isn't supplying? We can thank Him for what He has done in the past, claim His promises, and ask Him what He wants to teach us through the experience. He always has something important for us to learn.

Here at home when we find ourselves in a situation we don't like, what can we do instead of complaining? We can find out why things are as they are, and discover what we can do to make them what we want them to be. Usually if we ask the persons involved, we can uncover the root problem and can creatively see if there is any way to solve it.

If there is nothing we can do to get what seems best to us, what shall we do? We might just as well grit our teeth and say to the Lord, "Help me be strong enough to endure what I don't like. Even if I feel like grumbling, I will set my will on Your will and do what is required of me. Don't let me weaken. Make me into the kind of person You want me to be, a person You can depend on, a person others like to have around."

Guidance

IN OUR travels have we had the experience of engaging a guide to show us around a place that was new to us? Have we had good guides? Poor guides? How did the guide help us? He took us to the important places, arranged transportation, got tickets, and told us the background and interesting facts so that we spent our time wisely. What would have been the result if we had tried to get around the new place by ourselves? Why was the guide able to help us so much? The place was very well known to him; probably it was his home.

Imagine trying to take the greatest adventure of all—the adventure of life—without a guide! How is the Lord better than any human guide can be? He knows the future as well as the past, and has power to do anything that needs to be done for us. When He commands us to do His will, He also promises us that He will show us clearly what it is. He says, "I will instruct you . . . and guide you along the best pathway for your life; I will advise you and watch your progress" (Psalm 32:8, LB).

Today it isn't as easy for us to discover the Lord's guidance as it was for the people of Israel when He led them out of Egypt and through the wilderness. Then He used a pillar of cloud by day that became fire by night (Exodus 13:21, 22, Numbers 9:17). When the cloud moved, the people traveled, and when it settled down, they stayed there.

Today how does the Lord guide us into His best ways? What is our part?

The Steps in Seeking Guidance

I'll give you Scripture references that indicate what we should do to discern the Lord's will. See if you can infer what we should do from these Scriptures.

1. Probably most important of all is our attitude that is implied in Psalm 25. Look at verses 4, 5. If we expect the Lord to lead us, what must be our attitude? We must be ready to do His will, no matter what it is, whether it is hard or easy, whether it seems sensible or not, whether it would be our choice or not. Of course what we would like the Lord to do is to confirm what we feel like doing. Why may we have to wait to learn what God's will is? Until certain events take place we can't visualize the possibilities. In verse 9 why is it the humble or the meek that He will lead? These people are listening and ready to obey. In 10 what is our part? If we don't obey the leading we've had, we won't receive any more.

2. Verses 4, 5 give us an excellent prayer to memorize. It's in prayer that we tell the Lord our needs and the way the situation looks to us. What would happen if we asked the Lord only about the big decisions in our lives, the big steps? It would be very difficult to get His guidance. Why? Probably those decisions would already be made by the little ones that we make day-by-day. So how often shall we ask the Lord to lead us? At the beginning of every day, whenever we answer the phone, whenever we have a free minute, whenever we have a responsibility, etc. We're continually seeking His best.

3. Obeying the Word of God is so important that we better make a special point of that. Alice, do you remember the well-known verse about the Word's

being a light on our path (Psalm 119:105)? The Lord doesn't personally tell us things that are already written in His Book.

4. What is the implication for us in John 10:3 beginning with the words, ". . . the sheep hear his voice"? Our Good Shepherd leads us very individually and personally if we are listening to hear Him. He has things to say to each of us that no one else needs to hear.

5. What does John 16:13, 14 say about guidance? It is the Spirit who does the intimate inner willing and obeying in our hearts. So if we ask Him to take control, He works in the depths of our being.

6. What does Revelation 3:7, 8 add to our thinking about guidance? Though these words are addressed to a church, they are also true of our individual lives. When we are seeking the Lord's direction, He opens and shuts doors for us as He arranges providential circumstances. He closes some possibilities and beckons to us through some open ones. In Acts 16 when the Apostle Paul attempted to go into Bithynia, the Spirit of Jesus held him back, and in a night vision a man of Macedonia was beseeching him, "Come over [here] and help us" (7-9).

7. Sometimes the people mentioned in Proverbs 11:14 are helpful. Counselors can help us put the whole picture before the Lord, add aspects of the situation that we haven't thought of. But we would not rely on them alone, for all human beings make mistakes. Why is there safety in an abundance of counselors? If several people give the same suggestions, we better take them seriously.

8. Last and not first is the matter of feelings. Feelings are least reliable, but if all the other criteria focus on one course of action, it is most likely that our feelings will confirm them. Look at Isaiah 58:11. Let's read this verse in our various versions. Later if not sooner we'll thank the Lord that His way is the best way.

Let's thank Him in the song "My Lord Knows the Way through the Wilderness." All I have to do is follow.

The Weary Round

HOW MUCH of your life is composed of excitement, creativity, new experiences? Enough of it? How much of the weary round of routine, things you do over and over the same way day after day? Too much? Most people have too much routine because their jobs are monotonous—adding parts to an assembly line, selling the same products, washing the same dishes. So what do these people crave outside working hours?

Those who can't endure monotony use their brains to think up ways of doing the necessary duties quicker or better. What usually happens to these people? Their bright ideas get them positions that demand more—that demand far-reaching decisions and heavy responsibility. Some people don't want that much responsibility; it gives them ulcers and heart attacks. They'd rather go along comfortably in a rut.

Most of us have plenty of routine that we can't avoid, beginning with the simple daily habits of eating, sleeping, dressing, keeping clean. What routines do you get tired of? Are they all necessary? Let's not keep doing any that aren't necessary.

Since the Lord has ordained our regular patterns of daily living, what attitude should we take toward them?

Weariness Under the Sun—Ecclesiastes

Christians too get bored with the lives they are living. When they stand back and look at themselves, they think, "This isn't life. This isn't living." But they don't know what they can do about it.

A book in the Bible starts with this depressing note. A key phrase in this book is "under the sun." The writer is looking at life from the viewpoint of this world, under the sun. Turn to the Book of Ecclesiastes. Let's read 1:2 in our various versions. All seems to this writer to be vanity, empty, worthless.

Jim, read verses 1 through 11 to see how he feels about nature and events. As Jim reads, see what impresses you most in this section. In what sense is there nothing new under the sun? Yet if this writer should come back to earth today after hundreds of years, what would certainly seem new to him? How would you sum up his attitude? "What does all my work profit me? So what?" Do you think this attitude is justified?

Then the writer tries different interests to see what they do for him. Ted, read 2:1-3; what does he try first? A lot of people try pleasure, having a good time, escape to drinking.

What did he try next, in 4-10? Read that section, Sue. Apparently this wise man could get for himself anything his heart desired.

But in 11 what was his conclusion about all these things that he tried? Nothing satisfied him. Everything under the sun was empty, vanity.

Though this man under the sun sensed that wisdom was better than foolishness, what bothered him about wisdom? Mother, please read 12-18.

The first nine verses of chapter 3 are very interesting. Let's take turns around our circle, each of us reading a phrase that begins with "a time to . . . ." What value is there in the idea of a time for everything? There are times when things are appropriate and when they are not.

Though this book is mostly discouraging for the man under the sun, how does he end in 12:13, 14? The man who fears God and keeps His commandments is not this depressed soul, but one with great hope in the Son of God!

Doing All to the Glory of God

Personally I don't intend to spend my precious existence in vanity, emptiness, and boredom. How can we do otherwise? Turn to Colossians 3:16, 17. What a different spirit here! Just the opposite! What makes the difference? Why can the Word of God do so much more than the wisdom of men? The more grateful we are, the more the Lord can give us.

How can we do everything to the glory of God? If He is the center of our lives instead of ourselves, how will we take everything that comes? "Lord, You have a purpose in this; let me know what it is so that I can carry it out. If I have a routine chore, I will do it unto You. If someone needs to do it, I will do it because I love You." How can we keep our thoughts on the Lord when we're washing dishes or dusting a room or mowing the lawn? We can talk to Him about our own needs and the needs of others. We can memorize Scripture. These two verses in Colossians would be good ones to memorize. If we don't get some of these questions that we've discussed in family devotions thoroughly settled in our own minds, we can ponder them while we're doing chores and talk them over with the Lord.

Do you remember what happened to Joseph after he was put in prison because he would not sin? His life in prison was certainly not very exciting. But he performed his duties so well, because the Lord was with him, that he was made manager of the prison. Later he was brought out to become chief administrator of the food program for the whole country! There's no place in God's plans for vanity, emptiness, boredom!

Colossians 3:16, 17 is a good passage to memorize.

Death

PEOPLE WHO have not received Christ are often afraid of death, and they should be. Why? To them it is the great unknown, for they know nothing about what will happen next. Since they don't accept God's revelation, they have no source of information about death. Some believe that this life ends it all.

We believers are much concerned about the death of unbelievers. Why do we take it very seriously? Matthew 25:46 says that people not related to Christ will go away into eternal punishment, but those made righteous by Christ into eternal life. Since they have missed their greatest opportunity on earth, to belong to the only Victor over death, they will have to suffer eternal torment when they die. We don't like to think about that, but we better be doing something about it.

Therefore what is our chief concern about unbelievers? Are we doing all we can to lead them to Christ before it is too late? Even if they refuse the Lord's gracious invitation to come to Him, we must give them a chance to accept. They must realize how much He loves them and what a sacrifice He has made for them.

Resurrection—1 Corinthians 15

What attitude should we take toward the death of believers? The key to our future is the resurrection of Christ, which is an historical fact better substantiated than most historical facts. Because He came from heaven and went back to heaven, He is the only One who can tell us what will happen after death. He said to His friends, "Because I live, you will live also" (John 14:19 RSV).

1 Corinthians 15 is considered the great resurrection chapter in Scripture. Turn to 1 Corinthians 15:35. Here is a question that is often asked: What kind of bodies will we have after death?

Paul uses an illustration from the garden to answer this question. In 36, when we plant in soil a seed with life in it, what is the first step in the development of a plant? First the outer part of the seed dies, disintegrates.

Jim, read 37-41 from The Living Bible. How different is the pretty flower from the tiny brown seed that it grew from!

In 42-44 it tells us how our new heavenly bodies will be different from these earthly bodies. How many differences can we find? Die and never die, sickness or humiliation contrasted with glory, weakness and power, the physical and the spiritual.

In 45 who is the last Adam who is contrasted with the first Adam? Christ, the first of the new creation, not only lives Himself but becomes a life-giving spirit!

In 46-49, Mother, read the rest that Scripture tells about the kind of heavenly bodies we shall have. That's as specific as Scripture gets. For the rest we'll have to wait and see.

In 50 what is the reason why our present flesh and blood cannot get into God's kingdom? These bodies were not made to live forever; they wither and decay.

Wouldn't it be thrilling to be the people who don't die because we'll be here when Christ returns! In 52, how will that happen? Who will have their new spiritual bodies before we do? What a transformation God can accomplish in the twinkling of an eye!

In 54, 55 what are our victory exclamations? Let's all read those three sentences together. And also 57.

In 56 what is the sting of death? Christ has taken the sting out of the death of believers.

Our Attitude Toward Death

In the light of Scripture, how should we feel about believers who die? Usually there are both joy and sorrow. Why is there often sorrow at death? We miss our loved ones so much. Why joy? Paul said, "I would like to depart and be with Christ, which is far better, but I can be more help to you by staying here" (*see* Philippians 1:23, 24). Can you stretch your thoughts to imagine seeing the Saviour face-to-face in all His glory surrounded by the multitudes of heavenly hosts! Nothing on this earth will compare with that! None of us has ever seen heaven, but we can trust Christ's words about it. How do you visualize it? Scripture says that there will be no sin or sorrow (Revelation 21:4) and no night (Revelation 22:5), that heaven is extremely beautiful (Revelation 21:10, 11), it has places that the Lord is preparing for us (John 14:2, 3), that an inheritance is reserved for us there (1 Peter 1:4).

When is it that we're only glad to see believers leave this earth for heaven? When people are so old that their bodies are tired and sick, it is a great release for their spirits to be free from the worn-out frame.

How shall we feel about young people who die, especially parents who leave young children? This may look like a mistake on God's part, but no. How can that situation be for the best? Unless a believer dies because of sin, the Lord's timing is perfect, He sees the end from the beginning, He has the total perspective. If the other parent commits himself to the Lord, his heavenly Father will take care of him or her and the children. I believe that we are immortal till our work is done, until we accomplish all that God has planned for us.

When we see young people die, what does that do for the rest of us who live? It makes us take stock of ourselves. Are we living fully today? Are we ready to go today?

"Lord, we're so thankful that we look forward to eternal life in Your very presence! We're thankful that You hold the keys of life and death. Help us to live fully while we live here below, so that we may have no regrets when we leave."

11 WORKING TOGETHER

Each His Part

WHAT COOPERATIVE ventures have you experienced, when several or many people worked together to accomplish a certain purpose? Was it a satisfying experience? What made it so? Or was it a sad experience? Did the members work together as a good team? Were there any slackers, or people who withdrew? Did you have good leaders—wise people who steered and led without taking over and bossing? Was interest high until the project was completed?

All of us should have opportunities to work alone, to see what we can do by ourselves. But we should also experience the great things that people can do by working together—things that no individual could do by himself. Years ago when each worker in industry had to fend for himself, the individual didn't have much power; but when workers organized, they got great power, power enough to gain fair wages and even shut down whole industries. Sometimes unions aren't wise in their demands, but they show us the effectiveness of banding together. Some people don't make much difference in this world either individually or corporately. Don't we want to combine our efforts with those of others to make our influence felt?

Building City Walls—Nehemiah 2—3

Nehemiah was the honored cupbearer to the king of Persia. When one of his brothers came from Jerusalem and told him how difficult it was for the Jewish people in that city with its walls broken down and its gates burned, he wept and fasted and prayed. The Lord led him to ask the king if he could go back to rebuild the city, and led the king to let him go, even appoint him governor.

When he got to Jerusalem, he first inspected the ruins at night, so he knew just how bad they were. Then what did he say to the people of the city? Turn to Nehemiah 2:17.

How did Nehemiah encourage the people, in 18? It was amazing for a foreign king to let his servant go and even to give him lumber for the building. It was evident that the good hand of God had been upon the initiation of the project. How did the people respond?

In 19 how did the enemies of the Jews respond? They sneered, "What do these weak Jews think they are doing? Can they make stones again out of burnt rubble? If even a fox climbs up their walls, it would break them down" (see 4:1-3).

What was Nehemiah depending on, in 20? What faith and courage it would take to build in the midst of this opposition!

Chapter 3 lists the people who built the part of the wall nearest their own homes or shops. I'll make a list of the kinds of people, not all the individual names, as you find them, and another list of the gates that are mentioned in this chapter. The people: the high priest, goldsmiths, a perfumer, the two rulers of Jerusalem and the daughters of one of them, other rulers, Levites, priests, temple servants, keeper of the East Gate, and merchants. How can we summarize the types of people who built? Not only the ones who normally did manual labor, but rulers and priests and professionals who loved their city and their homes. Did you notice the only group of people mentioned who did not build? The nobles of Tekoa, in 3:5. The gates: Sheep Gate, Fish Gate, Old Gate, Dung Gate, Fountain Gate, Water Gate, Horse Gate, East Gate, and Muster Gate.

Though the enemies continually harrassed the builders, who had to be on the alert for attacks, how long did it take the people to finish the wall? Look at 6:15, 16. Fifty-two days is an incredibly short time! Even the enemies acknowledged that God had seen it through. His people too had worked together, each one doing his part.

My Part

Is each of us doing our part in the undertakings that we are involved in? Let's begin here at home. Do we all know definitely what are our responsibilities? Usually the various chores emerge from the members' interests and abilities. Can the others depend on our part? Of course in emergencies the rest of us are glad to pitch in and do extra. If we have a regular duty that is just a duty, that no one really likes to do, what is the easiest way to manage it? If we have a regular time for it, we can be free until that hour arrives, and don't have to have it hanging over our heads the rest of the time, feeling guilty because we don't want to do it.

(If your family is engaged in any family project, like improving the yard, gardening, making a collection, helping another family, etc., discuss the contributions of the members. If you are creative, you can no doubt find some significant part for the various ages and abilities. Don't lower the self-respect of anyone by suggesting for him busywork that is not really important.)

One problem for some people with wide interests is that they get involved in so many kinds of undertakings that they can't pursue any of them to a satisfying conclusion. What is the solution to this problem? It is better to do a few things thoroughly than many things superficially. We can appreciate many things without getting involved in all of them. Let's ask the Lord which projects in our home, church, school, business, and community He wants us to participate in. If His good hand is upon us as it was on Nehemiah, the results will be very satisfying.

The Church of Christ

CHRIST SAID, "I will build My church; and the gates of hell shall not prevail against it" (Matthew 16:18). That sounds as if the church would have strong opposition, but genuine triumph. What is the church? No, it is not essentially a building or an institution. Some churches don't own buildings. The church is the body of Christ, composed of every born-again person through the merits of His death and resurrection. An assembly, no matter what it is called, is not a church unless it is in living relationship with its living Lord.

Why did Christ leave His people here on earth when He returned to heaven? To demonstrate the immeasurable riches and wisdom of His glorious grace (Ephesians 1:6, 2:7, 3:10). How is it possible to accomplish such a tremendous purpose? How is our own head related to our body? Christ the Head is Himself at work in the church to give us directions and to carry them out (Philippians 2:13). As we partake of His divine nature, share in the very being of God, we escape the corruption and evil desires of this world (2 Peter 1:4).

The Relation of Its Members—1 Corinthians 12:15-26

We who belong to Christ have a special place in His body and are responsible for our own particular contributions according to our spiritual gifts (Ephesians 4:11, 12). How should we feel about the other members of the body? Turn to 1 Corinthians 12:15. Suppose your foot should see all the interesting things that your hands are doing, and should complain like this, how would you answer your foot?

And if your ear didn't think it was as important as your eye, in 16?

Why are the questions in 17 and 19 silly questions?

Who is it who has decided whether we shall be a hand or eye or ear or foot or a cell of our skin that no one notices? 18. God fits together all the intricate parts.

Regarding 20, we are more inclined to see the many individual parts than the whole body. Do we feel the oneness of everyone who is in Christ? Do we feel a kinship with each one, no matter what his color or race or station?

The idea of 21 might read, "The pastor cannot say to the caretaker, 'I have no need of you,' or the Sunday school teacher to the club leader, 'I have no need of you.' "

Sue, read how God feels about the weaker members of His body, in 22-24.

If we actually practiced what 25, 26 suggest, what would we do? Do we know which members of our local group are suffering, which are rejoicing? Let's thank God right now with those who are rejoicing, and pray for those who are hurting. How can we keep in touch with those we don't know? They belong to us, and we to them. Do you have one special person on your heart whom you support and care for daily?

The Life of the Church—Acts 2:42-47

Since the church is not just another institution, what should characterize its life? When we think of it in action, what should it be doing?

After Peter's sermon on the day of Pentecost when the church was born by the outpouring of the Holy Spirit, what did the radiant new believers do before they got bogged down with buildings and administration? Turn to Acts 2:42. What was their first interest? They couldn't find out enough about their Lord and His higher ways. They devoted themselves to the apostles' teaching. And fellowship. What is genuine Christian fellowship? What more is it than enjoying each other's company socially? Christian fellowship is enjoying Christ together, expressing our love and thanks and needs together. The breaking of bread refers to the taking of communion together, worshiping Him as they remembered all He had done for them. And they talked to Him in prayer.

In 43 what were the results of this kind of life? The new Christians didn't go about their business as usual. They felt awe and reverence as they realized that God Himself was in their midst, doing miracles through the apostles!

In 44, 45 how did they express the close bond of love and brotherhood that they felt for each other? "What's mine is yours," they said. If one of them had a financial need, someone sold a possession to meet that need. They knew who the others were whom the Lord had called to Himself and they treated them as brothers.

Because the Lord in them attracted them to each other, what else did they rejoice in doing together? 46. They worshiped in the temple, took communion in small groups in their homes, and shared meals with each other.

Enthusiasm like this is catching! It's great to have people praising God instead of griping and complaining. In 47 what effect did the Christians' praise have on other people? Their exuberance attracted outsiders. They were delighted to confess their faith and share it with all others! They had the very greatest in life to share!

Our Church

Is this the spirit that characterizes our church? Are we eager to learn more about the Word? Do we worship in spirit and in truth? Is our fellowship close and deep? Are outsiders attracted by our praise so that they come to Christ? If not, which of these elements of the life of the church should we begin to improve? What shall we do first, this week?

"Lord, we thank You that You are the head of the church, to give it direction and power. Don't let it get bogged down in organizing and maintaining itself. Rekindle our commitment until outsiders are attracted to our vitality and joy."

Being a Real Friend

IN YOUR mind list the people you call your friends. Which ones do you consider your best friends? How close are you to them? What are you ready to do for them?

All of us know people on various levels, from the very superficial to the depth level. Think of someone you know only by name; you know who he is when you see him, maybe a neighbor. Can you think of another person whom you know a few things about, maybe his regular habits, like when he comes and goes, or what church he goes to? You may know more about others, as the kind of people they are, the kind of student or manager or housekeeper, even what means much or little to them. We reach another level when we feel a spark of kinship with some, a bond is established between us when we find we have something personal in common. The next level is a sharing of values. We care enough to spend time together on mutual interests. Next comes a building of personal love and trust that sets some people apart as special people to us. Is this the last level of being a friend? No, one more is appreciation of the other for his own sake, without any benefit to ourselves. Even in love and trust there is often a trace of self-interest; the other person enhances our own self-concept.

On which of these levels of relationship are most of the people you call friends? What does it take to be a real friend?

David and Jonathan—1 Samuel 18:1-4, 19:1-7, 20:17, 30-34, 41-43

Jonathan was attracted to David at their first meeting, after David killed Goliath. Who was Jonathan? The oldest son of King Saul who would normally become king after Saul. Jonathan was a brave warrior, who, attended only by his bodyguard, climbed a rocky crag and killed twenty enemy soldiers, resulting in the panic of the whole army. Turn to 1 Samuel 18:1 to see how he felt toward David.

How did Jonathan seal the pact of being his blood brother, in 3, 4?

When the people praised David more highly than they praised King Saul, what did the king tell Jonathan and all his servants to do, in 19:1? When Jonathan realized that his father was jealous of David, and that David might become king instead of him, how did he feel toward him? That didn't seem to make any difference.

In 2, 3 why did Jonathan say what he did to David?

What did Jonathan say to his father, in 4, 5? He talked very frankly to him, saying that killing David would be sin.

King Saul respected this reasoning of his son, and David returned to the palace. But when an evil spirit came upon Saul, he tried to spear David as he was playing his harp for him. So David had to flee. Jonathan met him in a field in order to talk to him. What did Jonathan ask David to do again, in 20:17? Jonathan then tried to find out what his father's intentions toward David really were, and discovered that Saul was enraged at David.

How did the king treat his son when he excused David? Look at 20:30, 31.

When Jonathan asked his father what wrong David had done in 32, what did the king do in 33? Even threw his spear at his son!

How did that make Jonathan feel, in 34?

At their last meeting in the field, what did Jonathan and David do, in 41?

What was the last thing Jonathan said to David? 42. The two didn't have much time to enjoy their friendship, but the quality of it has been an example through the centuries. Soon Jonathan and Saul were both killed in battle, and David became king.

The Cost of True Friendship

What expressions were used about the way Jonathan felt toward David? Three times we read that he loved David as his own soul (18:1, 3, 20:17). Scripture also says that Jonathan delighted much in David (19:1), and that his soul was knit to the soul of David (18:1). How would two souls get knit together? We think of a person knitting first one strand of yarn and then another together to make a beautiful effect. What would be knit in friendship? First one person shares himself, his real inner self, then the other reveals more of himself, until the two are one in many of their thoughts and feelings. First one gives and then the other. Their interest is giving, not getting. What was there about David that Jonathan appreciated so much?

Are you a Jonathan to anyone? Whom do you love as much as yourself? Because you have much appreciated this friend, have you ever been jealous of him or her? It is very natural to be jealous. Hesitant to admit it, how do we often try to cover it up? We give various false excuses, rationalizations. What does this do to our friendship?

What is the root cause of our difficulties with friends? Our proud self, our lower nature wants to be first, to get for ourselves. Some people are just too selfish to be a friend. They like us as long as they get, but they are not ready to give.

Don't you think it is the Lord's best for us to have good friends? What else is likely to keep us from having them? There just isn't time to give to too many people. We have to be with people in order to know them, in order to enjoy them. But we can advantage of all the casual contacts we have to get to know people as people rather than talking about trivial things.

"Lord, we thank You for the joys of true friendship. Help us to be big enough to pay the price of being a true friend, of discerning the real needs of our friends and being ready to give all we've got to meet them."

Being Good Neighbors

IF WE could have just the kind of neighbors that we prefer, what kind would they be? Are we that kind? How do we feel toward our neighbors? Yes, we're thankful for the Christians with whom we have good fellowship.

How about our unsaved neighbors? The Lord has put us here near them for a purpose. If we thought mostly of our differences from them, we would become isolated from them, living in a different world. But the Lord has given us much in common with them, so that we have natural contacts. Let's see how many common needs and interests we can list, things that bring us together. With them we are fellow human beings made in the image of God, even if they have not yet entered into the fulness of spiritual *life* in Christ. As fellow human beings, how shall we treat them? We can show interest in them as people in their own right, with their own needs and interests and abilities. If they are going to learn to trust the Saviour, they may first need to learn to trust us. How can we bring that about?

How shall we pray for our neighbors? What shall we ask the Lord to be doing deep in their inner beings? He can work on them by His Spirit before they give Him a chance to work in them. How do we want them to think of us? As reflecting the Lord in all His gracious ways. We should ask the Lord to give us openings to speak of the Saviour to them, natural opportunities when they have been prepared by the Spirit. And we can learn another possibility from Philip the evangelist in the Book of Acts.

Philip's Obedience—Acts 8:26-40

The love of Christ had so filled the heart of Philip that he was preaching the gospel even to the Samaritans, with whom the Jews formerly had no dealings. Many believed and were baptized, and there was great joy in their cities. In the midst of all this rejoicing, what did the angel of the Lord say to Philip in Acts 8:26? How would you feel if the Lord told you to leave the cities where people were receiving Christ and go to a desert road?

In 27, did Philip hesitate? What did he find at the place where the Lord directed him? 27, 28. This treasurer had great authority under the queen. He must have been very eager for the Word of God to be reading it as he rode along.

How clearly the Spirit directed Philip, in 29! Do we hear Him speak to us that clearly?

In 30 what was Philip's question to the official?

And the man's answer? 31. When one of our neighbors needs a Christian's help, can the Lord direct us to him, like this?

Mother, read the Old Testament Scripture that the man was reading, in 32, 33. Would you be able to explain the meaning of this passage to someone?

How easy it is to present Christ when people ask definite questions, like these in 34. So Philip explained how Christ was the Lamb of God who takes away the sin of the world.

Again in 36, 37 how ready the man was to obey the Lord! His eagerness jumps out of the page at us!

Did Philip have any doubts about the readiness of this man to be baptized? 38.

The end of this event as recorded in 39 is as abrupt as was its beginning. How had this man been prepared for the gospel? No doubt his worship at Jerusalem. And why didn't he need follow-up? He had the Scriptures to teach him. Usually we need to feed newborn Christians on the milk of the Word, until they are strong enough to walk alone.

In 40 what did Philip continue to do? He kept bringing the joy of Christ to the villages.

Following the Lord's Leading

If one of our neighbors became interested in the Lord, could He direct us to this person, as He did Philip to the treasurer? If so, what would have to be true of us? Yes, we would have to be listening to His voice, be ready to leave what we were doing even if it was important, we'd have to be ready for the unexpected, and we'd have to be prepared to help the neighbor when we talked to him. How do we get prepared to help? In Philip's case it was being able to explain the Word of God.

When our neighbors are needing us, they may not always be reading the Word and seeking interpretation. What else may be needing? They may need someone to pour out their troubles to, someone who will listen to their inner struggles. They may need some material thing we can give or lend them. They may need to see more alternatives to a problem than they can think of. They may need someone to baby-sit.

Is each of us praying specifically for one of our neighbors? Do we know that person well enough to know what is happening to him so that we can pray definitely? What will it do for him if he knows that we are praying for him when he is sick, that he will be safe when he travels, that he will sell his house when he needs to move? Do we do extra things out of love, like taking him a new kind of cake, or book, or record? These extras sometimes speak volumes!

Yet how do people feel when the giving is all one way, when someone is always giving to us? As Jesus asked the woman at the well to give Him a drink, so we too can ask our neighbors for things they would like to give without its being a strain on them. We can try to put ourselves in their place and feel what they would like. The second great commandment is ". . . love your neighbor as yourself" (Matthew 22:39 RSV).

Outreach

SUPPOSE A boy that you know got lost in the woods or in the mountains. What would happen? Not only would his relatives and friends go out hunting for him, but many other people in the community would also. When many boys that we all know are spiritually lost in sin, what happens? Nothing. Most people don't realize that anyone without Christ is condemned to perish eternally.

But we, the people of God, who do realize how serious it is to be unsaved, how much are we doing? Do we conform to the way the unsaved feel, or do we feel the way the Lord feels about those who are lost in sin? Why are many believers doing so little about the salvation of unbelievers? Truly, it isn't as simple a matter to bring a person to Christ as it is to bring him back to his home if he has wandered away. We can't go up to an unbeliever and say, "Here, come with me, you need Christ." What can we do? We can be just as urgent in praying for him and using every opportunity the Lord gives us to help him see his need of Christ. Afterward those who come to Him are eternally grateful that we kept pursuing them even if they resisted at the time.

The last thing Jesus told his followers to do before He returned to heaven was to spread the good news of salvation to all nations. When the last person has been added to the body of Christ, He will come again. Are we obeying the great commission?

The Great Commission

Outreach to others is an important part of each of the four gospels that describes the life of Christ. Turn first to Matthew 28:18. When Jesus' friends met Him for the last time on the mountain, He gave them a directive that He never wanted them to forget. If we don't believe what He said first about Himself, we probably won't do as He asks. Do you believe it? If He has all power, full authority, all control in heaven and on earth, what difference does that make to us? He can overcome any kind of evil force that is mustered against us.

In His power what can we do in 19? All nations are to praise Him around His throne. And we are to make not converts, but disciples. What is the difference? Disciples continue to learn of Him and make more disciples. What is the significance of baptism? We are baptized into His death and resurrection in the name of the Trinity.

What are all nations to be taught to do? Everything that Jesus taught when He was on earth. And in the loneliest places on earth, we are never alone.

Now turn to the end of the gospel of Mark to see how the great commission is expressed there, in 16:15. How is this different from Matthew? Instead of "all nations," what words are used? And instead of "teaching"?

In 16 what is added to the words of Matthew?

Look also at Luke 24, beginning with verse 47. Instead of expressing what sinners should do, this writer begins with what the preacher should do—preach repentance and forgiveness to all nations. What is the significance to us of the words "beginning at Jerusalem"? Beginning at home; we can all begin right now wherever we are.

In 48 RSV Jesus says to us just as surely as He said to those disciples long ago, ". . . You are witnesses of these things" that I did.

In 49 what is the promise of the Father that He will send? The Holy Spirit in His power, who came to earth on the day of Pentecost. There's no use trying to witness in our own strength.

In the Gospel of John the emphasis on outreach is in different form. In 3:15-18 what word is used several times instead of "all nations"? God sent His Son that the *world* might be saved. And in all the world *whosoever* believes becomes part of the body of Christ.

Our Part

Every member of the body of Christ has a part, a responsibility for outreach, witness, missions. There are three things that we can all do. What are they? Yes, pray, give, and go.

Not much is accomplished when we pray very generally: "Lord, bless the missionaries, reach the heathen, help them believe." How should we pray for missions? If possible, we should find out all we can about a real person in another nation who needs Christ so that he is more than a name to us. Then pray every day about his particular needs, and keep in touch with someone who can report on his progress. (If your family gets prayer letters from several missionaries, see if there is one person who will interest each member of the family so that he can take that one as his special concern.)

Each year of our lives we ought to be able to give more for missions as long as we continue to get more each year. What can we give in addition to money? Missionaries never get enough mail, so letters are always most welcome. Also you may be able to help whoever in your community sends out missionary letters; see if you can help fold, stamp, and seal them. Sometimes collections or objects are appreciated. Sometimes churches need posters and exhibits made.

And all of us can go for Christ—yes, all of us. How can that be? We are each responsible for those with whom we have natural contacts in our daily living, for we can reach these people better than anyone else. How can we show these people that the Lord wants to give their lives a plus quality? How can they see by our lives that we have Someone they want? What is our part? We can ask the Lord to work in their lives and lead us to souls prepared, we can show interest in them as people, can put ourselves out to help them, can be ready to explain Christ to them.

Let's each mention one person here or abroad that you are now taking or will take as your special concern, and we'll pray for these individuals. Then you can report if they make any moves toward the Lord.

Matthew 28:18-20 is one passage we should all know by heart.

INDEX

INDEX

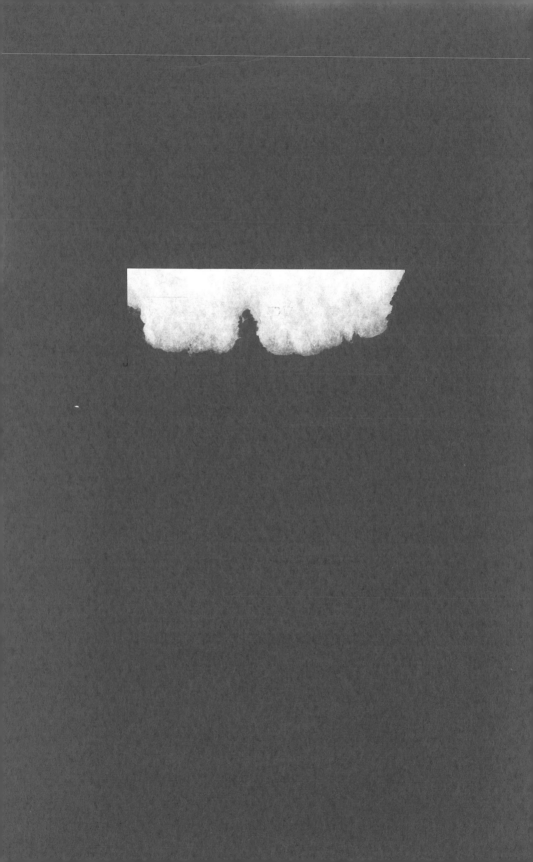